MANAGING
INTERNATIONAL
SCHOOLS

Managing International Schools is an accessible introduction to education management in international schools. It provides essential practical solutions based on real situations. Topics covered include:

- planning, implementing and evaluating the curriculum
- teacher recruitment, school leadership and middle management issues
- educational management: in particular, the cultural language, curriculum and staff management issues
- the management of change, curriculum development, assessment, leadership, middle management, professioanl development and staff recruitment, in the context of international schools.

Written by internationally renowned practitioners and academics with long-standing knowledge and experience of international schools, the emphasis is on management that enhances learning organisations set in the global community as determined by the ever-changing environment of the international school.

Managing International Schools offers a practical framework for management, support, development and improvement for practitioners at all levels in the school: teachers, middle and senior managers, headteachers, principals, patrons and boards. It will also be of interest to lecturers in higher education, trainers, researchers and other educational professionals.

Sonia Blandford is currently Director of Learning and Teaching at Westminster Institute of Education, Oxford Brookes University. She is also associate manager for ESCalate, the LTSN subject centre for education.

Marian Shaw is a Senior Lecturer in Education Management at the Westminster Institute of Education at Oxford Brookes University.

MANAGING INTERNATIONAL SCHOOLS

Edited by
Sonia Blandford
and
Marian Shaw

LONDON AND NEW YORK

First published 2001
by Routledge
2 Park Square, Milton Park, Abingdon, Oxon, OX14 4RN

Simultaneously published in the USA and Canada
by Routledge
270 Madison Ave, New York NY 10016

Routledge is an imprint of the Taylor & Francis Group

Transferred to Digital Printing 2009

Typeset in Garamond by
Prepress Projects Ltd, Perth, Scotland

British Library Cataloguing in Publication Data
A catalogue record for this book is available
from the British Library

Library of Congress Cataloging in Publication Data
Managing international schools / edited by Sonia Blandford
and Marian Shaw.
p.cm
Includes bibliographical references and index.
ISBN 0-415-22885-9
1. International education. 2. School management and organization.
I. Blandford, Sonia. II. Shaw, Marian.
LC1090.M36 2001
371.2–dc2   2001019474

CONTENTS

unit 1

CONTENTS

CONTENTS

vii

FIGURES

TABLES

BOXES

CONTRIBUTORS

Dr Sonia Blandford is currently Director of Learning and Teaching at the Westminster Institute of Education, Oxford Brookes University, UK. As a researcher, teacher and consultant, Sonia has worked with individuals, masters and doctorate cohorts and ministries of education from around the world in the development of educational management policies, procedures and practices. Sonia has published a number of education management books on generic issues relating to national and international schools. Her most recent research focuses on middle management and the management of discipline in schools. She is also course leader for the international EdD at Oxford Brookes University.

Simon Catling is Professor of Education and Deputy Head (Undergraduate and Initial Teacher Education Programmes) of the Institute of Education, Oxford Brookes University, UK. While he has a strong teaching interest in primary school geographical education, he also teaches curriculum theory and practice. For 10 years he has led and taught the curriculum component of the Institute's MA course for teachers in international schools. Before joining the Institute he was deputy head of an inner London primary school. He has published widely on primary geography and environmental education, both for pupils and for teachers. He is a past President of the Geographical Association. His research interests include children's understanding of geography and maps.

Dr Dean Fink is an international educational development consultant. He is a former superintendent and principal with the Halton Board of Education in Ontario, Canada. In his career he has taught at all levels of education from primary grades to graduate school. He has been a senior manager at both primary and secondary levels. During the past four years Dean has made presentations or conducted workshops in 27 different countries. He has published numerous articles on topics related to school effectiveness, leadership and change in schools, as well as co-authoring *Changing Our Schools*, *It's About Learning and It's About Time* and *Good Schools/Real Schools; Why School Reform Doesn't Last*. Dean is an associate of the International Centre for

Educational Change at the Ontario Institute for Studies in Education, a fellow of the University of Hull, UK, and The Queen's University of Belfast, UK, and a research associate of the Centre for Teacher and School Development at the University of Nottingham, UK. Dean lives in Ancaster, Ontario.

John Hardman was born and raised in Argentina and has been a primary and secondary teacher, secondary principal and headteacher at several international schools in Buenos Aires. His experiences with overseas staff during this time fired his interest in international education in general, and more particularly in the plights and delights of international teachers' lives. While taking an MA in International School Management at Oxford Brookes University, UK, he became keenly interested in carrying out active research into the motivation of international teachers, the dissertation which provided the raw material for the present chapter. To give credence to his interest, in August 2000 John took up a new appointment as Head of Colegio International SEK Ecuador-Quito

Jackie Holderness has worked in primary education for over 20 years. She specialises in the teaching of Language and Literature. She is a qualified OfSTED schools inspector and has worked at Oxford Brookes University, UK, for 10 years. She has worked overseas and has taught French and English as foreign languages. She has also published several coursebooks and supplementary language teaching materials in addition to books for mainstream primary teachers. She has worked with teachers from all over the world, providing CPD and running summer schools in Britain. Since 1992, she has been a core tutor on the Oxford Brookes MA in Education for International Teachers and is the current Course Leader.

Robin McClelland is a senior lecturer at the Westminster Institute of Education, Oxford Brookes University, UK. Prior to this, he was headmaster of a primary school, a schools' adviser and an OfSTED Inspector. He has worked on the Oxford Brookes International MA since its inception. Increasingly, he is working overseas with international schools developing school structures and good practice in planning and assessment. His chapter, Managing Assessment in International Schools, is developed from a key note address given at the Latin American Heads' Conference in Peru in May 1999.

Marian Shaw is a Senior Lecturer in Education Management at the Westminster Institute of Education at Oxford Brookes University, UK. When she is not leading the management track on the MA for International Schools, she is a trainer and consultant in education management, largely overseas, supporting development in international schools and ministries of education. Her doctorate research interest is in the application of management models in cross-cultural settings. She jointly led a recent research project and published a book on school inspection. She formerly taught science, became a local education authority adviser for personal and social education and qualified as an OfSTED inspector.

Martin Skelton has been a teacher and a headteacher. He is currently a director of Fieldwork Education Ltd, which he helped to co-found. Fieldwork works extensively with international schools around the world in a variety of different ways. Among Martin's current work he is director for the management of Shell English-speaking schools throughout the world and director of the new International Primary Curriculum. In addition, Martin offers consultancy and staff development on a wide range of issues to more than forty of the schools with which Fieldwork works. His main interest lies in helping schools use all the resources at their disposal to improve the way that children and students learn. In connection with this he is currently delivering a programme of seminars throughout the UK and overseas on 'brain-friendly learning'.

Linda Squire joined the Oxford Centre for Education Management (OxCEM) at Oxford Brookes University, UK, in 1993 after a successful career as a teacher, headteacher and senior Local Education Authority (LEA) inspector. Since then she has worked as a trainer and consultant in projects, government ministries, schools and LEAs in the UK and overseas. Her particular interests lie in the fields of leadership, organisational management, strategic planning and continuing professional development. She is leader of the Education Management Track in the Home and Distance Learning MA courses and is a member of the MA (International) team.

Professor John Welton has extensive experience of international education working for international schools and for agencies such as the United Nations (International) Children's (Emergency) Fund (Unicef), the Overseas Development Agency/Department for International Development and the European Union. He has worked on change in education for governments and individual schools in Africa, the Middle East, South Asia, the Far East, Europe and Latin America. Formerly head of the School of Education at Oxford Brookes University, UK, Professor Welton's experience in working with individual international schools convinced him of the need to start the MA for International School staff, the first in the UK. Professor Welton has written and edited books and articles on curriculum planning, policy and provision for special education, restructuring schools, managing teacher education and the future of cultural minorities in multicultural states. He retired early from Oxford Brookes University in summer 2000, and he is currently Representative for the Quaker Council for European Affairs, based in Brussels.

ACKNOWLEDGEMENTS

This book arose after seeing the enormous volume of excellent work carried out by our colleagues working with students on the MA for International Schools. The book was both inspired by them and written by them, and so it is to them that we are primarily indebted. They not only wrote their chapters, but did so cheerfully and without complaint during the tortuous process of the merger between the School of Education and Westminster College, forming the current Westminster Institute of Education at Oxford Brookes University, UK.

Our thanks also go to Martin Skelton from Fieldwork; already an 'honorary' member of Brookes in that he shares his experience every year with the management cohort, we are delighted that he agreed to do this for a wider audience. Dean Fink, a leader in the field of educational change, also shared his current thinking with us, and we are grateful to him for his insight. John Hardman, labouring under the delusion that his academic writing would end with his MA dissertation, was also prevailed upon to make the outcomes of his research available to other heads and teachers in international schools, and to him we owe our thanks as well.

Finally, our personal thanks go to Charlie and Derek, long-suffering 'academic widowers' left to fend for themselves while the computer whirred aloft.

SB and MS
May 2001

COPYRIGHT ACKNOWLEDGEMENTS

The authors and publishers would like to thank the following for granting permission to reproduce material in this work:

International Thompson Publishing for permission to reproduce Figure 1.1, originally published as 'Model for Self Management', derived from Caldwell, B.J. and Spinks, J.M. (1988) *The Self Managing School*, Lewes: Falmer Press.

Prentice Hall Australia/Pearson Education for permission to reproduce Table 2.1, originally published as 'Curriculum Orientations and Functions', adapted from Brady, L. and Kennedy, K. (1999) *Curriculum Construction*, Sydney: Prentice Hall.

Kogan Page Publishers for permission to reproduce Table 2.2, originally published as 'Categories of curriculum influence drawn on by international schools', adapted from Thompson, J. (1998) 'Towards a model for international education' in E. Hayden and J. Thompson (eds) *International Education: Principles and Practice*, London: Kogan Page.

Pearson Education for permission to reproduce Table 2.3, originally published as 'Curriculum Management Skills', adapted from Lofthouse, M., Bush, T., Coleman, M., O'Neill, J., West-Burnham, J. and Glover, D. (1995) *Managing the Curriculum*, London: Pitman Publishing.

Multilingual Matters Ltd for permission to reproduce Table 4.1, originally published as 'Types of Bilingual Education', simplified from Baker (1993) *Foundations of Bilingual Education and Bilingualism*, Clevedon: Multilingual Matters.

Dr B. Everard for permission to reproduce Figure 6.1, originally published as 'Systematic Approach to Change', Everard, K.B. and Morris, G. (1985) *Effective School Management*, London: Harper and Row.

Sage Publications for permission to reproduce Figure 6.1, originally published as Everard, K.B. and Morris, G. (1996, 3rd edn) *Effective School Management*, London: Paul Chapman Publications/Sage Publications.

Pearson Education for permission to reproduce Figure 6.2, originally published as 'Relationship between aims and objectives, strategic planning and school planning', adapted from Fidler, B. (1989) *Effective Local Management of Schools*, London: Financial Times Prentice Hall

Hay McBer for permission to reproduce Figure 7.1, originally published as 'Stages of learning in Kolb's "learning cycle" (1999)', Kolb, D. (1999) *Learning Style Inventory*, Boston: McBer and Co. © Experience-Based Learning Systems, Inc. 1999. Developed by David A Kolb. Reproduced with permission from Hay/McBer, 116 Huntington Ave., Boston, MA 02116, USA.

Pearson Education Ltd for permission to reproduce Figure 9.1, originally published as 'Middle management in context', Blandford, S. (1997) *Middle Management in Schools – How to Harmonise Managing and Teaching for an Effective School*, London: Pitman.

ABBREVIATIONS

AAIA	Association of Assessment Inspectors and Advisers
AICE	Advanced International Certificate of Education
A level	Advanced level
BICS	basic interpersonal communication skills
BoG	Board of Governors
CALP	cognitive and academic language proficiency
CERI	Centre for Educational Research and Innovation
CPD	continuing professional development
CSD	Commission on Sustainable Development
DfEE	Department for Education and Employment
EAL	English as an additional language
EB	European Baccalaureate
ECIS	European Council for International Schools
ESL	English as a second language
ESOL	English for speakers of other languages
GCSE	General Certificate of Secondary Education
HoD	head of department
IATEFL	International Association of Teachers of English as a Foreign Language
IB	International Baccalaureate
IBO	International Baccalaureate Organisation
ICT	information and communication technology
IEP	individual education plan
IGCSE	International General Certificate of Secondary Education
IiP	Investors in People
ISA	International Schools Association
ISCP	International Schools Curriculum Project
LEA	Local Education Authority
MA	Master of Arts (degree)
MBA	Master of Business Adminstration
MYP	Middle Years Programme (IB)
NASSP	National Association for Secondary School Principals

NATO	North Atlantic Treaty Organisation
NEAC	National Education Assessment Centre
NCATE	National Council for Administration and Teacher Education
OfSTED	Office for Standards in Education
OxCEM	Oxford Centre for Education Management
PD	power distance
PETA	Primary English Teachers' Association
PTA	parent–teacher association
PYP	Primary Years Programme (IB)
QCA	Qualifications and Curriculum Authority
R of A	record of achievement
SAT	scholastic aptitude test
SDP	school development plan
SEAL	Society for Effective Affective Learning
TESOL	Teaching English to Speakers of Other Languages
TQM	Total Quality Management
TTA	Teacher Training Agency
UA	uncertainty avoidance
Unesco	United Nations Educational, Scientific and Cultural Organisation

INTRODUCTION

The purpose of *Managing International Schools* is to provide practice-based management advice and guidance for all practitioners in international schools, thus raising the profile of school improvement within the international setting.

It arose out of necessity: students on the MA for International Schools at Oxford Brookes University, UK, were frustrated by the dearth of published material available to support them, not only in their studies but also in the development of their jobs in their international schools. This student body comprises teachers and headteachers in international schools throughout the world, all of them experienced in the international school circuit and clear about what they need. Over the last eight years, a wealth of knowledge and experience has built up, and conversations with students persuaded us to utilise this in order to benefit future generations of teachers in international schools.

Managing International Schools, therefore, is derived from the experience of both tutors and students, and it attempts to encapsulate some of the more challenging aspects of managing international schools. We do not pretend to cover systematically the whole range of school management topics. Other volumes do that more comprehensively. This book rather focuses on some of the specific issues that, through experience, we have found our students to need in particular. Hayden and Thompson published *International Education: Principles and Practice* in 1998, and Brookes' students have found that volume most useful in their studies; this book attempts to complement their volume.

In addressing management issues this book moves towards the international school of the future, where managers and teachers are leading educators and managers of the educational needs of their students. In providing the reader with ideas on how to manage themselves, their colleagues and the curriculum, this book aims to provoke thought and to enhance the good practice that exists in many schools on the international circuit. Thus, *Managing International Schools* focuses on the development of management thinking and practice within the international context.

Defining this context is a difficult task, and others have engaged with the nature of international schools and international education (for example Hayden and Thompson, 1998, 2000). In terms of phase, size and sex, international schools defy definition: they may include kindergarten, primary, middle and upper, higher or secondary pupils, or incorporate all of these in a combined school; they may range in number from twenty to 4500; they could be co-educational or single sex. The governance and management of such schools might be determined by the school, the owner, the board, the senior management team or head of school or a managing agency. Many argue over what constitutes an 'international school', and whether or not an 'international education' is provided: the range and variety is huge. At one extreme are the virtually single-culture schools, working to their own national curriculum and taught largely by own-national staff, but operating in a different country in order to educate children of expatriates working in that country; there are many British and American schools like this in capital cities around the world. Students from the local community who enrol do so very much on the founder's agenda. At the other extreme are the international schools which genuinely cater for many different nationalities, such as the European schools. Between these poles are others, such as the bicultural schools of Latin America or the English-medium schools of India and Africa, which provide an education mainly for local students with the help of teachers and some elements of curriculum and/or examination boards from overseas.

Suffice to say that *Managing International Schools* is addressed to the whole of this range: young people across the world need educating, and teachers have challenging jobs to do in managing this learning. This book is about understanding what management, in many different facets, is, and how effective management can lead to raising student achievement within an international context. But it is more: in addition to the challenges of managing schools, the book also addresses some of the features of international schools which make them special. One such example is the exciting mix of cultures represented among the staff: as well as producing unexpected delights and sociological advantages, this same characteristic can also present management challenges. The diverse and itinerant parent clientele is also a special case. Whether they are nationals of the country in which the school is placed or expatriates who are sojourning in the country for a limited time, as consumers – the 'new diaspora' of Willis et al. (1994) – they have particular expectations of the international schools in which their children are educated in terms of language teaching, information, communication and technology skills – as well as external examinations. Parents may be very conscious of the need for their children either to return to a national education system or to transfer to the next international school in another part of the world, and they need to be sure of the appropriate curriculum and the right assessment procedures to smooth this move. Language is a further particular issue, and needs specialist and sensitive attention. It is expectations such as these, together with the frequently rapid – even abrupt – staff turnover, that put pressure on international schools and their managers to adopt practices that accommodate these established patterns.

In this context, then, *Managing International Schools* addresses issues real to practitioners at all levels in the school, providing teachers, middle and senior managers, headteachers, principals, patrons and boards with a practical framework for management, support, development and improvement. Aimed at teachers, managers, trainers and educators, *Managing International Schools* provides guidance on the development of senior and middle managers and teachers by drawing together the best practices from a range of international schools through school-based research. The philosophy of the book is that the reader should have unambiguous 'takeaways', or practical ideas, from each chapter.

In addition to serving a need for school practice, we hope that lecturers in higher education, trainers, researchers and other educational professionals will also find *Managing International Schools* useful in understanding and supporting life in international schools. In practice, school managers create, maintain and develop conditions which enable effective learning to take place, and it is within this framework that this book seeks to provide both practical advice and food for thought.

In order to meet this agenda, most of the authors of the chapters in *Managing International Schools* are teachers and tutors who lead tracks and modules on the international MA programme. The authors are also experienced consultants in international schools and the international setting. In addition to the staff at the Westminster Institute at Oxford Brookes, we are privileged and delighted to have three guest authors. Ex-student John Hardman was persuaded to share with a wider audience his interesting and relevant MA research findings of what makes teachers apply for, and remain in, jobs in international schools. Dr Dean Fink, who hardly needs an introduction on the international circuit, has been kind enough to give us an update on his thinking on change in schools. Martin Skelton, Director of Fieldwork Ltd, also needs no introduction: his wisdom derives from many years of experience in international schools, and he is also a regular teacher on the MA programme.

Using *Managing International Schools*

By placing practitioners at the centre of each chapter, we aim to provide recent and relevant material that will assist you in developing professionally within the international school setting. You should therefore know and understand your role and the role of your students within your own setting, and be aware of your own needs and personal goals.

As a practitioner, you will have your own agenda when using this book. You may like to read it through in its entirety, or you may find it more useful to dip and select. In order to help you find your way around, the remainder of this chapter gives an outline of each of the other chapters, explaining how they relate to each other.

The general layout of the book is uncomplicated: after an initial chapter on the nature of international school leadership, Chapters 2, 3 and 4 look at specific aspects of curriculum management; Chapters 5–11 then address broader management issues.

The first chapter sets the scene for the rest of the book by exploring *the nature of international school leadership*. Management texts are filled with theory, models and advice on how to improve leadership in general commercial settings, but how applicable are these to life in school, with its relentless throughput of students and its complex human relationships? More importantly for this publication, is it possible to characterise leadership of *international* schools? The chapter identifies ways in which international school leadership is special, and draws on research to examine the pivotal relationship between headteacher and board of governors.

In Chapter 2, Simon Catling writes about *developing the curriculum in international schools*. His broad experience derives from interacting with international schools and teaching on the MA programme since its inception. What pupils learn in international schools is in part the result of what the school sets out to teach them but is also the result of what happens incidentally, even accidentally, as it is never possible to control the variety of experiences that pupils have in school. Catling believes that an international school should provide an opportunity for its pupils to learn in an environment which is concerned with developing their capabilities, understanding, emotions and social relationships with an international dimension in mind. This chapter examines the nature of curriculum with a view to indicating some of the possibilities for internationalising the curriculum, while recognising that often the influence of the home nation can be very strong. It argues that the choice of curriculum will depend on key decisions about the basis for the curriculum and that the management of the curriculum and of changes to it depend on an appreciation of the responsibilities of curriculum managers and an analytical approach to curriculum development. In providing an insight into the international curriculum, Catling highlights values based on intercultural learning, the use of culturally varied teaching strategies and teaching materials gleaned from a variety of cultural sources, drawing on the experience of a diverse school community (Sylvester, 1998; Thompson, 1998). Managing the curriculum is more than just a matter of agreeing content, teaching strategies and materials: it involves the whole process of schooling and reflects the nature of the decisions about staffing, resources, priorities and directions.

The next chapter is written by an experienced specialist in assessment, Robin McClelland. He describes how *managing assessment in the international school* can be improved by theoretical and pragmatic ideas that are challenging and engaging. He debates the validity of the traditional pattern of assessment – measuring achievement at the end of a phase of education – interrogating whether this is relevant to the future of today's students, who could enter the world of work to jobs that we are only beginning to imagine. The attitudes, skills and knowledge valued in the new work place could be difficult to teach and assess in an examination system that is still largely based on a nineteenth century understanding of education. McClelland argues that assessment is an integral part of planning and teaching in all schools, and that it is at its most effective where there is a whole-school approach. Assessment information must be meaningful and specific to parents and students. Parents whose work requires them to be residents of a number of different countries while their children are of school age expect comparative data that allow them to gauge progress and compare standards with specific national education systems. McClelland's wealth of sound advice stems from years of experience working with international schools on assessment.

Another experienced author, Jackie Holderness, concludes this first cluster of curriculum-focused chapters with her practical analysis of *teaching and managing English as an additional or second language in international schools*. Examples of language provision are taken from American, British and Australian systems, and also from recent research by international school teachers studying at Oxford Brookes University which focused on managing and teaching 'global nomads' (McCaig, 1992). Holderness's experience as an international schools consultant, and her writing of language texts, leads her to conclude that international schools are interlingual and intercultural institutions, and that one of the main challenges to school management, therefore, is ensuring that every international school teacher sees him- or herself as an English as an additional language (EAL) teacher.

The second cluster of chapters is introduced by one of our guest authors, Dr Dean Fink. In the management of an international school, perhaps the only consistent feature is the expectation of change, and Fink has chosen *learning to change and changing to learn* as the theme of Chapter 5. An established senior manager and researcher in international settings, Fink begins by asking international colleagues, 'What is our core business?' As McClelland raised the issue of the changing world, so does Fink; practitioners are now responsible for preparing pupils for another century. Critically, Fink advises that 'innovation is something you do instead of – not on top of'. In a world of rapidly changing social forces in which every aspect of society is experiencing pressure for change, Fink advises that schools must keep their mandate to promote student learning as the 'holy grail' towards which all their efforts are directed. To this end, his chapter emphasises how school communities need to review continually what it takes to prepare students for this shifting world into which they have been born. Fink concludes that, to achieve the changes necessary to promote new and more challenging approaches to learning, schools will have to learn how to change through asking better questions, and his 'change frames' model is introduced as a vehicle for this interrogation. His chapter provides both the complexity of argument and simplicity of practical pointers required for the management and sustainability of change.

Sustainability is also central to the next theme, in which Professor John Welton highlights the complexities and difficulties of *planning: the art of the possible*. He develops the theme that planning and management are processes of successive approximations. When planners become really effective, they have a greater chance of achieving something like their original intention. Dwight D. Eisenhower is alleged to have said, 'planning is everything, plans are nothing'. For the individual child, the outcomes of planning are crucial: school-age years are not repeatable, and children need schools to respond flexibly to meet their individual needs as they occur. Based on the author's experience of working with senior and middle managers of international schools over the last 15 years, in addition to leading a university department, this chapter develops the principle that organisations can work well or badly as either loosely or tightly coupled systems (Weick, 1976). However, lack of shared planning can make it very difficult for board members, staff and parents to communicate effectively, and to understand how changes in one part of a school may affect other parts. In practice, Welton concludes that while good planning may not guarantee success it will at least increase the chance of success and reduce risk. By planning the future of a school, from money to staffing, from curriculum to governance, the chance of success is multiplied and the risk of failure is drastically reduced. The aim of planning, then, is not to predict the future precisely but to improve the chances of achieving future objectives.

Linda Squire takes the theme of *school improvement and professional development in international schools* for Chapter 7. This is a practically based chapter which sets out to explore a model based on the concept of concentricity, in which 'best value' principles of economy, effectiveness and efficiency are met through the careful alignment of individual and institutional development goals. Writing as an ex-headteacher and an educational consultant, Squire examines the ways in which schools that choose to do so may become 'learning organisations' through their approaches to professional development. She presents a rationale for investing in continuing professional development (CPD), introduces a specimen school policy for CPD which can be adapted for use in any school and discusses the concept of personal professional development planning. Squire addresses squarely the knotty issue of financing staff development – a notoriously inconsistent commodity in international schools. She offers a 'best value' rationale for use in persuading funders, administrators, budget holders and directors that structured investment in the development of human resources is crucial to the success of international schools as businesses.

Improving recruitment and retention of quality overseas teachers is the topic of Chapter 8. Building on his experience as an international school head, the second of our guest authors, John Hardman, notes that 'outside the home, international children's most important relationships and activities are centred around the school, with their classmates and their teachers. For the children, the international school and its microcosm, the classroom, is their community.' But how stable and consistent *is* this community if the teachers themselves are part of a transient population, rarely in any one school for more than two years? Can quality teachers be persuaded to work at the school, and then be retained beyond their short contract? If so, how? Hardman seeks to address this issue, offering an insight based on his MA research into the successful staffing of international schools, arguably one of the most important functions in any manager's job description. He identifies the incentives and conditions that might motivate good teachers to remain in a school beyond their original contract and to become keenly involved in school affairs within and outside the classroom, promoting that desired sense of stability and consistency. Hardman found that a pattern in the profiles emerged, which made it possible to identify various categories of teachers applying to work in international schools and to formulate some practical guidelines that may serve to increase managers' effectiveness in recruiting, sustaining and retaining good overseas staff.

The emergence of *middle management in international schools* is addressed in Chapter 9, in which Sonia Blandford provides an insight into the 'player–manager' role of a practising middle manager, exploring the hybrid role of teachers who manage. As an established researcher and practitioner, she relates modernist theoretical views to practice relevant to all practitioners. After a brief introduction to the international school setting, a description of middle management is followed by a discussion on practical issues relating to the role of middle managers. There is a particular focus on team leadership and management, and the chapter concludes with a 'framework for practice' derived from the literature that is helpful for aspiring and practising middle managers.

One of the key characteristics of international schools is the mix of cultures represented among the staff, and Chapter 10 explores some implications for managers who wish to obtain the best from teams of students and teachers. *Managing mixed-culture teams in international schools* is a chapter which is based on Marian Shaw's own research, and her management training and consultancy experiences in many international schools. The chapter largely consists of ten real cases of misunderstanding which are analysed by reference to cross-cultural social psychology research. It emphasises the need for the creation of a positive organisational culture in the school itself, and concludes with a practical framework for investigating misunderstandings which might be due to culture. It is hoped that the examples given, together with the theory summarised, will heighten awareness of the complexities of cultural issues.

Central to *Managing International Schools* is the issue of *creating standards and raising performance*. Martin Skelton, the third of our guest authors, draws on his vast experience of managing, supporting, training and consulting in international schools to present this topic in Chapter 11. The chapter examines some of the difficulties particular to international schools, and then points the way to some of the standards and elements of consistency which might matter more to international schools than schools in other contexts. Skelton explores how standards might be created, and identifies the key questions that schools should ask themselves. He concludes by describing different contributions that students, teachers, schools and boards can make to raising performance in international schools. The concepts described in this chapter can be applied to almost any aspect of international school life, and, if implemented with professional rigour, can help to create a culture of improvement.

This summarises the chapters ahead. We hope you will enjoy the eclectic mix of styles adopted by different authors. Some give an overview of the current scene, some use a self-help approach with materials useful in training, some write an essay to present their own perspective on an issue, and some augment their arguments with outcomes from their own research. Whatever your preferred approach and topics, we wish you fruitful browsing.

References

Hayden, M. and Thompson, J. (eds) (1998) *International Education: Principles and Practice*, London: Kogan Page.

Hayden, M. and Thompson, J. (2000) 'International education: flying flags or raising standards?', *International Schools Journal* 19 (2): 48–56.

McCaig, N.M. (1992) 'Birth of a Nation', *The Global Nomad Quarterly* 1: 1–2.

Sylvester, R. (1998) 'Through the lens of diversity: inclusive and encapsulated school missions', in E. Hayden and J. Thompson (eds) *International Education: Principles and Practice*, London: Kogan Page.

Thompson, J. (1998) 'Towards a model for international education', in E. Hayden and J. Thompson (eds) *International Education: Principles and Practice*, London: Kogan Page.

Weick, K.E. (1976) 'Educational organisations as loosely coupled systems', *Administrative Science Quarterly* 21: 1–19.

Willis, D., Enloe, W. and Minoura, Y. (1994) 'Transculturals, transnationals: the new diaspora', *International Schools Journal* 14: 29–42.

1

THE NATURE OF INTERNATIONAL SCHOOL LEADERSHIP

Sonia Blandford and Marian Shaw

Introduction

The effective running of schools has been subject to scrutiny in recent years, but there is a paucity of documentary evidence concerning leadership of *international* schools. There is a real need of such educational provision in order to service the needs of what Willis et al. (1994) term 'the new diaspora': those expatriates who find themselves working in different parts of the world, bringing with them their children who need to obtain an education that will serve them well for the next stage in their development, whether this is a return to a school in their home country, a transfer to another international school or progression to higher education.

Leadership of any school is determined by its function, which in turn is affected by its patrons, usually the board of governors, directors or trustees. The structures, systems and policies on which each school is based are all designed, in theory at least, to achieve the most desirable outcomes for students in terms of quality delivery of curricula and student outcomes. Many research projects based on national systems (for example Rutter et al., 1979) highlight the importance of the school leader in the effectiveness of the school, and there is a strong probability that this also applies to international schools, although research on the subject is scarce. Unlike national schools, however, international schools are often 'islands' with minimal reference to authorities beyond the local community, sustaining more autonomy. But does this make the task of school management any easier? Malpass (1994: 22) is relatively pessimistic about the way in which international schools are run: 'despite many years of independent management experience, it is still the case that certain schools continue to run into management difficulties. Many heads and boards, it seems, have either forgotten, or indeed have never learnt, the basic principles of good school management.' The mention of the board here is central: several studies of international schools have demonstrated that problematic relationships between the board and the school make the task of the school leader more complex.

It is in this context that the chapter attempts to explore the parameters of international school leadership. It does not set out to be a text on leadership *per se*, but rather to investigate how some of the leadership theory applies to international schools with their very specific environments. The role of the board of governors is also addressed, looking especially at the relationship between the board and the school leader (henceforth termed the 'headteacher' or 'head', but also embracing the term 'principal').

School leadership theory

Throughout the twentieth century, leadership in the administration of organisations was a popular subject to pursue in business and industry, but, predictably, education, underfunded as ever, came at the impoverished end of research. Greenfield (1991), however, made a special study of the administration of schools, focusing closely on how this differed from administration elsewhere. His study finds that 'school principals rely much more extensively upon leadership than do their administrative counterparts in other settings' (Greenfield, 1991: 5) because of features unique to schools: student character, student subculture and the nature of the teacher–student relationship.

Greenfield also identifies other specific features of managing in school settings which influence the way that the head leads the school: 'most of the work of the principal involves face-to-face communication; it is action oriented; it is reactive; the presented problems are unpredictable; the principal must rely on others for information and frequently must make decisions without accurate or complete information' (ibid.: 6).

Perhaps it is helpful here to differentiate between management and leadership. Many have offered definitions but they may be summarised by Zaleznik (1977), who classifies managers as people who define themselves and others by their own roles in their organisation and who are relatively impersonal. Leaders, on the other hand, are portrayed as more person-focused, relating to others empathetically and intuitively, generating excitement and being imaginative in developing options and seeking opportunities for change. Others have described management as coming from the *head* (getting things done by logical systems) and leadership as coming from the *heart* (generating enthusiasm so that people want to succeed). One might draw a parallel here between what Bass (1985), based on the ideas of Burns (1978), describes as the *transactional* way of leading an organisation compared with the more exciting *transformational* way. The transformational leader motivates others to higher levels of interest and performance through enthusiasm, inspiration, intellectual stimulation and a personally oriented approach.

So, what does a headteacher need in order to inspire and lead an international school community? Can a transformational style be learned, or is it innate? Various theories and models have been developed which analyse leadership styles effective under different circumstances. If we accept Greenfield's analysis, the 'situational leadership' model of Blanchard et al. (1985) would appear to be particularly appropriate for school leadership in that it focuses closely on choosing the *appropriate style* for a *particular individual* who is undertaking a *specific task*. It reflects and augments the work of Tannenbaum and Schmidt (1958), who defined appropriate leadership styles in terms of the needs of the leader, the led, the task and the organisation, relating this to a continuum of management influence.

One approach to identifying and analysing the contribution that different headteacher attributes make to the quality of their administration has been the competencies movement, such as the US-based National Association for Secondary School Principals (NASSP), and the UK-based National Education Assessment Centre (NEAC). They produced lists, against which practising or aspiring headteachers could be assessed (see Box 1.1).

Some argue that leadership cannot be defined by lists, and that these do, in fact, limit the horizons of imaginative leadership. Grace (1995: 5) describes 'the commodification of school leadership' as reductionist, and categorises it more as management than leadership. He argues for the more flexible 'policy scholarship' approach to deepen understanding offered via the school's 'historical, theoretical, cultural and socio-political setting' (ibid.: 3).

The job of leading a school into the future, conducting it safely through change, has been likened to conducting an orchestra, ensuring that all instruments play in harmony. Huberman (1992) projects this one stage further with his jazz metaphor, pointing out that change is continuous, 'the metaphor is not the orchestra, with its methodological rehearsals, but rather the jazz group, improvising continuously within the bounds of implicit understandings, even rituals, among its members about melodic progression' (ibid.: 9).

Box 1.1 The twelve competencies of the National Educational Assessment Centre (UK)

- Problem analysis
- Judgement
- Organisational ability
- Decisiveness
- Leadership
- Sensitivity
- Stress tolerance
- Oral communication
- Written communication
- Range of interest
- Personal motivation
- Educational values

Source: Green et al. (1991).

While systems, logic and planning for the future are clearly necessary as a guide, or a map, writers who have studied the phenomenon of school leadership acknowledge that the job is too complex for its components to be limited by definitions. In Chapter 6 of this book, Welton writes about the necessity of leaders breaking the rules, intuitively getting the best out of the situation for everyone – but only once they have a thorough grounding in what 'the rules' are. Jones (1987) also concluded in her study of headteachers that a break from logic was necessary: 'strategic management has to take account of the psychological, sociological, political and systemic characteristics of complex organisations. Logic and rational argument are certainly not enough' (Jones, 1987: 195). Fink's 'change frames', introduced in Chapter 5 of this book, develop this theme further, providing a structure for the examination of school complexity through 'multiple lenses'.

In his work on leadership, Greenfield (1991) identifies five 'situational imperatives', or dimensions, which apply in particular to those leading schools, pointing out that it is the first of these, the managerial dimension, which has received the most attention, but that the other four dimensions are also central to the successful fulfilment of the role of headteacher. The five dimensions characterise 'role demands' (Box 1.2) encountered by school leaders which are 'interactive and constitute the very fabric of the school administrator's milieu' (ibid.: 12), although 'the nature of the relationships among these five role-demands is not entirely clear' (ibid.: 13).

These writers on educational leadership all appear to be saying the same thing in different ways: although the skills of management are essential for school leaders in order to maintain daily school operations, good leadership is more than that. Books focus on management skills because they are easier to identify, to rationalise, to train for and to reproduce. But true leadership qualities are more elusive. So where does this leave the leader wishing to develop his/her skills?

Box 1.2 Greenfield's five role demands of school leaders

> *Managerial:* managing the daily school operations necessary to sustain the enterprise
> *Instructional:* supporting and improving the school's instructional goals and activities, and the associated work of teachers, parents and students
> *Political:* developing and utilising power to influence the allocation of resources and the conflicting and competing special interests of school participants
> *Social:* working through people, directly and indirectly, to accomplish the daily work of the school
> *Moral:* making normative judgements regarding standards and moral values that shape school life

Source: Greenfield (1991: 13).

The ability to observe, analyse and reappraise everyday actions is a skill which can be practised. Sometimes known as critical reflection, 'it seeks to infuse the teaching profession with a new set of insights and understanding about school process' (Hargreaves, 1989: 57). Perhaps it is the process whereby Greenfield's five dimensions are brought together through lateral thinking? As Berlak and Berlak (1987: 169) describe it,

→ Generative ?

> critical thought is a process of freeing oneself from dependence upon taken-for-granted ways of viewing and acting in the world, and seriously entertaining and evaluating alternative possibilities... to evaluate alternative courses of action we must see connections among every day events, patterns of behaviour, and cultural, social, political and economic forces. In a phrase, it is to seek the relationship of 'micro' to 'macro'.

Whatever this elusive quality of leadership is, a strong focus on people emerges very clearly. If the leader's job is to achieve through the actions of others, then s/he must act in such a way as to earn the respect and personal loyalty from staff. Indeed, Etzioni (1965: 690) defines leadership as 'the ability, based on the personal qualities of the leader, to elicit the follower's voluntary compliance in a broad range of matters.' This concept of 'voluntary compliance' must be earned – it cannot come from status alone. Greenfield (1991: 3) identifies two sources of influence available to the headteacher, 'position power and personal influence', and points out that both are used. Personal influence is more substantial, however, as 'a principal who must resort to influence on the basis of authority derived from position or office ... diminishes his or her ability to lead. This is especially true in a school' (ibid.: 26).

At an implementation level, Jones (1987: 193) found that in order to carry out innovation through others 'you have to show trust, suspend disbelief, recognise problems and risk-taking as inevitable, give people full credit for their achievements and support if they run into difficulties.'

The skill of the headteacher, then, is to get teachers *voluntarily* to change practice for school improvement, but, as Greenfield (1991) points out, school leaders are only likely to do this if it will either make their own work easier or be in the best interests of the students. It therefore becomes essential to know one's staff well enough to be able to understand what motivates individual members, and what therefore might elicit voluntary changes in teachers. Greenfield places the responsibility on the followers: they take action according to the behaviour of the leader: 'consent is temporary, it must be earned, and it can be both given to and taken away from leaders by followers' (ibid.: 25). This he describes as 'leadership-as-consent'.

If leadership of today's schools, then, is heavily dependent on micropolitical interactions, what sort of people make the best headteachers? Many studies (for example Marshall, 1984; Ozga, 1993) indicate that leadership traits displayed by women tend to be both more flexible and more person-oriented, relying on their interactions with people to build loyalty into their relationships at work, thus inspiring Etzioni's (1965) 'voluntary compliance'. There is much in this stereotypical management style which is consistent with the rationale for the interpersonal approach to leadership described above. Does this mean that women make better headteachers? Statistically, women occupy a small percentage of the senior posts in education, and international schools would appear to be no different. In Thearle's (1999) study, less than 20 per cent of international school headteachers were female, although more than 50 per cent of the staff were female. In Hawley's (1994) survey, only 12 per cent of the 336 heads in his sample were women. Why is this? The statistics are similar to those in national schools, but are the reasons the same? Certainly, there are special circumstances surrounding many of the international schools, such as women following male partners to overseas contracts, leaving their own career development to serendipity. It may be that some of these circumstances have a significant effect on who chooses to apply for headship overseas, but more research is needed before the reasons are fully understood.

 Sexism?

Is leadership of international schools different?

The discussion to this point has focused largely on the complexities of school leadership in general. We turn now to identify ways in which leadership of international schools might be different. Although the school as an organisation may be similar to national schools, this does, of course, give a huge scope or variety. As pointed out in the introduction, 'the standard international school' defies description – there are so many different categories and constitutions. Nevertheless, certain features tend, in general, to distinguish international schools in terms of the way in which they work:

- *Differing parental expectations:* Pearce (1991) highlights the dissonance that can occur between the parents' *belief* of what schools are about and the *reality*. Some of this dissonance may be due to cultural differences, and some may concern misunderstandings of the aims and methods of the school.
- *Staff and student turnover:* when this is very high, it may have a destabilising effect on the school (Hawley, 1994, 1995; Malpass, 1994).
- *The head's own precarious position:* there is less security of tenure for a headteacher in an international school than in most national schools: being fired is a frequent occurrence.
- *Over-involvement of board members in school business:* this is another common challenge to the leadership of international schools, and a major reason for heads leaving their posts, as discussed later.
- *In-country laws/education policies:* these may, depending on the country, influence the curriculum offered and/or the ages at which examinations can be taken; they may therefore influence student destinations.

- *Ephemeral and itinerant membership of the board of governors:* this may result in sketchy attendance at board meetings and lack of continuity. Members may be replaced with such frequency that the lack of continuity becomes a seriously debilitating feature of school management.
- *The mixed-culture nature of staff, students and board,* all of which present extra challenges to the school leader. Not only do they have to manage the consequences of intercultural interaction, but there may also be difficult decisions and judgements to be made about staff recruitment in the interests of achieving the right balance for the school community.

  Selecting another example, if Etzioni's 'voluntary compliance' is to be harnessed in the staff, is the task for the school leader compounded by the mixed-culture nature of the staff? 'Standard' motivation theories do not apply to everyone equally: Maslow's (1943) well-known hierarchy of needs makes the assumption that the goal is self-actualisation, but this theory was developed in an individualist and masculine culture (see Chapter 10) and is not necessarily appropriate in other cultures. As Hofstede says, the order of Maslow's categories would need to be shuffled according to culture before school leaders might identify what motivates the people in their team of staff (Hofstede, 1991: 126). This example of potential mismatch extends to areas of training too: staff development co-ordinators in school would do well to consider the cultural origin of models, theories and even training techniques before applying them in their schools, or before introducing them via brought-in consultants and training experts (Shaw and Welton, 1996).
- *Choosing the right balance of curriculum:* the international school has a broader menu of possibilities to select from than national schools: should it be international, such as International Baccalaureate (IB), Advanced International Certificate of Education (AICE), International General Certificate of Secondary Education (IGCSE), or national, linking into a single country's examination systems to enable easy transition back in the home country? Or should it be a combination of these? The choice may not be straightforward, as discussed by Catling in the next chapter.
- *The headteacher's relationship with the board of governors:* this may be more challenging than in many national schools, although, whatever the nature of the school, much hinges on individual characters and the climate of the school. There does appear to be a change in the pattern of tenure in international schools from long-term board members and heads to much shorter term, but, in Littleford's (1999) view, the pendulum has swung too far, resulting in short-termism and instability.

Values and school culture

Values underpin the entire operation of the school. They may be implicit, in which case they risk not being recognised, or explicit, which leaves less to chance. In either case, they establish the environment for everything that happens in the school. In Greenfield's (1986: 166) words, 'organisations are built on the unification of people around values'. But values cannot be seen, so how does anyone know what they might be? Boards and headteachers may articulate these, but unless they are manifestly 'lived' they are meaningless. A school might commonly articulate its 'vision' (where the school is heading) and its 'mission' (its sense of purpose), and from these a set of values may – on paper at least – be derived. It is more likely, however, that people make judgements about school values by observing the reactions and behaviours of the people who make up the school community. This, in its turn, creates the school culture or climate, which reciprocally influences future actions (see Chapter 10).

It is interesting to observe that whenever a group of international school teachers is asked what their school's mission is, a very common response is, 'I know we've got one, but I can't tell you what it is.' Headteachers, on the other hand, usually *can* cite their mission. Cambridge observes that in the school there are diverse expectations of this concept: a mission may be seen as something the board of governors invents, and 'it is doubtful if this has the wholehearted support of all the staff. Different educational values are expressed by various members of the school community' (Cambridge, 1998: 199). This is true in any school: roles and positions flavour perceptions. But how much more complex this is where the school community is pluralistic as well. Rodger, studying moral values in such an international school setting, is convinced that 'we need to move beyond merely competing convictions and (especially) clashing ideologies to meet each other in our fundamental nature as human beings – not so as to obliterate our identities, rather to recognise the fact that they are particular ways of being human' (Rodger, 1995: 53).

Headteachers need to be aware of these differing perceptions and values, as their moral judgement affects the morale and willingness of the staff to collaborate. If, for example, a school leader sets up a façade of consultation for change when all concerned know that a decision has already been made, staff may be understandably demoralised, which will affect their future attitude towards the school, the system or the head. On the whole, people prefer honest dictatorship to autocracy dressed up as democracy. Hargreaves (1994) describes the problem of manipulative headteachers who attempt to contrive collegiality.

As discussed in Chapter 10, many international schools are constituted, either deliberately or by default, on Western-centric cultural assumptions, even though the school community itself may embrace a huge range of pluralistic values. One might argue that parents who decide to educate their children at the school are *de facto* selecting and subscribing to the values that this particular school upholds. But parents choose international schools for many different reasons, not least being the best option in the region to provide their children with a privileged start in life. Once there, however, they may perceive ideological differences that make them uncomfortable. Some parents, and teachers also, may see that their own traditional values are, as Cambridge puts it, 'being overwhelmed by the "international style" of Western liberal humanism that embodies the so-called internationalism of the school. Their attitude is that tolerance of all points of view, or cultural relativism, is not the hallmark of having strong values but, rather, the outcome of a lack of values' (Cambridge, 1998: 199).

If parents disagree in some way with the school, they have several possible alternatives: they can take action, which often means lobbying the board of governors – even getting elected to it; they can mutter about the school outside its boundaries – judging it through a 'trial by gossip'; or they can decide to do nothing in complicit acceptance. The last of these options quite often pertains, as it is the easy way out, and parents may in any case be intimidated by the school. But the first option, which demands most energy, and is therefore taken up least frequently, may present headteachers with some of their biggest challenges. Hawley's (1994, 1995) research on American-style international schools indicates that a significant number of parents join the board of governors in order to press for changes in some way. While sometimes being uncomfortable for the head, this approach is at least visible, unlike the second of the three options above. Muttering outside the school has the disadvantage that the headteacher may never get to hear what is being said in the community, particularly where there are factions of culture or language, and this is fertile ground for suppressed dissension to fester.

School values are subtly affected by the way language is used to describe everyday school activities. Davies posits that the use of military language applied to leadership of schools mitigates against establishing a collaborative or enquiring culture: 'steering a tight ship, marshalling the troops, patrolling the corridors' depict schools as battlefields 'where the enemy is the children'. This has an effect on school outcomes, as 'one thing a military regime will not try to produce is questioning participants' (Davies 1994: 5).

School management issues

The discussion turns now, albeit briefly, from leadership to management issues – those organisational features that enable the school to function. A plethora of school management texts can be found on the shelves of bookshops and libraries, and this chapter does not attempt to replicate them; its purpose is rather to interrogate the issues of structures, planning and accountability through the eyes of the international school leader.

Structures

Deciding on the most appropriate structure for the functioning of the school is a matter of both management and leadership, and is settled at the board/senior management team level. Most headteachers find that they inherit a management structure on arrival in post – which is not to say that it cannot be changed. In fact, international school structures are good candidates for change at present. There is increasing evidence that the structure needed to serve the International Baccalaureate's Primary Years Programme and Middle Years Programme is at odds with the traditional structures of international schools, and that a structural review is overdue.

The structure itself is, perhaps, less significant than the way it operates, which can be summarised as the way people communicate inside the system. Do, for example, deputies and other teachers accept real responsibility for leadership at levels below headship, or does the head feel the need to control everything closely? As Jones found, in her research on headteachers, 'the very difficult skill to arrive at is the ability to empower and motivate the deputies and staff as a whole, without at the same time weakening and undermining one's own authority as head' (Jones, 1987: 77). If a headteacher misjudges this, s/he increases the gap between intended and actual teacher empowerment.

If the school operates to an agreed structure, tasks, roles and responsibilities as well as channels of communication are all defined (Mullins, 1999), which gives people a better chance of understanding the parameters of their own jobs. The degree of team autonomy or of decentralisation in any school is a matter of choice of what is most appropriate under the circumstances: the important thing is that it is well understood and consistent.

Caldwell and Spinks (1988), in their work on self-managing schools, developed and refined (Caldwell and Spinks, 1991) a model that seemed to encapsulate the best practice in schools which they considered to be effective. This model (Figure 1.1) allows sufficient autonomy within school teams for people to be creative about the team tasks, while at the same time operating within an agreed policy framework.

Being able to make decisions about one's own area of work is more motivating than carrying out handed-down instructions, and the tasks tend to be performed more successfully as a result. Such team tasks in an international school might include delivering an area of the curriculum, looking after the personal and social development of a year group or co-ordinating a cross-curricular area, such as language development, or community service.

This is not a model which can be imposed, unrehearsed, on a staffroom; it would seem to need:

1   a board of governors that understands the model and has sufficient confidence in the headteacher and the staff to allow them to fulfil their designated roles without interference;
2   a headteacher prepared to delegate with authority;
3   a school climate which helps staff to grow through their mistakes;
4   staff prepared to take risks;
5   a degree of stability in order to develop over time.

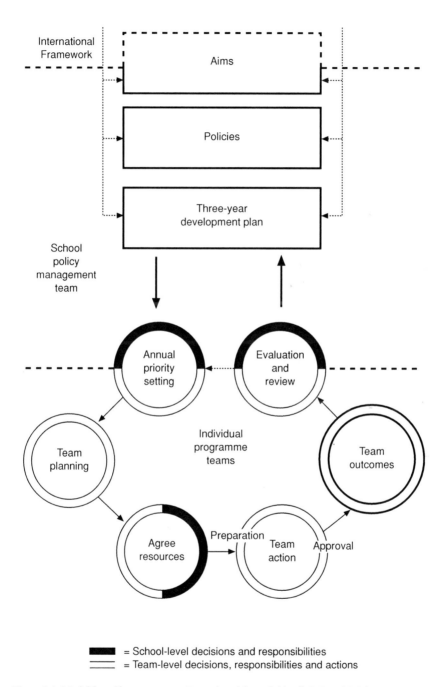

International
Framework

Aims

Policies

Three-year
development plan

School
policy
management
team

Annual
priority
setting

Evaluation
and
review

Team
planning

Individual
programme
teams

Team
outcomes

Agree
resources

Preparation

Team
action

Approval

Team
outcomes

■■■ = School-level decisions and responsibilities
= Team-level decisions, responsibilities and actions

Figure 1.1 Model for self-management. Reproduced from Caldwell, B.J. and Spinks, J.M. (1988)
The Self Managing School, Lewes: Falmer Press, with permission from International
Thompson Publishing.

Where there is a high degree of instability in the school leadership and staff turnover, far from improving the operation of the school, the introduction of a decentralised system such as this might be more confusing than helpful.

The structure described in the Caldwell and Spinks model is consonant with Kanter's (1983) 'participative' organisation, and, given the conditions outlined above, conducive to change in the school. Kanter identifies participative behaviours and flatter organisational structures as being more capable of responding flexibly to new situations, and of taking responsibility at team level. The greater formality of hierarchical organisations, on the other hand, while being useful to maintain routines, may become a barrier to change. But, as discussed later in the book, international schools, with their mixed-culture staff, students, board and parents, exhibit a range of different responses to consultative leadership behaviours. The international school leader therefore needs to tread a very fine line of judgement in selecting and using appropriate structures and styles: what appears to be a strength in one culture can appear to be a weakness in another (Hofstede, 1991).

Structure also has an effect on communication, controlling the way it flows upwards, downwards or sideways. A particular point of interest is the 'gatekeeper' post, such as B in Figure 1.2.

B might be, for example, a deputy head (where A is the head and C the teachers or heads of department), but the way schools work, unlike other organisations, means that virtually every teacher in the school occupies this position to some extent, including the classroom teacher. This person controls the flow of information down from above and upwards from below. Gatekeeper *positions* are inevitable, but they only become dangerous if the people occupying these posts *behave* as gatekeepers: information may be distorted, manipulated or withheld in either direction, sometimes deliberately and sometimes through ignorance or misunderstanding. The potential for abuse is huge, and schools

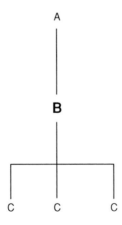

Figure 1.2 The 'gatekeeper' position.

must seek to minimise the potential of such 'gatekeeper behaviour'. The strongly hierarchical pattern makes it easier for information to be controlled and manipulated, while the participative approach allows freer flow of information in all directions – upwards, downwards and laterally. Once more, the manifestation of school values is paramount: if those in power lead by example, there is less likelihood of communication problems at lower levels.

Planning

Many texts provide information to help with planning (for example Everard and Morris, 1996; Fidler, 1997), but a classic model of strategic school planning for optimal effect might be summarised as:

1 *Conceptual level:* values→vision/mission→strategic plan→policies.
2 *Transducer level:* school development plan (SDP), which includes decisions about timing, staffing, budget and professional development needs.
3 *Operational level:* tasks, responsibilities and short-term targets for individuals, in the context of the whole SDP, so that individual members of staff understand precisely the parameters of their jobs.

In this model, level 2 is a crucial link, a functional interface between the conceptual and the operational levels. A 'transducer' is a device which changes one form of energy into another; in this model it is needed to change policy into action. Too many schools assume that, once they have created the strategic plan and the policies, all teachers will be both willing and able to put these into practice in their classrooms and other areas of responsibility. It is a matter of grave disappointment to school leaders to find that this is not the case. Unless staff personally engage with the process of helping to turn policy into action, it is unlikely that they can make policy work effectively. A transducer is needed: a democratically hatched school development plan which enables staff to carry out policy with both motivation and competence.

Each level can then be evaluated against the targets in the SDP; the key issue for the school is the educational outcome, which must be closely related to the success of the operational level. It takes time, however, for the fruits of school planning to mature, and so it is clearly preferable for the governors, senior management and staff to be relatively stable; it is doubtful whether a headteacher can be effective in carrying out longer term plans when s/he may be in post for a short time. Littleford (1999) maintains that the head starts to make a difference after 5 years, but that it is the head's contribution over the subsequent 5–10 years which makes the greatest contribution to the life of the school.

Accountability

Headteachers are accountable to the board members, who pay the headteacher's salary; middle managers are accountable to the head; and teachers are accountable to their leaders at every level. But the ultimate point of accountability in any business must be to the customers – in this case the parents, who are paying fees. Parents need to know whether the school is giving value for their money, and they hold the school to account for the performance of individual teachers educating their child.

The effectiveness of school accountability systems is dependent on both policy and school culture. While policy establishes the mechanism for staff support, staff development and, eventually, procedures to deal with underperformance, it is school culture which dictates how this will actually work in practice. Is underperformance treated as wilful, or as an indication of support needed? Is the school culture supportive, treating mistakes as learning opportunities? Or does it take draconian and punitive measures in an effort to 'tighten things up'? If the policies for support and development are effective, dealing with underperformance, one of the most difficult tasks to manage, should be an exception. But it only takes an apparently small change in the conditions under which staff work to trigger opposition and lose willingness. To take one specific example, there are several cases of international schools where an appraisal system becomes linked to performance-related pay, a change introduced by the board, imported from an industrial model, and upsetting previously harmonious relationships on the staff. This is a prime example of how interference with one part of the system can have unintended consequences on staff morale and motivation in the broader job.

Another example of a management dilemma might be the staff development policy: should a teacher in need of development be sacked, or should the board invest in professional development? Again, this depends on the philosophy of the school, the make-up of the board of governors and whether or not they are taking a long-term versus short-term view. In schools where the board is dominated by parents of children on roll, the longer term benefits of staff development, when their children are already in the system, may not be apparent, resulting in a dismissive approach. On the other hand, long-term orientation boards may see continuing professional development as a sound investment for greater stability and higher quality of education.

Board of Governors

The success of an international school depends partly on the actions of its Board of Governors (BoG), so there is a need to invest some time in understanding and developing them because 'the strength of the governing body lies in the collective knowledge, experience and expertise of its members' (Barber et al., 1995: 2). Malpass (1994) feels that the best size for a BoG to work effectively is ten to fifteen members. The composition of the BoG varies enormously, depending on the constitution of the school. At one extreme, a school set up by a parents' co-operative may state that only parents can be voting members of the board. At the other extreme is the stance typified by this headteacher's comment to one of the authors: 'I am the chair, and the rest of the board consists of my daughter and my son-in-law … parents are nothing but trouble'.

Whatever the composition, a challenge is to attract the best people for the running of the school, which might include: the founder/owner, parents, interested members of the community, specialists from local business, headteacher, teacher representative and others. Each of these may have a different reason for wishing to be on the board, and this determines their behaviour, both as individuals and as a group.

Recruitment patterns may differ from national schools, where parent representatives are sometimes difficult to attract. In international schools, parents may be keen to join the governing body in order to play an active role in the life of the school on behalf of their children, but their enthusiasm to change things quickly may not always be in the best interests of the school – particularly in terms of harmonious relationships on the board if they have 'a particular axe to grind' (Malpass, 1994: 23). Not only might this sort of parent member lose enthusiasm once they realise the hard work involved, but also the effect on the board of short-term parents who create waves may have an ultimate impact on the duration of the school head in post.

Although functions of boards of governors vary from school to school, in general a board should:

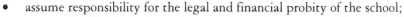

- assume responsibility for the legal and financial probity of the school;
- concern itself with the formation, revision and monitoring of general school policies;
- support the school in all its aspects;
- approve the budget and set school fees;
- appoint, supervise and evaluate the head;
- develop and monitor short-, medium- and long-range plans;
- seek to build up financial reserves (Malpass, 1994: 25).

This might be summarised as needing:

1 to provide a strategic view;
2 to act as a critical friend;
3 to ensure accountability (Barber et al., 1995: 2).

Or, as one head, with the experience of several international schools, expressed it – with feeling – governors should hire the head, set the long-term goals for school, maintain overall budget control – 'then get out and let the professionals get on with it'.

In order to carry out their functions as a collective body, individual members also have responsibilities, which are to:

- understand the school;
- act as a link between the school and the community;
- support the school at all times;
- seek information and partake in important decision-making;
- listen to the head and staff;
- defuse playground gossip;
- devote time and attention to board meetings (Malpass, 1994: 26).

Barber et al. (1995: 6) add to these responsibilities maintaining a good relationship with their headteacher and undertaking training and development as needed.

In some international schools, attendance at board meetings may be problematic, especially for people who travel a lot. This is compounded if meetings are inefficiently run, which Malpass (1994: 27) sees as a real issue: 'many board meetings lack structure. The agenda is not clearly defined, major issues are introduced without warning, trustees are given insufficient time to prepare for meetings, discussions become rambling and repetitive, meetings do not finish on time.'

Relationship between the board and the headteacher

Littleford (1999) found that as much as 40 per cent of headteacher time may be spent on BoG-related activities. The headteacher is employed and evaluated by the board, is responsible to the board and has the task of executing board policies, so heads need to take a major responsibility in treating the board fairly. Malpass recommends that heads should 'deal openly, honestly and courteously with the board at all times, encourage the support and proper involvement of board members, provide trustees with a positive role and welcome their proper contributions, and seek to achieve teamwork and unity of purpose' (Malpass, 1994: 26).

The relationship between the board and the headteacher is not always an easy one. In Hawley's (1995) research, of the 81 headteachers in his sample who gave their reasons for leaving post, 75 per cent had done so because of something to do with the board. Malpass (1994: 24) concurs: 'the lack of understanding of the different but complementary roles of the board and the head of the school goes to the heart of school management problems.'

It is therefore vital to get this relationship right, and the few studies that exist help to throw light on the issue. One of the common misunderstandings about roles and degree of involvement which emerges is the over-involvement of board members in the everyday business of the school. Malpass (1994) suggests that this may be due to the wrong terminology in some cases. Where a school has 'a board of directors', members may be tempted to 'direct', causing interference in the day-to-day running of the school and failure to fulfil their function as policy-makers and advisers to the head. A more helpful terminology

better term

may be 'board of trustees', as members then tend to 'hold the school in trust, now and for the future' (ibid.: 25).

Littleford (1999) outlines how a self-repeating pattern of quick turnover may become established in a school. A power vacuum is created when a school has a weak head. This person is asked to resign, and the board selects the new head, giving very firm instructions about the direction and pace of change. The new head follows the board's prescription, and in doing so disrupts school life – and so is fired, creating a new power vacuum. Sometimes the thread of continuity in a school is provided by a few of the more senior members of staff. But this layer of leadership is not necessarily immune, and may also be removed by a board's instructions to the new head to 'clean out the dead wood' (ibid.: 27). In doing so, the institutional memory of the school is lost, and the school is now in a self-perpetuating cycle of short-termism, lurching from one crisis to the next.

Another particular challenge for the relationship between international school headteachers and their boards is the mixed-culture board membership. Although desirable and necessary for the representation of all sectors of the school community, where the cultural relationships are not well understood disagreements may be caused by misinterpretation when members do not understand the different philosophies and cultures. Hawley goes further, finding in his research that 'the more multi-national the school board is, the shorter will be the school head duration' (Hawley 1994: 15).

Hawley's (1994, 1995) research was carried out on US-style international schools and may therefore not necessarily represent faithfully other types of international schools, but, in the absence of data on a broader range, the findings might nevertheless be interesting and potentially useful to headteachers of international schools generally. There seems to be a consensus of opinion that it is beneficial to the school to have headteachers who stay long enough to work through the planning cycle, as this creates an atmosphere more conducive to school stability than rapid turnover (Hawley, 1994; Malpass, 1994; Littleford, 1999). Hawley's research focused on the factors that affected the duration of the head in post, several of which concerned their relationship with the governing body. Headteacher tenure was increased:

- with low board membership turnover;
- where the board was relatively disinterested, i.e. fewer board members had children enrolled in the school;
- where there was a written set of policies to guide the school and minimise misunderstandings;
- when the board gave feedback to the headteacher about his/her performance;
- where there was less multinational membership of the school board.

Some of these factors may be less relevant to international schools which are *not* US style, and other factors may not be negotiable, but there are clear pointers starting to emerge from the literature. Some of these may be addressed through training, a relatively rare but much-needed occurrence for boards of governors of international schools. Such training as there is commonly focuses on the tasks and responsibilities of the board, but there is a particular need for boards to be trained in the *process* of working effectively together, through such programmes as *The Effective Governing Body* developed by Oxford Polytechnic (1992) as a result of research into governor training.

Conclusions

The leadership of schools is different from the leadership of other types of organisations, being more complex and dealing with students, parents and the community. The international context adds yet another layer of complexity as it entails dealing with many cultures, rapid turnover and, sometimes, isolation. Studies of successful headteachers show that, as well as being able to manage their schools on an administrative level, they understand and interact closely and sensitively with their staff and their board members, drawing the best out of each individual. Furthermore, those headteachers of international schools who demonstrate an understanding and a sensitivity towards the cultures represented in their school community are not only more successful in maintaining harmonious relationships but also, on a personal level, may remain in post long enough to work through one or two complete planning cycles – which builds a school's stability and ultimately benefits the students in the school (as discussed further by Hardman in Chapter 8).

It would seem to be essential to nurture a positive school culture, underpinned with sound and shared values, and an expectation of continuing professional development, turning the school into Senge's (1992) 'learning organisation', as discussed by Squire in Chapter 7. The actions and influence of the board of governors may have a dramatic impact on the ability of the head to lead effectively, and so it makes some sense to both manage this relationship and invest in training for boards, as the European Council for International Schools (ECIS) is currently suggesting.

Experience in international schools is starting to be shared more widely. As yet, we do not perhaps know enough about how different types of international schools are led. There is such huge diversity that it is difficult to project outcomes from one type of school onto another. Nevertheless, the more research that can be undertaken in this field the more likelihood there will be that a common body of sound practice will be established. At an individual school level, there is no shortage of school-based research projects being undertaken by students as part of their studies for higher degrees. If more of these students, having graduated successfully, can be persuaded to publish their findings in such journals as ECIS's *International Schools Journal,* or disseminate them at conferences, more pieces may be added to the jigsaw, and a more complete picture would start to emerge.

References

Barber, M., Stoll, L., Mortimore, P. and Hillman, J. (1995) *Governing Bodies and Effective Schools*, London: Department for Education and Employment.

Bass, B. (1985) *Leadership and Performance Beyond Expectations,* New York: The Free Press.

Berlak, A. and Berlak, H. (1987) 'Teachers working with teachers to transform schools', in J. Smyth (ed.) *Educating Teachers: Changing the Nature of Pedagogical Knowledge*, Lewes: Falmer Press.

Blanchard, K., Zigarmi, P. and Zigarmi, D. (1985) *Leadership and the One Minute Manager*, Glasgow: Fontana/Collins.

Burns, J.M. (1978) *Leadership*, New York: Harper and Row.

Caldwell, B.J. and Spinks, J.M. (1988) *The Self-Managing School*, Lewes: Falmer Press.

Caldwell, B.J. and Spinks, J.M. (1991) *Leading the Self-Managing School*, Lewes: Falmer Press.

Cambridge, J. (1998) 'National and organisational culture', in M. Hayden and G. Thompson (eds) *International Education: Principles and Practice*, London: Kogan Page.

Davies, L. (1994) *Beyond Authoritarian School Management: the Challenge for Transparency,* Ticknell, Derbyshire: Education Now Books.

Etzioni, A. (1965) 'Dual leadership in complex organisations', *American Sociological Review* 30: 690–1.

Everard, B. and Morris, G. (1996) *Effective School Management*, London: Paul Chapman.

Fidler, B. (1997) *Strategic Planning in Schools*, London: Paul Chapman.

Grace, G. (1995) *School Leadership: Beyond Education Management; an Essay in Policy Scholarship*, London: Falmer Press.

Green, H., Holmes, G. and Shaw, M. (1991) *Assessment and Mentoring for Headship: New Approaches to Senior Management Development in Schools*, Oxford: Oxford Polytechnic.

Greenfield, T. (1986) 'The decline and fall of science in educational administration', in T. Greenfield and P. Ribbins (eds) *Greenfield on Educational Administration: Towards a Humane Science*, London: Routledge.

Greenfield, W. (1991) 'Towards a theory of school leadership', American Educational Research Association paper, Chicago, April 3–7.

Hargreaves, A. (1989) *Curriculum and Assessment Reform*, Milton Keynes: Open University Press.

Hargreaves, A. (1994) *Changing Teachers, Changing Times*, London: Cassell.

Hawley, D. (1994) 'How long do international school heads survive? Part 1', *International Schools Journal* 14: no. 1: 8–21.

Hawley, D. (1995) 'How long do international school heads survive? Part 2', *International Schools Journal* 14: no. 2: 23–36.

Hofstede, G. (1991) *Cultures and Organisations*, London: Harper Collins.

Huberman, M. (1992) 'Critical introduction', in M. Fullan (ed.) *Successful School Improvement*, Oxford: Oxford University Press.

Jones, A. (1987) *Leadership for Tomorrow's Schools*, Oxford: Blackwell.

Kanter, R. (1983) *The Change Masters*, London: Unwin.

Littleford, J. (1999) 'Leadership of schools and the longevity of school heads', *International Schools Journal* 19: 23–34.

Malpass, D. (1994) 'School boards need management training', *International Schools Journal* 14: no. 1: 22–8.

Marshall, J. (1984) *Women Managers: Travellers in a Male World*, Chichester: Wiley.

Maslow, A.H. (1943) 'A theory of human motivation,' *Psychological Review* 50: 370–96.

Mullins, G. (1999) *Management and Organisational Behaviour*, 5th edn, London: Pitman Publishing.

Oxford Polytechnic (1992) *The Effective Governing Body* (training pack), Oxford: Oxford Polytechnic.

Ozga, J. (ed) (1993) *Women in Educational Management*, Milton Keynes: Open University Press.

Pearce, R. (1991) 'Understanding national education systems to facilitate transition in international schools', in P. Jonietz and D. Harris (eds) *The World Yearbook of Education*, London: Kogan Page.

Rodger, A. (1996) *Developing Moral Community in a Pluralist School Setting*, Aberdeen: Gordon Cook Foundation.

Rutter, M., Maughan, B., Mortimor, P. and Ouston, J. (1979) *Fifteen Thousand Hours: Secondary Schools and Their Effects on Children*, London: Open Books.

Senge, P.M. (1992) *The Fifth Discipline*, London: Century.

Shaw, M. and Welton, J. (1996) 'The application of education management models and theories to the processes of education policy making and management: a case of compound cross-cultural confusion', paper presented at the Indigenous Perspectives of Education Management conference, 19–24 August, Kuala Lumpur.

Tannenbaum, R. and Schmidt, W.H. (1958) 'How to choose a leadership pattern', *Harvard Business Review* 36 (2): 95–101.

Thearle, C. (1999) 'Women in senior management positions in international schools', *International Schools Journal* 18: no. 2: 38–47.

Willis, D., Enloe, W. and Minoura, Y. (1994) 'Transculturals, transnationals: the new diaspora', *International Schools Journal* 14: 29–42.

Zaleznik, A. (1977) 'Managers and leaders: are they different?', *Harvard Business Review* 55 (5): 67–78.

2

DEVELOPING THE CURRICULUM IN INTERNATIONAL SCHOOLS

Simon Catling

Introduction

What pupils learn in school in part happens because of what the school sets out to teach them but also happens incidentally, even accidentally, since it is never possible to control the variety of experiences that pupils have in school. Nonetheless, it might reasonably be considered that an international school should provide an opportunity for its pupils to learn in an environment which is concerned with developing their capabilities, understanding, emotions and social relationships with an international dimension in mind. This chapter examines the nature of curriculum with a view to indicating some of the possibilities for internationalising the curriculum, while recognising that often the influence of the home nation can be very strong. It argues that the choice of curriculum will depend on key decisions about the basis for the curriculum and that the management of the curriculum and of changes to it depends on an appreciation of the responsibilities of curriculum managers and an analytic approach to curriculum development.

Viewing the curriculum

At the heart of the schooling process lies the curriculum. It is the key focus for effective schools around which decisions are taken about teaching activities and resources, staffing and staff development, and ways to respond to external demands, opportunities and constraints. For the international school, the curriculum provides messages to its prospective and current parents and to the local community about its market, its stance and its strengths. Not least, the curriculum speaks loudly to its pupils. But, what is the curriculum, who is it for and what influences it?

What is the curriculum?

There are many views about the nature and use of *curriculum*. While Ross (2000) considers it to be a statement about what must be learnt, others argue that curriculum covers much of what children learn in school, including the attitudes and behaviours that might be unintentionally acquired (DES, 1985; Print, 1993; Wragg, 1997). Others extend this view by referring to the way that teachers teach and to the materials that they use (Reid and Johnson, 1999). There is no doubt that the curriculum is a contentious arena about which there is conflict because the curriculum reflects social and/or individual values and its development is never, for internal school reasons and because of external factors, a completed exercise (Kincheloe, 1998; Brady and Kennedy, 1999). In this respect, we can see the curriculum as a culture, which reflects the knowledge that counts, the beliefs and mores, and the practices of the school community (Joseph, 2000). On this basis, the *curriculum* includes the following *elements*:

- The *values* that are espoused by the leadership of a school and that lie behind such intentions as to foster the intellectual, emotional, physical, personal and social development of pupils or to ensure entry into higher education or to develop global citizens.
- The *structure of knowledge* which is used to organise what is to be learnt, e.g. by using subjects or core themes or elements of learning.
- The specific *content* which it is decided to set before pupils, i.e. what subject matter will be taught in, for instance, science, geography and art.
- The *balance* between the different subjects and content in the curriculum, e.g. the time given to mathematics or to a pupil's first language as against music or history.
- The *organisation* of the school day and the timetabling of sessions.
- The *resources* which are used in teaching, including not only the materials that pupils use but also the physical environment in which they work.
- The *teaching methods*, strategies and activities which are used to plan, teach and assess the content of the curriculum.
- The *expectations* of pupils and staff in the way they behave towards each other and to the wider community, i.e. the nature and quality of relationships, the standards in work and behaviour and the image presented to the outside world.

As such, the curriculum is seen to be more than the course of study that the school provides for pupils. It covers the formal, the informal and the hidden dimensions of schooling, including the timetabled periods, the school rules, the extracurricular activities, the unspecified attitudes of heads and teachers, and the explicit ethos of the school.

Curriculum functions

In reflecting the culture or cultures of the school community, the curriculum serves a number of functions, linked to the *stakeholders* in the schooling system (Brady and Kennedy, 1999; Ross, 2000). This is no less true for international schools than for national schools, perhaps just the opposite. International schools reflect a variety of cultural contexts and identities, drawing as they do on families from a variety of nationalities who bring a range of expectations regardless of the focus of education publicly espoused by the school. These might be economic and vocational and/or to do with values such as internationalisation. The pupils likewise will have aspirations, perhaps of a personal and social nature or about higher education and particular jobs. School owners, whether charities or individuals, will have views about the purpose and nature of their school, whether as a business and/or in terms of a focus and style of education. Teachers, equally, will bring their own perspectives, interpretations and agendas to an international school. Their knowledge, skills and experience influence the way in which a school will give messages, for instance, about the balance between academic and vocational emphases in the curriculum. Teachers' backgrounds and perspectives will have an impact on the way they approach, for example, a particular national curriculum content to develop international understanding. The business community may well be interested in and want to have some influence on the curriculum of the school because multinational companies may be a key source of families who use the school and because national families have aspirations to send their children to an international school. The local and wider host country community may well have interests because they see the potential of the school to provide an education which meets their aspirations for greater global accessibility for their children, perhaps through language learning or through access to higher education in other countries. Not least, the national government may have an interest arising from its own educational agenda and, for instance, require the curriculum of private schools to provide specific content and time for national pupils who attend the school in subjects such as religious education or the first national language.

Brady and Kennedy (1999) argue that it is vital to take into account the range of these stakeholders in shaping the curriculum. They see the curriculum as providing the opportunity for children and students to develop the knowledge, understanding, skills, values and attitudes which will enable them to be both informed and productive citizens, which from an international school perspective would be in their own national and an international context. This is balanced with the recognition of the need for personal and social dimensions, fundamental to developing positive values and to promoting personal responsibility (Tomlinson, 1995). This includes the pupil, the family and the society among the stakeholders. Brady and Kennedy (1999) see the curriculum reflecting the interests of stakeholders in a complementary way, encouraging curriculum planners and managers in school to take the variety of individual and group needs into account. To do so, they propose that the key curriculum functions are identified and considered. In the context of the international school, these are outlined in Table 2.1.

Table 2.1 Curriculum orientations and functions

Key curriculum orientations	Curriculum functions for an international school
	The curriculum should include the knowledge, skills and values that:
Cultural orientation	ensure pupils encounter and can learn from a selection of cultures
Economic and vocational orientation	enable pupils to develop their ability and competence to contribute to the national and international community and to participate productively in work
Personal orientation	equip pupils to be able to clarify their own understandings and values and to make decisions and take actions to meet their personal needs in the context of international awareness and understanding
Social orientation	equip pupils to participate positively and responsibly in groups and the wider society so that the international community functions beneficially for all

Source: adapted from Brady and Kennedy (1999) *Curriculum Construction*, with the permission of Pearson Education Australia Pty. Ltd. Copyright 1999.

Curriculum experiences

The curriculum consists not just of what might be explicitly planned or even unintentionally provided, but also includes the experience of the participants, both the teachers and the pupils; it draws on the ideals that those who developed the curriculum had in mind (CERI, 1998). In examining the nature, quality and effectiveness of the curriculum, it is essential to evaluate the range of intentions and experiences. For an international school this is vital since its appeal and success depend on it meeting its stated aims and in maintaining a public image of achievement. Understanding curriculum experience involves consideration of three key dimensions: the formal or *intended* curriculum, the operational or *observed* curriculum and the experienced or *received* curriculum.

The *intended curriculum* describes, at one end of the continuum, what the school sets out to provide, and, at the other end, what the individual teacher has planned to do. It includes the explicit aims and timetabled subjects and/or topics and the stated school rules and requirements, in its brochure perhaps, as well as the subject syllabuses and the unit and lesson plans which teachers prepare for use during the year and term, and daily. In effect, the intended curriculum sets out the formal, stated curriculum intentions of the school. However, the curriculum is mediated by teachers. Each teacher brings their own interpretation and understanding of what is to be taught and will draw on the strategies and activities in their teaching with which they feel most comfortable, that excite them and/or that they feel are most appropriate to the subject matter they are teaching.

The *observed curriculum* is what we see happening in the classroom; in other words, it is the curriculum (in its widest sense) that we see put into practice. It concerns the emphasis placed on particular content, on expectations of pupil involvement in the lessons, on how pupils are to engage with the materials they are given to use, on the behaviour expected of them and on ways in which such matters as rewards or sanctions are carried through. The observed curriculum examines both the formal, intended curriculum and the hidden or unintended curriculum, the latter being those aspects of school life which children learn about but which are not spelt out or which may not even be consciously realised by teachers. If an international school intends to help pupils achieve in a particular national curriculum, whether the English national curriculum or a variation of a USA state curriculum, observation and evaluation of what is taught, how it is taught and what other activities and expectations occur is vital.

The *received curriculum* is the knowledge, understanding, skills, values and attitudes that pupils take away from their experience of the curriculum. It relates to the extent to which pupils have engaged with and learnt from the intended curriculum, and even any observed aspects of the hidden curriculum. It relates also to what pupils feel they have gained from their experience of the curriculum. While the former can be gauged to some extent from pupil behaviour and expressed attitudes and from the quality of their assignments and examination outcomes, the latter requires seeking pupils' views directly. Yet, there are other stakeholders who can contribute to an understanding of the received curriculum. These include parents, who will comment on what they feel their children have or have not gained from their schooling, higher education institutions, who may or may not offer places for further study, and employers, who may offer jobs to individual pupils or who may make statements about the overall levels of achievement of their new employees and generalise these into views about schooling. It is not, of course, unknown for governments to offer a view too! In effect, appreciation of the received curriculum requires the international school not just to look inwardly at its own pupils but also to the community on which it draws and to the wider national and international context.

Understanding the impact of curriculum does not end here, however. An important outcome for the pupil in later years is the *residual curriculum*. This is the learning that is applied in employment and in leisure and personal life. It is also the memories of schooling, the knowledge that surfaces from time to time and, most particularly, the values which help shape a life (Fail, 1996). Although the curriculum in school may be strongly focused on the cultural, economic and vocational orientations and foundations noted in Table 2.1, it is more often the personal and social dynamics of curriculum experience that shape pupils' values and attitudes and the contribution they make to the wider world. This implies that what the school sets out to do is vitally important. The curriculum is not a matter for quick decisions at the heart of the educational experience.

A basis for an international school curriculum?

There are international schools of many different guises and styles, and, indeed, there is considerable diversity in international education (Waterson and Hayden, 1999; Hayden and Thompson, 2000). Yet there is strong common ground to most national and international schools in terms of the formally expressed curriculum (Meyer et al., 1992). At the core of the curriculum in most schools lie first-language teaching, mathematics and science, and beyond these are included the humanities or social studies, the arts and physical education. Information technology is making its way, in some cases, into the core of the curriculum. There are few schools where a subject approach in one form or another does not prevail. In many cases the structure of the curriculum is driven by externally adopted syllabuses, whether the IB or another that is nationally based. Indeed, the organisation of the curriculum often tends to reflect the notion of curriculum held by teachers and school owners, as well as by parents. Their experience of curriculum is largely that of a subject-structured curriculum.

It is unlikely that the relatively traditional structure of the curriculum will change to any great extent. Nonetheless, it is important for international schools to identify the values and direction they want to underpin the ethos of their curriculum, in order to:

- help teachers select subject content examples;
- influence the way people treat, interact with and respect each other;
- indicate to the external world (to the school) the view of the world that the school is trying to foster in its pupils.

Various phrases have been coined and used as umbrella terms to specify the international, more global and forward-looking sense of curriculum. These include international education (Hayden and Thompson, 1998), global education or perspectives (Osler, 1994), global citizenship or global civic culture (Boulding, 1988; Oxfam, 1997), global multicultural education (Lynch, 1989), intercultural education or literacy (Fennes and Hapgood, 1997; Heyward, 2000), and even futures education (Hicks and Slaughter, 1998). Common to many of the proponents of the internationalisation of the curriculum in all schools are a number of *principles* that might underpin the internationally oriented curriculum:

- the development of openness towards all cultures;
- the appreciation of similarities within cultural diversity;
- the overcoming of cultural bias and ethnocentrism;
- the development of thinking and decision-making skills in culturally divergent contexts;
- the appreciation of globalisation and global issues.

In effect, the heart of an international curriculum, indeed of all curricula, lies in the attitudes, values and behaviours that are developed by pupils. Fennes and Hapgood (1997) argue that positive attitudes, values and behaviours must be fostered through the learning goals set out within the curriculum. For these to have any impact, they must be put into practice throughout the school, a point strongly reinforced by Oxfam's (1997) view of the key elements of global citizenship and the International Schools Association (ISA) curriculum framework for education for peace (Thomas, 1998). Box 2.1 draws on these sources to outline an example of learning goals for an internationally oriented curriculum.

Hayden and Thompson (2000) make the point that international schools should not be automatically linked with the concept of international education. Inevitably, international schools will decide on the curriculum they wish to offer to the clientele they intend or need to attract. The term 'international' can mean little more than that a school accepts pupils from more than one cultural or ethnic background, in some cases to follow a common single national curriculum in a given language, probably English. Alternatively, 'international' can refer to a school that challenges its pupils to work bilingually at school, to develop intercultural understanding and to be global in outlook, while respecting the cultural dignity and identities of its pupils and their families and its staff (Walker, 2000). The perspective offered in Box 2.1 supports the view that an international school curriculum should shape pupils' values and world view 'in the widest and most inclusive manner' (Sylvester, 2000: 24). This requires taking up the challenge to work for consistency and coherence in meeting the elements of curriculum outlined above.

Examining the international curriculum

Exploring the idea of an international curriculum, Thompson (1998) outlines a general typography of influences that have been used as a basis for curriculum organisation in international schools. These identify the sources of the curriculum that a school adopts and indicate its focus of attention. The four categories which Thompson uses are outlined in Table 2.2. What is clear from the examples of each category is that the influence of external syllabuses is strong. Furthermore, they indicate the emphasis on meeting the interests of client parents in offering the opportunity for their children to meet the examination needs of their home country and of university entrance criteria. As Thompson notes, often this produces a 'backwash effect' throughout the curriculum. A conclusion that can be drawn from this process of curriculum influence is that, unless and until examination syllabuses and national curricula are developed from a set of values that foster international education, it will be difficult to encourage international schools to adopt fully a truly international perspective to their curricula.

The requirement for school leaving accreditation is central to almost all

Box 2.1 Learning goals for an internationally oriented curriculum

The curriculum of an international school which sets out to enable pupils to develop intercultural understanding and a sense of global citizenship could do so by enabling pupils to:

Self-knowledge and perception
- develop their understanding of their self-perception and self-esteem and of their own identity and attitudes
- develop insight into and an understanding of other cultures
- become conscious of their own stereotypes and prejudices and recognise stereotypes and prejudices as superficial images
- recognise the influences of their perceptions of their own culture/self on their perceptions of other cultures and other people
- recognise perceptions of other cultures having an influence on their own perception of themselves and their own culture

Knowledge and understanding
- know and understand something of their own culture, including its values, lifestyles and patterns of behaviour
- know and understand something of other cultures, their similarities to their own and of their diversity
- realise that (cultural) values influence behaviour
- recognise cultural differences as enriching and appropriate
- understand something of the nature and role of social justice and equity, and peace and conflict
- know and understand something about globalisation and interdependence
- know and understand something about sustainable development

Attitudes and values
- accept and value (cultural) diversity
- be open and respectful towards the 'foreign'
- be concerned to tackle conflict
- have a sense of common humanity
- tolerate ambiguity in themselves and others
- have a commitment to social justice and equality
- have concern for the environment and a commitment to sustainable development
- believe that people can make a difference

Skills and behaviours
- communicate with others using their ways of expression, both verbally and non-verbally
- think critically and argue effectively

- analyse their own culture, including data gathering, in order to contrast it with other cultures
- show respect for people and things, and empathise and be sensitive to others
- work co-operatively, and listen actively to those from a different culture
- give and receive feedback honestly and with sensitivity
- consider proposed solutions to problems and concerns and examine their potential impacts
- challenge injustice and inequalities and negotiate tension and conflict that is culturally based
- adapt their behaviour in another cultural setting
- adapt to changing social/environmental factors

Sources: adapted from Fennes and Hapgood (1997), Oxfam (1997) and Thomas (1998).

school systems. National assessment systems, such as the scholastic aptitude tests (SATs) in the USA and the General Certificate in Secondary Education (GCSE) in the UK, although markedly different, are focused strongly on school certification and influence the nature of the curriculum to ensure that pupils are given the opportunity to take them and to achieve well. The IB Diploma was developed with the same intention, essentially to enable academically able pupils to gain entrance to higher education. This rationale is also behind the development of the International General Certificate of Secondary Education (IGCSE) and the Advanced International Certificate of Education (AICE) (Findlay, 1997). Inevitably, not just the 14–16 and 16–18 curricula are influenced by these examination syllabuses. Schools and teachers, particularly in secondary and junior high schooling, look to prepare their younger pupils for the coming syllabus. The use of a national curriculum, such as that for England (DfEE/QCA, 1999a,b) from age 5 to 14 years, can give an international school, basing itself on English lines, a clear programme to work through.

The notions of curriculum continuity and coherence underpin the development of the Primary Years Programme (PYP) (for 5–12 year olds), which leads into the Middle Years Programme (MYP) (for 11–16 year olds), which in turn links with the IB Diploma (Peel, 1997; Barnes, 1998; Bartlett, 1998; Ellwood, 1999). Home-based national curricula, although they may take some account of the wider world, do not set out to be international in either flavour or content. Their interest lies in meeting their own perceived needs nationally, often with an economic and vocational emphasis, while accepting the need for cultural, social and personal dimensions. National curricula are intended for the whole school population, to provide a common curriculum. The development of the IB PYP and MYP to complement and lead through to

Table 2.2 Categories of curriculum influence drawn on by international schools

Curriculum influence category	Curriculum source and focus	Examples of curricula or syllabuses
Exportation	The use of existing national or state curricula and examination syllabuses as set out and used in the home nation with which the school regards itself connected	English national curricula and their key stage tests for 5–14 year olds English and Welsh General Certificate in Secondary Education (GCSE) or Advanced level (A level) Board examinations and syllabuses Curricula drawn from states in the USA
Adaptation	The use of a modified national curriculum or examination syllabus which draws on a variety of contexts	International General Certificate of Secondary Education (IGCSE) Advanced International Certificate of Education (AICE) Curriculum modification to take into account host county curriculum interests, e.g. in language or religious education
Integration	The use of a curriculum developed from the best practices from a number of sources (particularly countries) which are brought together	The European Baccalaureate (EB) syllabus
Creation	The use of a curriculum which is developed from first principles	The International Baccalaureate (IB) Diploma syllabus The IB Middle Years Programme (MYP) curriculum The IB Primary Years Programme (PYP) curriculum International Schools Association (ISA) Education for Peace curriculum framework

Source: adapted from Thompson (1998) 'Towards a model for international Education', in E. Hayden and J. Thompson (eds) *International Education: Principles and Practice,* London: Kogan Page, with permission from Kogan Page.

the IB Diploma, although constructed at different times and in reverse order, are focused on a holistic view of education which:

- has an international focus to the curriculum;
- provides experience and development in key areas of knowledge and understanding, including languages, mathematics, sciences and social studies throughout, and the arts and physical education and technology in the PYP and MYP;
- fosters enquiry and critical thinking skills and the ability to apply developing knowledge and understanding to encourage learning how to learn;

- encourages co-operative approaches to learning, such as through group work, and the capacity to work independently;
- uses assessment both formatively and summatively to show development and understanding in PYP and MYP and end of schooling achievement in the IB Diploma.

What distinguishes the IB MYP from the GCSE and IGCSE programmes is the IB's holistic perspective founded on a philosophy concerned with providing a curriculum to develop the whole pupil rather than a series of syllabuses about individual subjects (Fox, 1998; Ellwood, 1999). However, the AICE programme and the IB Diploma share the intention of providing a broad and balanced curriculum. The English/Welsh A level programme is a full subject option programme, the available selection of which depends on the school and the choice of the pupil within the school's framework. There is much in common between the requirements in the IB subject curricula and the individual Examination Board subject syllabuses. It is the perspective from which any examination structure comes that must be taken into account by an international school in determining its curriculum offer.

Choosing and managing the international school's curriculum

The continuing debate about the nature of an international curriculum, and the way in which many international schools continually reconsider their approach to their curriculum offer, indicates that curriculum and external examination decisions are not set but are monitored, reviewed and modified. The increasing number of schools taking up the IB programmes and looking to the IGCSE and AICE is testament to this. The bases on which curriculum selection and management decisions are made influence strongly how successfully curriculum development can be maintained.

Selecting the curriculum

The issue of selecting the curriculum focuses on the purpose for setting up, maintaining and developing an international school. The views and needs of the variety of stakeholders in the school need to be taken into account. These indicate several key questions that are likely to inform and, perhaps, guide the selection of curriculum, focused on the aims, client group and financial circumstances and aspirations of the school:

- What is the company or individual owner's view about the nature and purpose of the education to be provided in their school?
- Who is the client group?
- What age are the pupils?

- What expectations of the pupils are held?
- What is the financial position of the school?
- What sort of reputation does the school expect to develop and retain?

Where a school exists to serve a particular home clientele, perhaps from the UK or the USA, whose aspirations are that their children will move on to higher education in their home country, decisions have usually been to provide the home country curriculum (for the UK this means an English curriculum) and/or examination syllabus. If that client group begins to change, particularly if there is a considerable increase in host nation pupils, decisions about the curriculum provision need to take account of the host government's interests as well as host nation parents' aspirations for their children in deciding on modifications to the curriculum. Where a particular international school has been set up with the concern of its board to provide an environment in which the development of international perspectives and qualities (such as those outlined in Box 2.1) is to the fore, the curriculum will be developed to meet these intentions.

The selection of the curriculum of an international school depends on the aspirations of the school board or owner and those with influence. In effect, the focus of the school on its clientele will lead to decisions about its curriculum, a point reinforced by the curriculum influences typology in Table 2.2. Indeed, as Bartlett (1998) has explicitly stated, there is no need for an international school to devise its own curriculum for international education because the PYP, MYP and IB Diploma structure provides a formula for a school to achieve this without 'reinventing the wheel'. In effect, the key questions for choosing the curriculum of an international school move towards being:

- Is the curriculum to be based explicitly around a perspective on international education?
- To what extent will the curriculum to be provided meet the needs of home country clients?
- How far should the curriculum provide for and introduce the pupils to the host country?

Added to these might well be a question about the extent to which the school will provide access to higher education in the international environment.

In making decisions about curriculum structure and content, it will be important to supplement the key questions above with such practical questions as the following:

- Which subject areas are to be offered and at what levels in the school?
- Which subject areas are to be compulsory and which optional?
- Which national or international opportunities are to be available in non-examination and examination syllabuses?

- What is the range of teaching styles that will need to be used to teach the subject areas?
- Which resources are to be used to teach the subject areas?
- What are the staffing needs to teach these subject areas?
- How are the pupils to be grouped for teaching, taking account of their needs and parental expectations?

Such questions are valuable to use not only in deciding to adopt, for example, a home nation curriculum or in developing one's own curriculum but particularly where drawing on the curricula of different nations, for instance, in selecting components from the English national curriculum, from a state curriculum framework in the USA and from the host nation. National and internal state (in the USA) curricula are constructed around particular sets of expectations and ideas about purpose, content and standards (Marsh, 1997). Much of the set of curriculum subjects (home language, mathematics, science, technology, social studies, arts, physical education) is used commonly around the globe (Meyer et al., 1992), but content may be only superficially similar. For example, in mathematics one nation might focus largely on number skills while another includes geometry, measurement and statistics. In history the focus in each country is usually strongly on its national past. In science and religious education, what is argued to be acceptable to be taught varies even within some nations. In constructing an international school's curriculum, considering using, adapting or selecting from the curricula on offer from more than one country to meet the needs of the variety of clients in the school requires delicate considerations. Neither the different curricula nor the related resources necessarily match well together. In this respect, it is worth keeping the following additional questions in mind:

- To what extent can published curricula, or elements of them, from particular national or state contexts provide and fulfil what is needed for this school?
- In what ways and to what extent can different curricula be integrated or used side by side helpfully to meet the pupils' needs and interests?

These and related questions will need to be considered and reconsidered periodically as a key element in the process of evaluating the curriculum available within a school and in order to guide the decisions that need to be made as to whether to continue with, modify or fully replace the current curriculum offer. Choosing the international school's curriculum, even where that might be the IB's PYP, MYP and Diploma for ages 5/6 to 18 year olds, can never be set in stone. The mobile nature of the international school's families and pupils, the changing composition of a school's population with increasing host nation pupils and shifts in subjects and examination syllabuses, for instance, will each influence the choices available and contribute to the decisions about the curriculum that it is most appropriate to offer.

Managing and developing the curriculum

Curriculum management focuses on a number of key areas within a school. These include:

- the specific format and timetabling of the curriculum;
- the particular subjects or topics on offer;
- the staffing to teach and support the curriculum;
- the materials to be used in teaching;
- the assessment processes to be used;
- the monitoring and evaluation approach.

While key decisions about curriculum provision and resources will be made at owner, board, head or deputy head levels, the general management of the curriculum for the pupils will happen at the middle-management level of department heads and curriculum co-ordinators. Curriculum leaders need a mix of curriculum and interpersonal skills to maintain and development curriculum provision and quality (Lofthouse et al., 1995). These are outlined in Table 2.3.

Managing an international school's curriculum requires for all those involved a clear understanding of the nature of the curriculum as a whole and, in addition for the subject leader, of their subject responsibilities. In the appropriate context, this will include a clear appreciation of the values and perspectives underpinning international education. Where a school or department needs to continue to make progress towards an international curriculum, to modernise its internationalism or to update its subject or thematic curriculum, it will be important to take a considered and analytical approach to curriculum development. One approach to examining the current curriculum in order to foster change at whichever appropriate level is outlined in Box 2.2.

Managing *curriculum development* is a challenging but rewarding responsibility. The importance of curriculum development in the international school lies particularly in keeping abreast of research and innovation and in influencing the nature and quality of teaching through the use and development of good practices. This can certainly involve curriculum change, just as much as the introduction of more stimulating and appropriate teaching techniques and materials. Purchasing teaching resources which support the internationalisation of the syllabus and/or adopting available international syllabuses, such as those of the IB programmes or the IGCSE and AICE, can be important ways to support development. But for curriculum development to be undertaken successfully, it requires a clear sense of what ought to be done, a clear idea of how to go about it, an understanding of what enables change to happen and an appreciation of what needs to be done to influence change (Fullan, 1993). Hence the importance of both curriculum and interpersonal skills.

Curriculum development implies the need for staff development. At a basic level, it is essential to keep the teaching staff informed and to involve them in

Table 2.3 Curriculum management skills

Curriculum management skills	*Curriculum management roles and responsibilities*
Curriculum skills	
Knowledge of subjects	Keep up-to-date in the subject(s) for which responsibility is held
Professional skills	Develop the scheme(s) of work; manage implementation; maintain and evaluate effectiveness
Professional judgement	Be informed about teaching strategies and teaching materials in relation to scheme of work needs and children's development; purchase and manage resources; develop the match between pupils' abilities and the schemes; manage assessment and records; support pupils' option decisions
Professional leadership	Be thorough in preparation for teaching and work with colleagues; teach to a level of high quality; be proactive in developing the subject(s) in the school
Interpersonal skills	
Social skills	Work co-operatively with and teach alongside colleagues from a variety of cultural and language backgrounds; observe and listen; be open minded; lead discussion groups; organise and manage professional development activities; build the confidence of colleagues; empathise with the interests, concerns and needs of colleagues
Communication skills	Provide and maintain an effective communication process with colleagues; disseminate information; tackle concerns quickly; inform parents, bearing in mind cultural and linguistic diversity
Management skills	Ensure that colleagues are working to agreed approaches and content in schemes of work, while drawing on and valuing their expertise; maintain standards and expectations with pupils; delegate; be able to forward plan
External representation	Represent and defend the subject(s) to outsiders such as governors, advisers and inspectors and colleagues in other schools; develop networks; disseminate practice from within the school; identify good practices from elsewhere to bring in

Source: adapted from Lofthouse, M., Bush, T., Coleman, M., O'Neill, J., West-Burnham, J. and Glover, D. (1995) *Managing the Curriculum*, London: Pitman Publishing, with permission from Pearson Education.

the debates that lead to decisions about curriculum change, whether of changes in resources to be used, a change of subject syllabus or change to the nature and focus of the school's whole curriculum. Since their role will be to plan, teach and assess in the context of the new developments to the curriculum, it will be vital to provide time for discussion and, quite probably, in-service training to introduce and identify good practice to be put in place. In internationalising the curriculum, through the use of resources from different cultures and places,

Box 2.2 Key questions in managing curriculum development

1. *What is the current practice?*
   Identify: policies and priorities in place, syllabuses and teaching methods currently used.
   Key question: Does it need changing?

2. *What is the purpose of curriculum development?*
   Identify: focus, rationale, gains.
   Key questions: What is the need for change? What are the arguments for change? What will be lost as a result of change?

3. *Who gains from the development of the curriculum?*
   Identify focus of gain: pupils, parents, school staff, governors, local community … .
   Key question: Where will the gains best be?

4. *What is to be done to develop the curriculum?*
   Identify: how to go about change.
   Key question: How will this will help individuals, whole school … ?

5. *Who needs to know about the development?*
   Identify: staff, governors, parents, pupils … .
   Key questions: Who gets left out? Who is brought in?

6. *Who is to manage the development?*
   Identify: responsibilities, personnel, limitations, decision-making powers.
   Key question: Is an appropriate person able to lead the development?

7. *What is needed to enable the development to take place?*
   Identify: 'moral' support, training, materials … .
   Key questions: What is the level of support needed? What will the cost be?

8. *What is the time span involved in the development?*
   Identify: time needs, time scale, sequence of 'time needs'.
   Key questions: How realistic is it? What timescale is needed? When might there be an impact on the curriculum?

9. *How is the development to be evaluated?*
   Identify: who will evaluate, when will it occur, focus of evaluation.
   Key question: Will the monitoring and evaluation be carried out internally or externally.

10. *What will be the next stage in the development process?*
    Identify: long-term planning context.
    Key question: What is expected or planned to follow this development?

Sources: adapted from Day et al. (1993) and Hargreaves and Hopkins (1991).

through broadening the mix of teaching styles and through recognising and planning for the variety of culturally contextualised learning styles, teachers need time to trial and adapt their approach. Where the curriculum development is considerable, it will be important to provide staff development over time. This enables change to become 'bedded in', enabling staff to make it part of their own perspective on the curriculum and to contribute to making the development a success.

Conclusion

There is no singular definition of the curriculum (Ornstein and Hunkins, 1998). Nor is there any agreed understanding of an international curriculum. There are a number of elements in the idea of curriculum that might be agreed, essentially to do with content that is planned to be taught to pupils and its organisation. The elements of an international curriculum would seem to include values based in intercultural learning, the use of culturally varied teaching strategies, teaching materials gleaned from a variety of cultural sources and drawing on the experience of a diverse school community (Sylvester, 1998; Thompson, 1998). Ideally, the curriculum of an international school will be taught by teachers who are not only internationally minded but are also drawn from a variety of cultures, so that the notion of intercultural learning is seen to be for the staff as much as for the pupils. This supports the notion of the curriculum as the holistic experience of the pupil, in other words the view that 'the school is the curriculum' (Lofthouse et al., 1995). Managing the curriculum is not, then, just a matter of agreeing content, teaching strategies and materials. It involves the whole process of schooling and reflects the nature of the decisions about staffing, resources, priorities and directions. No simple matter to define or implement, the curriculum is what education is entirely about.

References

Barnes, D. (1998) 'And then there were three … IB programmes, that is …', *International Schools Journal* 18: 44–9.

Bartlett, K. (1998) 'International curricula: more or less important at the primary level?' in E. Hayden and J. Thompson (eds) *International Education: Principles and Practice*, London: Kogan Page.

Boulding, E. (1988) *Building a Global Civic Culture*, New York: Teachers College Press.

Brady, L. and Kennedy, K. (1999) *Curriculum Construction*, Sydney: Prentice Hall.

CERI (Centre for Educational Research and Innovation) (1998) *Making the Curriculum Work*, Paris: Organisation for Economic Co-operation and Development.

Day, C., Hall, C., Gammage, P. and Coles, M. (1993) *Leadership and Curriculum in the Primary School*, London: Paul Chapman Publishing.

DES (Department of Education and Science) (1985) *Curriculum Matters 2: the Curriculum from 5 to 16*, London: Her Majesty's Stationery Office (HMSO).

DfEE/QCA (Department for Education and Employment/Qualifications and Curriculum Authority) (1999a) *The National Curriculum: Handbook for Primary Teachers in England*, London: DfEE/QCA.

DfEE/QCA (Department for Education and Employment/Qualifications and Curriculum Authority) (1999b) *The National Curriculum: Handbook for Secondary Teachers in England*, London: DfEE/QCA.

Ellwood, C. (1999) 'IGCSE and the IB Middle Years Programme: how compatible are they?', *International Schools Journal* 19: 35–44.

Fail, H. (1996) 'Whatever becomes of international school students?' *International Schools Journal* 15 (2): 31–6.

Fennes, H. and Hapgood, K. (1997) *Intercultural Learning in the Classroom*, London: Cassell.

Findlay, R. (1997) 'A guide to international qualifications', in R. Findlay (ed.) *International Education Handbook*, London: Kogan Page.

Fox, E. (1998) 'The emergence of the International Baccalaureate as an impetus for curriculum reform', in E. Hayden and J. Thompson (eds) *International Education: Principles and Practice*, London: Kogan Page.

Fullan, M. (1993) *Changing Forces: Probing the Depths of Educational Reform*, London: Falmer Press.

Hargreaves, D.H. and Hopkins, D. (1991) *The Empowered School*, London: Cassell.

Hayden, M. and Thompson, J. (1998) *International Education: Principles and Practice*, London: Kogan Page.

Hayden, M. and Thompson, J. (2000) 'International education: flying flags or raising standards?', *International Schools Journal* 19 (2): 48–56.

Heyward, M. (2000) 'Intercultural literacy and the international school', *International Schools Journal* 19 (2): 29–35.

Hicks, D. and Slaughter, R. (eds) (1998) *Futures Education*, London: Kogan Page.

Joseph, P.B. (2000) 'Conceptualising curriculum', in P.B. Joseph, S.L. Bravmann, M.A. Windschitl, E.R. Mikel and M.S. Green (eds) *Cultures of Curriculum*, London: Lawrence Erlbaum.

Kincheloe (1998) 'Pinar's 'Currere' and identity in hyperreality: grounding the post-formal notion of intrapersonal intelligence' in W.F. Pinar (ed.) *Curriculum: Toward New Identities*, New York: Garland Publishing.

Lofthouse, M., Bush, T., Coleman, M., O'Neill, J., West-Burnham, J. and Glover, D. (1995) *Managing the Curriculum*, London: Pitman Publishing.

Lynch, J. (1989) *Multicultural Education in a Global Society*, London: Falmer Press.

Marsh, C. (1997) *Key Concepts for Understanding Curriculum. 2. Planning, Management and Ideology*, London: Falmer Press.

Meyer, J.W., Kamens, D.H. and Benavot, A. (1992) *School Knowledge for the Masses*, London: Falmer Press.

Ornstein, A.C. and Hunkins, F.P. (1998) *Curriculum: Foundations, Principles and Issues*, Boston: Allyn & Bacon.

Osler A. (1994) 'Introduction: the challenges of development education', in A. Osler (ed.) *Development Education: global perspectives on the curriculum*, London: Cassell.

Oxfam (1997) *A Curriculum for Global Citizenship*, Oxford: Oxfam.

Peel, R. (1997) 'International education comes of age', *International Schools Journal* 17 (2): 12–17.

Print, M. (1993) *Curriculum Development and Design*, St Leonards: Allen & Unwin.

Reid, A. and Johnson, B. (1999) 'Contesting the curriculum', in B. Johnson and A. Reid (eds) *Contesting the Curriculum*, Katoomba: Social Science Press.

Ross, A. (2000) *Curriculum Construction and Critique*, London: Falmer Press.

Sylvester, R. (1998), 'Through the lens of diversity: inclusive and encapsulated school missions', in E. Hayden and J. Thompson (eds) *International Education: Principles and Practice*, London: Kogan Page.

Sylvester, R. (2000) 'The unintended classroom: changing the angle of vision of international education', *International Schools Journal* 19 (2): 20–8.

Thomas, P. (1998) 'Education for peace: the cornerstone of international education', in E. Hayden and J. Thompson (eds) *International Education: Principles and Practice*, London: Kogan Page.

Thompson, J. (1998) 'Towards a model for international education', in E. Hayden and J. Thompson (eds) *International Education: Principles and Practice*, London: Kogan Page.

Tomlinson, J. (1995) 'Teachers and values', *International Schools Journal* 14 (2): 8–21.

Walker, G. (2000) 'One-way streets of our culture', *International Schools Journal* 19 (2): 11–19.

Waterson, M. and Hayden, M. (1999) 'International education and its contribution to the development of student attitudes', *International Schools Journal* 18 (2): 17–27.

Wragg, E.C. (1997) *The Cubic Curriculum*, London: Routledge.

3

MANAGING ASSESSMENT IN THE INTERNATIONAL SCHOOL

Robin McClelland

Introduction

The role of assessment is traditionally viewed as measuring achievement at the end of a phase of education – infant, junior, secondary or elementary and high and providing access to the next level of schooling or university. This is usually measured by externally set examinations. The enormous changes that have taken place and continue to take place in the telecommunications industry in the late twentieth and early twenty-first century have demonstrated the need for a broader interpretation of both curriculum and assessment.

Students in schools now could enter the world of work to jobs that we are only beginning to imagine. Skilled graduates no longer see job security as their most important goal. Instead, building up a range of experience and expertise in short-term contracts and working globally may have greater significance to them. Mortgage lenders now recognise that short contracts are a way of life for an increasing number of working people and acknowledge this with more flexible lending packages for house buying purposes. The attitudes, skills and knowledge valued in the new work place could well be difficult to teach and assess in an examination system that is still largely based on a nineteenth century understanding of education.

International schools often have as their clientele parents, whether nationals of the country in which the school is placed or expatriates who have embraced many of the work place changes. As consumers they have particular expectations in terms of language teaching, information, communication and technology skills in addition to external examinations. Parents who are working in another country on a short-term contract will also be conscious of the need for their children to return to a national education system or transfer to the next international school in another part of the world. It is their expectations and the changing nature of employment and the job market that is putting pressure on international schools to adopt curriculum planning and assessment systems that accommodate these new patterns.

This chapter looks particularly at the consideration and management of:

- quality control in assessment in the school;
- an assessment policy that reflects an education philosophy that accepts both the need for successful external examination outcomes and a broader interpretation of curriculum and achievement;
- testing in the school;
- teacher assessment in the day-to-day role of supporting pupils' learning;
- reliability and validity in assessment;
- the use of assessment information to promote the school.

The head of school will have responsibility for all of these areas, although some will be delegated to members of the senior management team. The head will also have an overview of how the school should function, which will be shared with the teachers. It is effective heads who create and sustain effective schools. It is their active involvement in developing ways of planning and assessing that will bring about a whole-school approach. Through active involvement and support the teaching staff will be encouraged to try out ways of planning and assessing possibly different from their normal way of working, discussing progress together and evaluating the outcomes. In doing this the head enables teachers to see strengths in new approaches and adopt these into their daily routine. An agreed system of planning and assessment by necessity must be part of school policy.

Quality control

One of the most important roles the head of school exercises is assuring the quality and consistency of the teaching and learning in the school. A school will want to ensure that it delivers education of high worth across all subjects throughout the age ranges. Quality control issues in assessment are essential in marketing the school; parents will want to know that the assessment results are reliable and hold up well to schools of similar standing. No less important will be the extracurricular activities that the school supports and the pastoral system, both of which can facilitate learning by creating for the needs of the pupil beyond the academic. A range of information should be available to provide a broad and comprehensive picture for this purpose. The senior management of a school should be able to answer the following questions:

- How is our school performing now?
  - Do we have assessment information for all sectors of the school?
  - What subjects are we assessing?
  - Are we using a range of assessment tools?
  - What aspects of learning beyond the formal curriculum do we value?
  - Do we acknowledge achievements outside school?
  - How do we make judgements about this?

- Do we know what we do well?
    - Are these in broad areas; humanities, sciences, sports, arts?
    - Can we identify why we do well?
    - Can we use this information in other areas of the school?
- How reliable is our assessment information?
    - What external/published tests do we use?
    - Why have we chosen these?
    - What skills, concepts and understanding do they assess?
    - Can we use this information to improve pupils' performance and teachers' teaching?
    - How much use do we make of teachers' ongoing assessment in the classroom?
    - How regularly do we analyse pupils' achievement to identify learning needs?
    - How often do we analyse patterns of achievement in a class to identify planning and teaching areas to be addressed?
- Are we certain of what our assessment tells us?
    - Can we interpret assessment outcomes?
    - Do we allow time for re-teaching learning that has not been achieved?
    - Are we sure we know what published tests are measuring?
- Are some aspects of our work more effective than others?
    - Is this the result of good teaching skills?
    - Do we have good resources?
    - Are they well used?
    - Are there areas where resources should be improved?
    - Can we identify what makes the difference where teaching and learning is effective?
    - Do we have an in-service programme for teachers?
    - Does it address identified deficiencies in the school?
    - Is it effective?
- Are some ethnic groups doing better than others?
    - Are we able to retrieve this information?
    - Does a pattern emerge over time?
    - Are there anxieties at particular points in the school?
    - Are there concerns within any subjects?
- Are boys and girls achieving equally?
    - Are gender outcomes analysed?
    - Do any trends emerge?
    - Are they similar to outcomes from published research?
    - Can specific action be taken in the school?
- Are some classes performing better than others?
    - Can we detect what makes the difference?

- – Are we able to use this information for the benefit of other classes?
- Are there variations in performance in different subjects or departments?
  - – Is the variation consistent over time?
  - – What changes could be considered within the school to bring about improvement?
- How do our school's present achievements compare with its previous achievements?
  - – What has changed in the last 5 years?
  - – Have specific measures been introduced that have effected change?
- How does our school's performance compare with other international schools of similar character?
  - – Have we identified schools we can compare with?
  - – Have we agreed to exchange assessment outcome information?
  - – Allowing for similar resourcing and numbers, how do our outcomes compare, measured using similar external assessment systems?
  - – What factors might be causing any variations?
  - – Do we discuss this with other schools not competing for the same pupils?

McClelland (1999)

These are probing and interrogative questions; few heads would be able to answer them instantly. It is to be hoped that they are acknowledged as important questions that will provide the range of information necessary to plan for improvements in the quality of education provided. Senior management teams might be asking:

- Is this information valued?
- Are the systems in place to enable this information to be retrieved?
- How are we responding?
- If we have undertaken this exercise before what has changed since then?

All schools would argue that they monitor standards, and the most obvious way of doing this is through examination results. Knowing where the strengths and weaknesses of the school are and how these appear over time enable a development plan to be produced to put strategies in place to bring about desirable change and ultimately improve standards. Using these questions as an agenda within the senior management team on a regular basis will produce comparative data that will prove useful in tracking change and indicating trends.

Some information for school improvement will be easily obtained from external examination results, and by comparing results over time these can be analysed to show consistency or change. Knowing the useful questions to ask of the data can produce surprising outcomes, if we look beyond the numbers of passes and grades. Other questions can only be answered by observing practice in the school and having agreed approaches to pupils' learning, planning and assessment that all teachers work within.

Assessment policy

The purpose of a policy in the school situation is to inform all those who have an interest in what the official view is on an aspect of the school's responsibilities. It should define the responsibility and indicate how it will be performed. This is important not only for prospective parents in helping them come to a decision about the most appropriate school for their children but also for both new and established teachers who know what is expected of them professionally.

- An assessment policy needs to explain the school's philosophy about assessment. It relates to the school's view of how pupils learn and the teaching approaches that are used to encourage learning. It is the product of wide consultation to ensure that teachers', parents', governors' and pupils' views are represented.
- Unlike other school policies, the assessment policy has an impact on all departments and subjects. Its contents are reflected in the curriculum policies. The policy will include:
  - what planning is required;
  - the different forms of assessment that will be used;
  - what information the different forms of assessment will provide;
  - how assessment information will be returned to pupils to inform them how they can improve their work in the future.
- There are always tensions in the purposes of assessment. The policy needs to acknowledge the accountability role and concede the necessity of testing to safeguard standards and secure high levels of achievement across the school. There is a requirement for a clear statement of what information the tests will provide and how this is to be used by the teachers.
- A greater emphasis is placed in the policy on the use made of assessment on a day-to-day basis by the teachers to provide information about pupils' learning and how this assessment information enables teachers to support the pupils' learning needs.
- If testing has a role in guaranteeing the quality of the teacher assessment then this should be stated with an explanation of when the testing takes place and how the information it provides is used.
- The relationship between planning and assessment is given prominence. A statement about assessment informing the teacher in regard to each pupil's attainment and learning needs is made either because the pupil is

having learning difficulties or is very able and should be stretched academically. It needs to explain how this advises the teacher in making changes to planning.

- The assessment policy stresses the importance attached to enabling the teacher to be flexible enough to take account of individual's learning requirements.
- Where pupils are arriving from schools from other countries, a statement is made that informs the reader how the new pupils are accommodated in the school at the appropriate academic levels to ensure a smooth transition and minimum delay in the continuation of learning.
- A policy needs to include how parents are involved in the process:
  - transferring information from one school to another;
  - parent–teacher consultations;
  - contacting teachers on other occasions;
  - written reports.
- Policies need to be reviewed regularly to check that:
  - everyone understands the contents;
  - it reflects the practice in the school;
  - it is realistic;
  - it enables planning and assessment to be effective;
  - pupils' learning outcomes have benefited from the process.

Testing in school

The use of published or external tests plays a part in the life of most schools. Many national systems use a range of standardised tests at different points in a pupil's compulsory education. The main purpose of these is accountability. The test will check that the assessment the teacher is making in the classroom is at the appropriate level against a national standard. It can also be used to judge the effectiveness of the whole school against a standard and enable one school to be compared with another.

Many international schools buy into a national assessment system, e.g. British International Schools. In doing so they are adopting the highly structured British curriculum (National Curriculum) and undertaking the elaborate assessment system that is an essential part of it, beginning at age 5 years and continuing until age 16 years. Increasingly, international schools are recognising the very positive values in working with a broad range of nationalities and want a curriculum that reflects this. The International Baccalaureate has now introduced a Middle Years Programme and a Primary Years Programme for this purpose. Other schools undertake courses leading to university-recognised examinations, such as International General Certificate of Secondary Education (IGCSE), Advanced International Certificate of Education (AICE), International Baccalaureate (IB) and Advanced Level (A level), but before that make their own decisions about an appropriate curriculum and assessment.

International schools often feel quite vulnerable about assessment as they are frequently isolated schools trying to ensure that the standard of education they provide is of the same quality as that in national systems possibly thousands of miles away. Published standardised tests are used to demonstrate that quality is being maintained.

A large number of tests are available, developed and produced commercially to measure some aspect of competence or learning attainment such as in tests of numeracy and reading (Levy and Goldstein, 1984). Tests are usually 'standardised'; they have been tested on a large particular sample. The test user will then know that the test outcome is reliable compared with that sample.

The buyers of such tests in international schools need to ensure that the sample is a meaningful one for their clientele. If the purpose of the test is to allow teachers in the international school to compare outcomes with a standardised sample then the reservations of Corbett and Wilson (1990: 14–15) should be noted:

> Outcome measures stated in terms of student learning do not provide direction as to what school systems should do to produce different results.

> Testing programmes, both in terms of results and the implications for action, ignore variations in district contexts that may affect the importance of the results, and the appropriateness of certain responses from community to community.

Tests may provide information about quality of learning, but they do not help the teacher in analysing poor outcomes and deciding what can be done to improve the situation. It should also be noted that the context in which the tests were originally standardised were different from those in the international school and this will have a bearing on the results.

Airasian (1988) comments that tests carry with them a feeling of traditional values and are respected symbols of a broad range of administrative, academic and moral values. Whether or not they have any impact on pupils' learning they have an important perceptual impact on the public. Schools need to recognise this and use such tests when they are sure that they will be in support of the learning they are promoting and to support the teachers' own assessments. Test results appear to have greater significance than teachers' day-to-day assessment for some parents. Using test results to confirm teacher judgement can give greater emphasis to teachers' more detailed knowledge of progress and understanding.

The use of published tests that do not relate to the curriculum and teachers' learning objectives take up valuable teaching time and are unlikely to inform the teachers how to make their teaching better and learning more accessible. The tests may not be set in a meaningful context for the pupils. The questions will probably not relate to work they have been doing in class. They often test isolated aspects of knowledge or understanding. Their alien nature can confuse pupils. Some teachers respond to this by providing more experience of tests to provide familiarity, but in doing so reduce the amount of time available for teaching.

The use of a standardised test over a period of years with the same age groups may be of value to the school in comparing achievement patterns. By scrutinising the results it should be possible to say whether the standard in the aspect of learning has improved over the period of time. Considering what has changed in the teaching context may enable reasons for the change to be identified. It also needs to provide data on changes in outcome for gender and ethnic groups in the school.

Teacher assessment in the classroom

Assessment is undertaken in schools for a number of purposes, sometimes in tension with one another. In this section, the different purposes will be considered.

The main functions of assessment are:

1   formative;
2   diagnostic;
3   summative;
4   evaluative;
5   informative.

Assessment for formative purposes

Formative assessment is in support of learning. Shepard (1992) stresses the significance of this function:

> ...the teacher has need of constant information about what the student knows and the strategies being used to process and comprehend new concepts. By embedding diagnostic teaching in instructional activities, teachers can preserve the integrity of assessment tasks (the wholeness of the task and natural learning context) and protect instructional time that would otherwise be diverted to testing.
>
> (Shepard, 1992: 312)

All teachers have the opportunity to use feedback from assessment to discover how effectively the pupils have learned from their teaching. By regularly checking understanding, teachers can modify their planning to accommodate difficulties that the pupils may be experiencing. This may mean repeating work or differentiating work so that some pupils are challenged to extend their learning and some are given extra support to achieve the basic learning requirements. Not all teachers make use of these opportunities to reflect on the success of both the learning and teaching, and in not doing so much is lost. Regular assessment enables the teacher to recognise problems and deal with them quickly so that progress can be maintained. Formative assessment usually takes place while a unit of work is ongoing rather than at the end.

The important issue arising from formative assessment is how teachers feed back information to their pupils so that they know what to do to improve. It is not enough to say that they must do better; they need to know what 'better' looks like rather than trying to guess what is required. In a problem-solving exercise this may require a range of questions suggesting possibilities:

- What would happen if ...?
- If you did A instead of B what would be the outcome?
- Are there any other ways of approaching this task?

These are questions that probe and prod and cause the pupil to reconsider ideas or strategies, which require them to think again, or enquire further.

In a writing task it might be helpful to show the writer an example of a piece of work that demonstrates the quality of outcome desired. Many teachers are now maintaining portfolios of work, good examples of different types of writing and different grades to show to students. A pupil achieving a B grade would benefit from seeing A-grade work. A pupil achieving C-grade work might be downhearted at seeing A-grade work, but motivated by seeing B-grade work. It is important that the improvement proposed is attainable for each pupil. Where pupils are very grade conscious, they may appreciate the opportunity to submit work as a first draft to be graded and be given advice on how to improve it. In this way, they can respond to the comments and possibly improve upon their grade by resubmitting a finished product.

In a move away from external testing regimes, many schools and education authorities are turning to 'performance assessment' or 'authentic assessment', both of which are based on assessment of the learning that takes place on the classroom. Darling-Hammond et al. (1995) describes authentic assessment as having the following characteristics:

- You can see how students learn as well as what they have learnt.
- One tries to assess complex tasks which call for integrating knowledge.
- Students are challenged to generate new knowledge and products.
- Tasks call for the ability to engage in intellectual, interpersonal or intrapersonal work.
- Tasks reflect the reality of the field of study being explored in the curriculum.
- Tasks can last for a variety of time periods, both long and short.
- Tasks are embedded in the curriculum and an assessment is made of a pupil's response to a genuine learning experience, not a contrived one.

- Tasks are set in real contexts that connect school work to real world experience.

All of these characteristics except for the last two are shared by performance assessment. Black (1998: 87–8) explains the difference between the two:

> A performance assessment can be an *ad hoc* assessment exercise, whereas an 'authentic' assessment is a performance assessment in the normal learning context.

Authentic assessment is planned into the topic or scheme of work and is an essential part of the learning experience. Performance assessment, although still assessing understanding and application in a realistic situation, may be planned as an isolated assessment task.

Only a few schools would be prepared to adopt such an approach to deliver the whole curriculum. It nevertheless offers many advantages to pupils for demonstrating a range of interrelated skills that fit very much with the requirements of the changing workplace discussed in the introduction. The teacher also has the opportunity to assess a broad range of skills in the learning context. Although assessment should be high in validity, there could be difficulties in achieving a level of reliability.

Assessment for diagnostic purposes

If formative assessment is used to discover what pupils have learned and at times to identify a learning difficulty then diagnostic assessment is used to enquire further into the nature and cause of the difficulty. The intention is to suggest strategies to overcome the difficulty. This evaluation is usually undertaken by the teacher, possibly in consultation with other professionals within the school. On occasions a teacher may call a meeting of all teachers who work with the pupil to discover whether the learning difficulty spreads across a number of subjects. Using the shared expertise within the school an individual education plan (IEP) may be drawn up for the pupil with short-term learning goals to be achieved within defined time blocks. The IEP would be reviewed at intervals to judge its effectiveness. Occasionally, outside expertise may be called upon to provide advice. Diagnostic assessment is closely associated with formative assessment.

Formative and diagnostic assessment has many advantages over published tests, as it is:

- *Ongoing.* The teacher is carrying out assessment every day, noting progress and development, acting upon this knowledge in supporting the pupils and altering planning where necessary. The assessment skills teachers will be using are:

- observing;
- listening;
- asking questions;
- setting tests concerning work covered;
- assessing work.

- *Integrated within the learning and teaching context.* The teacher knows what outcomes are expected of the planning and asks questions that give direction to pupils' thinking and provide information about levels of understanding. Teachers' knowledge of each pupils' attainment is added to on a daily basis as questions are asked and support is given in the classroom.
- *Context and skill based.* The assessment is within the topic context that the pupils are working in, and the questions being asked make sense within the unit of work. Skills, such as using the Internet, are meaningfully being used for research within the unit of work and can be assessed for their effectiveness. Assessment provides a broader picture of the pupils' understanding of a range of interrelated skills within the topic context.
- *Developmental.* Whereas a test provides a snapshot of what a pupil is able to do at a particular time, teacher assessment builds up a picture of growth and development regularly over a period of time. Teachers do not record and act upon everything they see a pupil do but look for evidence of progress. They can thus not only find out what a pupil understands, but also learn about the rate of development, what consolidation may be necessary and the next steps which should be taken.
- *Building a picture of the whole child.* All skills and concepts are seen together in a range of contexts. The teacher knows what skills the pupil can transfer to other contexts and what knowledge and concepts can be used in problem-solving situations, this being a good measure of understanding.

Assessment for summative purposes

External tests and examinations are usually considered as summative assessment when they come at the end of a taught syllabus. Teacher assessment can also be summative when it draws together what a pupil has achieved at the end of a period of time, often the end of term or year. It is used to provide a description of broad achievement, possibly for a new teacher or for parents. It has formative value for a new teacher, enabling decisions to be made about starting points for beginning a new year's teaching or for a new school when a pupil transfers. This is particularly important when a pupil transfers from one international school to another and from one country to another. Test results and teacher assessment are complementary.

The information needs to be clear and precise about:

- work covered;
- skills/concepts achieved;

- broad and balanced achievements covering academic, cultural, sporting and social areas;
- needs for the future.

Not all tests are summative alone, a teacher may devise a test of a unit of work to summarise achievement but also to note where there are deficiencies. Using this information some aspects may be re-taught to the whole class or some pupils may be given additional work to consolidate understanding.

Assessment for evaluative purposes

The evaluative function of assessment relates closely to the formative. In reflecting on the effectiveness of pupils' learning the teacher will need to consider and evaluate the quality of the teaching, and particularly the planning. It is sometimes hard to admit that the problem lies not with the pupils' ability to learn but with the appropriateness of the planning and the clarity and enthusiasm of the teaching.

There are several questions that are useful for teachers to ask of themselves:

- Are the learning objectives clear and precise?
- Do the pupils understand what they mean?
- Are they realistic for the time available?
- Do I have the necessary resources?
- How am I going to make this interesting?
- What questions will I ask to engage the pupils?
- How will I know that they understand what I want them to undertake?
- What methods of assessment will I use?

Self-reflection on effectiveness of teaching is a powerful tool in professional growth.

Assessment for informative purposes

This function of assessment concerns providing information to a range of people or groups who are entitled to it. These include firstly and most importantly the pupils, whom we have already discussed, parents, receiving teachers, heads of department/school and school board members. They all require information for different purposes:

- for pupils to enable them to do better in the future;
- for receiving teachers so that future teaching can be as effective as possible;
- for parents so they can appreciate their child's progress and development;
- for heads of department to assure standards and organise class groupings in the future;

- for heads of school to know about both individual achievement and patterns of achievement within the school;
- for school board members to know that the school is functioning appropriately and to take an interest in individual/department success.

Issues of validity and reliability

The issue of the quality of an assessment test is usually described in terms of reliability and validity. Gipps and Stobart (1993: 22) discuss reliability:

> ... if the test were given on a number of occasions to the same child, or was marked by different people, would we get the same score? This is important for teachers because it answers the question: Would this pupil achieve the same score if the test had been taken yesterday instead of today? The greater the reliability of the test, the more closely the scores on the two days would coincide.

For published tests the reliability factor is important to guarantee outcomes in different schools, under different conditions. Cultural differences are factors that may affect the reliability of tests. Most are standardised with sample student populations quite different from that of an international school. Senior management needs to be aware of this in choosing published tests.

Validity is a measure of how well the results of the assessment task reflect the purposes that it was intended to assess. For teachers this means that the assessment should match as closely as possible their learning objectives for the taught unit. In reality it is difficult to attain high reliability and validity together. Tests are often considered to be high in reliability but low in validity; they measure limited or narrowly defined aspects of learning in attempting to retain reliability.

Teacher assessment is generally thought to be high in validity, as it is tied closely to the learning objectives taught, but low in reliability, as the results could be very different if another teacher used the same test. A balance between the two must be sought, but assessing what has been taught must be the most important. Harlen (1994: 13) states that 'the usefulness of an assessment is directly related to its validity, providing it is not so low in reliability as to call this into question.'

Greater reliability of teacher assessment can be sought within a school where teachers in a department:

- plan together with clear learning objectives for the units of work;
- devise assessments which reflect these learning objectives;
- use the tests with the same age group of pupils and explain and set them in the same way;
- share the marking so a common understanding is achieved of what different levels of achievement look like;

- share expectations of outcomes.

This is again a useful in-service experience within the school in sharing an understanding of standards, and raises the status of teacher assessment by combining validity of assessment with greater reliability. This aspect of assessment should be recognised in the assessment policy document and be developed as a whole-school approach.

Using assessment information to promote the school

With international schools it is unlikely that assessment information will be used to compare schools in the same city or in the rest of the country. It is nevertheless useful to be able to use assessment results to promote the positive outcomes of the school. In using the questions set out in the section on Quality Control, a range of information can be presented to both existing and prospective parents. This will provide information not only about attainment in academic areas of the school but also cultural, sport and community aspects that are measured. Gender and ethnic outcomes provide important messages about the school's values to parents on the importance attached to equal opportunities in the school.

The analysis of the data on the success of the teaching of EAL and of information and communication technology (ICT) and its resources will be welcomed by most parents, both nationals and expatriates.

Where the analysis shows shortcomings, these can be turned to the school's advantage by demonstrating how it is planning to develop resources to further enhance opportunities for pupils' learning.

Assessment information alone will not promote a school, but well-presented and broad assessment information will add greatly to its appeal.

Summary

Assessment is an integral part of planning and teaching in all schools. It is at its most effective where there is a whole-school approach. This chapter began by stating that the workplace and job opportunities are changing dramatically. Teaching and assessment must be flexible enough to accommodate the skills necessary for the twenty-first century. Assessment information must be meaningful and specific to parents and students. Parents whose work requires them to be residents of a number of different countries while their children are of school age expect comparative data that allows them to gauge progress and compare standards with specific national education systems. The management of assessment in international schools is everyone's responsibility. The main points of the chapter are summarised:

- The head of the school must be actively involved in changing attitudes to assessment and supporting new approaches to teaching and assessment.

- The assessment information should be able to be analysed to answer questions about the effectiveness of the school.
- All schools should have assessment policies that make clear statements about how assessment is used to support pupils' learning.
- Although published tests are highly regarded by the public they rarely provide teachers with information that will improve their teaching or the pupils' learning.
- Five functions of assessment are: formative, diagnostic, summative, evaluative and informative. Formative and diagnostic are the functions of which teachers make most use.
- Assessments on a continuing basis in the classroom allow the teacher to reflect on the quality of planning and teaching and make adjustments for the benefit of the pupils' learning.
- The issue of reliability and validity is important in assessment. Published tests are high in reliability. Teacher assessment is high in validity. Reliability can be improved in teacher assessment.
- The analysis of assessment data can be effective in promoting the success of the school to existing and prospective parents.

References

Airasian, P. (1988) 'Symbolic validation: the case of state-mandated, high stakes testing', *Education Evaluation and Policy Analysis* 10: 4.

Black, P. (1998) *Testing: Friend or Foe? Theory and Practice of Assessment and Testing*, Lewes: Falmer Press.

Corbett, D. and Wilson, B. (1990) 'Unintended and unwelcome: The local impact of state testing', paper presented at the AERA Conference, April, Boston.

Darling-Hammond, L., Ancess, J. and Falk, B. (1995) *Authentic Assessment in Action: Studies of Schools and Students at Work*, New York: Teacher's College Press.

Gipps, C. and Stobart, G. (1993) *Assessment: A Teachers' Guide to the Issues*, London: Hodder & Stoughton.

Harlen, W. (ed.) (1994) *Enhancing Quality in Assessment*, London: Paul Chapman Publishing.

Levy, P. and Goldstein, H. (eds) (1984) *Tests in Education: A Book of Critical Reviews*, London: Academic Press.

McClelland, R. (1999) 'Managing assessment in the international school', paper presented at the Latin American Headteachers' Conference, May, Lima.

Shepard L.A. (1992) 'Commentary: what policy makers who mandate tests should know about the new psychology of intellectual ability and learning', in B.R. Gifford and M.C. O'Connor (eds) *Changing Assessments: Alternative Views of Aptitude, Achievement and Instruction*, Boston: Kluwer.

4

TEACHING AND MANAGING
ENGLISH AS AN ADDITIONAL OR
SECOND LANGUAGE IN
INTERNATIONAL SCHOOLS

Jackie Holderness

Introduction

This chapter explores practical ways in which international schools can effectively deal with the management and teaching of students who are learning English as a second or additional language (EAL). Examples of EAL provision have been taken from the American, British and Australian systems and from recent research by international school teachers studying at Oxford Brookes University. This research focuses on managing and teaching 'global nomads' (McCaig, 1992) – people who tend to typify the international school population. It has been argued that the term 'trans-language learners' may be a more appropriate term for international school bilinguals who are accustomed to crossing language boundaries.

It may be helpful at this stage to define some of the terms:

- *Mother tongue*: a child's first, or preferred, home language (L1).
- *Target language:* one which is being learned at school as an additional language (L2).
- *Host language:* the majority language spoken by the population of the country in which the international school is based.
- *EAL:* the term currently preferred, in the UK, is English as an additional language (EAL) rather than English as a second language (ESL) or English for speakers of other languages (ESOL). EAL is the term used in this chapter.

Most international schools still speak of their ESL department and many would feel that terminology does not make a difference. However, one international school in Europe recently switched terms to EAL and discovered that the change of terms generated a more positive attitude among staff towards students' linguistic backgrounds and abilities. English may be, for some children, a third or even fourth language, and international school staff need to recognise pupils' achievements in their home languages.

Contexts for English as an additional language (EAL)

EAL provision varies widely across international schools, from dual-language programmes which are designed to develop bilingualism (for example Spanish/ English) to monolingual schools (for example a company-based English-speaking school for children of American expatriates). There are schools with several school languages, as in the European Union's European School system, where children are taught in one of the nine European Union languages but also learn two or three languages. Most typical, however, are the UK- or US-style international schools, where children learn in English and where a large proportion of the school is English-speaking, but where many children from diverse language backgrounds are learning English as an additional language. These potential bilinguals bring their language(s) and culture(s) to school, where they may encounter one of the following forms of bilingual education:

- *Immersion:* children are taught in their second language (L2), but their first language (L1) is accepted, and there is some effort made to maintain the mother tongue.
- *Submersion:* children are surrounded by English and the mother tongue is not welcomed – 'sink or swim'. Instruction is in L2 and most of the students are L2 speakers.
- *Partial immersion:* children are offered some curriculum subjects in their second language. In some cases there may be two parallel curricula so that children have an element of choice. On the whole, the curriculum is shared between two languages, e.g. Atlanta International School, USA.
- *Bilingual programmes:* children spend almost equal time learning in two languages.
- *Mother tongue maintenance:* many international students attend mother tongue classes on Saturdays or in the evenings to sustain progress in their L1. Some students will need to return to their home country school system and most wish to maintain cultural links with their home country. Teachers are beginning to realise that using L1 does not jeopardise progress in English. The International Schools Curriculum Project (ISCP, 1996) suggested that being able to use L1 is vital if children are to maintain their cultural identity and remain emotionally stable.

Baker (1993) identifies the characteristics of weak and strong forms of bilingualism, shown in a simplified version in Table 4.1.

Schools which see the range of languages in their school as an asset rather than as a problem are most likely to nurture the self-esteem of their students. Several schools display posters, in as many languages as possible, to welcome

Table 4.1 Types of bilingual education

Type of bilingualism	Language of classroom	Language aims
Weak forms of bilingualism		
Submersion	Majority language	Monolingualism
Withdrawal/sheltered L2 instruction	Majority language with pull-out L2 classes	Monolingualism/limited bilingualism
Mainstream	Majority language with L2 support	Limited bilingualism
Strong forms of bilingualism		
Immersion	Bilingual with emphasis on L2	Bilingualism/biliteracy
Maintenance/heritage language	Bilingual with emphasis on L1	Bilingualism/biliteracy
Dual language	Bilingual – some subjects in L1, others in L2	Bilingualism/biliteracy

Source: simplified from Baker, C. (1993) *Foundations of Bilingual Education and Bilingualism*, Clevedon: Multilingual Matters, with permission from Multiligual Matters Ltd.

visitors to the school. One school, with over 40 languages represented, has started to highlight one language per week, in a special display area or the entrance hall.

Key principles of English as an additional language (EAL)

Despite the diversity of setting and approach to be found in international schools, there are some key principles which underpin effective language teaching and learning. The first of these is the need for relevance and motivation. If L2 learning can be made *near, dear* and *clear* to the children, they will succeed. The students' developmental levels of maturity, cognition and social interaction can influence their levels of concentration and motivation. They will also influence their learning strategies and their approach to learning.

The second principle relates to culture. The EAL teacher has a responsibility to support the EAL student's induction into the culture of the school, whatever it may be. The ECIS Guide to School Evaluation and Accreditation (ECIS, 1997: 58) points out that an EAL programme should include 'songs, nursery rhyme, games and stories of Anglo-American cultural heritage to enrich the student's understanding of that culture and the colloquial use of its language.'

The third principle relates to the developmental nature of language learning. According to Cummins (1986), children have first to develop basic interpersonal communicative skills (BICS). Communicative skills are those which enable one to operate successfully on a day-to-day level, as shown in Table 4.2.

Developing BICS takes between 1 and 2 years. Children then progress and

Table 4.2 Some common language functions for communicative competence

Agreeing	Apologising	Asking for permission	Asking for help
Classifying	Comparing	Commanding	Criticising
Denying	Describing	Enquiring	Evaluating
Expressing preferences	Expressing obligation	Explaining	Giving directions
Hypothesising	Identifying	Inferring	Making plans
Predicting	Refusing	Reporting	Sequencing
Suggesting	Warning	Wishing	Wondering

aim to reach cognitive and academic language proficiency (CALP), similar to GCSE or High School levels, but this may take between 5 and 7 years. It is also accepted (Mills, 1993; Genesee, 1994; Hester, 1994; Baker, 1996) that all learners of English follow a similar continuum of development, and that learners make similar mistakes in English, for example 'He goeded home yesterday', irrespective of their language origins.

Finally, over time it is essential that EAL and subject teachers find ways to introduce problems and challenges to enable students move from things to ideas because, as this notice – seen on an international classroom wall in Sao Paulo, Brazil – points out, it is by exploring ideas that learners learn most:

> *GREAT PEOPLE TALK ABOUT IDEAS*
>
> *AVERAGE PEOPLE TALK ABOUT OTHER PEOPLE*
>
> *SMALL PEOPLE TALK ABOUT THINGS*

Managing the EAL department

The EAL department represents incoming students' first interface with the English-speaking culture of the school. Its ethos, dynamism and effectiveness will create an important first impression of the school. The calibre of its staff, if good relationships and systems are fostered, will indirectly influence the teaching quality and effectiveness of all the other teachers, and thus have an impact on the climate of the whole school.

One aspect of the role of the head of the EAL department is to ensure that there is some reference in the school's mission statement to the EAL language learning objectives and approaches which are currently being adopted by the school. An example of such a statement is offered in the ECIS Policy Planner:

> It is a policy that the basic language of instruction shall be English. In order to help students who do not have an adequate working knowledge

of English, the school will provide appropriate ESL, bilingual and multilingual assistance. When staff members are not available to provide such assistance, parents and other persons in the community may be asked to serve as resource persons.

(ECIS, 1997, section 7.50: 1)

It is up to the head of EAL to then ensure that the educational practice *as experienced by the students* accurately reflects the mission statement of the school.

Ellis (1985) laments that, because EAL is not an examination subject but a servicing subject, it makes EAL marginal to the mainstream life of a school in the eyes of policymakers, school administrators and even the staff themselves. Clearly, such views need to be challenged through continuing professional development (CPD) and discussion. The EAL department, often undervalued and under-resourced, has the potential to be a centre of innovation with regard to teaching styles and to cross-cultural awareness. Most EAL pupils may only need its services on an intensive level for a short period of time. However, carefully funded and structured support for intermediate and advanced students is essential if EAL children are to fulfil their potential, perform well in examinations and achieve genuine bilingualism and bicultural identity.

The management tasks and responsibilities that the head of an EAL department has and many other areas of responsibility are summarised in Box 4.1.

Whole-school issues: withdrawal or inclusion?

Many EAL decisions will need to be taken at school level, e.g. colleagues will have to agree whether to stream or group EAL students according to their level of English or according to their cognitive ability. One of the most pressing issues for the head of EAL is deciding whether to operate a withdrawal model of language learning, with increasing levels of mainstream experience, or whether to introduce EAL students into the mainstream from the very beginning. Traditionally, EAL pupils at secondary and primary levels were given a 'crash course' of intensive language teaching, with daily withdrawal into small focused groups. This is still the model used in many international schools and there are many reasons why, in some schools, the model may be entirely appropriate. At one international school, in Europe, students from different year groups were grouped together for specialist beginners' or intermediate withdrawal classes (1.5 hours each group) during their first year of EAL. If withdrawal classes do exist, it is important to decide which subjects students should miss, e.g. it would be better not to withdraw a primary student from the language arts class or the literacy hour (in UK curriculum schools) when he/she would receive dedicated exposure to written and spoken English.

Many teachers have now begun to revise their views on withdrawal. As Levine (1990: 29) points out, withdrawal can negatively affect students' status

Box 4.1 The roles and responsibilities of the head of the EAL department

---

The roles and responsibilities of the head of the EAL department:
- assessing and reviewing new arrivals and designing programmes for EAL support within and without the mainstream classroom;
- providing subject and class teachers with materials and support, e.g. a 'survival box' to help settle newly arrived students, with picture dictionaries, cassette stories and picture books, flashcards of basic vocabulary, etc.;
- teaching students, individually and in groups, in a dedicated teaching space and/or mainstream classrooms;
- advising colleagues about EAL students' language needs;
- helping colleagues appreciate the linguistic demands of their curriculum subjects, and advising on ways to ensure maximum access to the curriculum for EAL students;
- devising and refining language activities, which will encourage communicative competence and collaborative group work;
- team-teaching with class or subject teachers;
- choosing, ordering and disseminating resources, e.g. visual materials, appropriate dictionaries, books for teachers, textbooks, etc.;
- negotiating a budget to sustain a rolling programme of EAL INSET, which will enable all colleagues to improve their skills as language teachers, whatever their specialist subject;
- inducting and supporting newly recruited colleagues who may not have previously worked in an international school;
- looking for ways to celebrate the language groups represented within the school, so that all students become more aware of language;
- being a good model of EAL practice;
- planning departmental development;
- being the visible 'leader' in all of the above.

---

and achievement in school. She suggests that 'mainstreaming increases the possibility of ending the isolation of specialist language teachers and makes way for the productive integration and sharing of their expertise in the mainstream.' Bourne's (1994) model of partnership teaching in the UK, in which EAL colleagues work alongside class teachers at the planning, teaching and assessment stages, can work very well for both EAL and mainstream students.

Syanen (1993: 80) also makes a case for team teaching, based on her experiences in Oregon. She advises 'Don't pull out the kids, pull in the teacher' and suggests that pull-out programmes were 'disruptive to the classroom and the learners'. In her work she found that, where the EAL teacher and class teacher decided to team teach, all children benefited from the EAL teacher's input, extra visual support and carefully differentiated work.

In summary, many schools around the world are moving from the notion of withdrawal towards a policy of inclusion, just as they are moving from their nationally based curriculum towards a more international one.

Assessing and teaching new arrivals

EAL students are at their most vulnerable when they first arrive at an international school. They may experience a form of 'culture shock'. Not only is the language of instruction often different but also both the ethos and pedagogy of the new school may be at variance with the school they have come from in, for example, the status of women, relationships between children and adults, responses to behaviour, social and academic expectations and styles of interaction. In an American school in London, middle-school students expressed concern about social issues rather than academic ones (see Figure 4.1).

EAL staff can help their colleagues to achieve greater consistency about their responses to shyness, use of mother tongue, name-calling, inappropriate behaviour, parental concern and so on. EAL teachers can encourage colleagues to collect information on the student's language and literacy skills in L1 and operate a peer-support system, in which the new arrival is given a few special 'buddies'. Teachers can also recruit all members of the class to take on the responsibility of helping the new arrival to learn English, find their way around and feel welcome, as in the case that Sherman (1993: 62) describes. A teacher

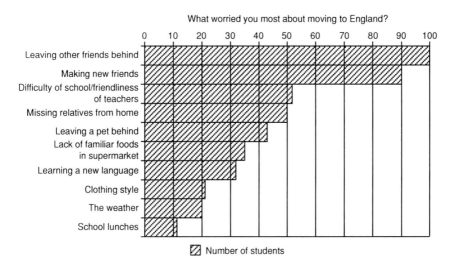

Figure 4.1 Students' concerns about moving country; language here came relatively low as the countries concerned were USA and England (Eriksen, 1997: 57).

was trying to integrate a newly arrived Vietnamese child, Tam, and turned a discipline lapse (children not getting into their listening positions before a story) into a learning point, 'Get into your listening positions so that Tam will learn from seeing what you do.'

Managing teaching, learning and the curriculum

There are differences between primary/elementary and secondary/high school departments in their management of EAL provision. The optimum age for learning an additional language has remained controversial (Singleton, 1989). Young children are less self-conscious as learners and tend to make rapid progress. They tend to make friends very quickly and focus on the 'here-and-now' of wanting to belong. Older learners can bring more conscious learning strategies, analytical abilities and study skills to their learning, but can be hampered by shyness, resentment towards being removed from old friends or pressure from their understanding of the need to succeed in examinations. International schools need to recognise that 'ESL teaching is developmental, allowing students to acquire English to their full potential at a pace appropriate to their age and developmental levels' (ECIS, 1997: 136).

Secondary EAL usually involves more explicit teaching of language features, together with subject-specific content and support across the curriculum. At secondary level, since the 1960s students have been able to follow a curriculum designed specifically for international learners: the International General Certificate of Education (IGCSE) and the International Baccalaureate (IB). More recently, the IB has introduced its Middle Years Programme (MYP, IBO, 1995).

During the middle years, in the MYP programme, students study language A and language B. One of these may be English. There are four main language objectives in the programme:

- memory;
- attitude;
- understanding;
- doing (for example producing a class newspaper or giving a speech).

Primary EAL is often based upon mainstream English mother tongue teaching, e.g. cross-curricular links, apprenticeship reading and literacy hours (UK) whole-language programmes or basal readers (US). The International Baccalaureate Organisation (IBO) Primary Years Programme (PYP) was introduced in 1998, based upon the International Schools Curriculum Project (ISCP, 1996). PYP favours a holistic approach to developing language skills and encourages an enquiry-based approach to learning, suggesting that the following questions might provide a valuable framework for learning, irrespective of curriculum content:

- What is it like?
- How does it work?
- Why is it like it is?
- How is it changing?
- How is it connected to other things?
- What are the points of view?
- What is our responsibility?
- How do we know?

The PYP curriculum framework is 'an expression and extension of three inter-related questions: What do we want to learn? How best will we learn? How will we know what we have learnt?' (IBO, 1998: 12).

Supporting EAL students in their reading development

Since reading skills underpin learning across the curriculum, all subject and class teachers need to be aware of strategies used by readers, which are:

- *Semantic strategies: searching for meaning.* The EAL student may find cross-cultural information gaps a problem. For example, a Nigerian child who has never seen snow before could have difficulties with a poem about a Canadian winterscape.
- *Graphophonic strategies: identifying words by their letter patterns and how words would sound, if read aloud.* EAL students whose mother tongue uses another alphabet will have to master a new system, which may be written and read in a different direction, e.g. right to left, bottom to top.
- *Syntactic strategies:* using familiarity with spoken language to predict sentence structure. EAL students are clearly disadvantaged here until they have heard a great deal of English read aloud. The EAL student needs to hear the syntax of fiction and non-fiction read aloud expressively and with clear pronunciation.

To support EAL students' reading development, teachers can analyse provide EAL students with a diagram of the key concepts and key vocabulary to look at before the text is read and prepare visuals of keywords. EAL departments may find it useful to give subject and class teachers model planning proformas, where they can identify language features within a forthcoming lesson (Gibbons, 1991).

Assessment and record keeping

EAL students can be adversely affected in examinations and tests because of cultural reasons (for example unfamiliarity with topics chosen) or because of linguistic reasons (for example unfamiliar vocabulary and the way questions are framed). Authentic, classroom-based assessment (for example running records or miscue analysis in reading) is more useful to plan effectively for students' learning. The use of the following procedures can be helpful:

- Think-alouds: Garcia (1994) claims that the use of 'think-alouds', in which students share their thoughts as they attempt to perform a task, can help teachers who work with second language students. Through 'think-alouds', teachers can discover not only the types of challenges that students encounter with a task or a text but also how they deal with such challenges.
- Reading logs and diaries, where students record and evaluate the books that they have read.
- Writing folders, where students keep work in process, together with the draft stages of completed work.
- Teacher conferences, where students discuss their progress and set targets for the short-term future.
- Target-setting (QCA, 1999), where teachers identify specific targets for each student or group of students. These are recorded and monitored, so that students' progress is carefully reviewed.

Support for more advanced students

Debate often arises about the length of time over which the EAL student should receive language support. There is no hard and fast rule, but students who have made good progress in communicative English (BICS) and who seem to be able to cope in the mainstream classroom may still need explicit teaching to extend vocabulary, develop academic English skills (CALP) and refine their language-learning strategies.

Implications for examinations

Where examinations are involved, the EAL student is, inevitably, going to encounter an extra challenge. Time spent on revision, memory and study techniques, although useful to all students, will be particularly valuable for EAL students. Ideally, an EAL student should not be entered for an examination if the chances of success are minimal. Realistic appraisals of potential performance are essential to protect students and their parents from disappointment.

Managing teaching approaches

Inevitably, any school may be a 'melting pot' of different, sometimes contradictory, teaching styles. This is even more true for international schools, where colleagues may have been trained in different educational systems. Language teaching approaches have changed over time, and the last 20 years have seen a shift from the direct method (no L1 allowed in L2 lessons) to a more interactive communicative approach. Sears (1998: 67), in describing current methodology, suggests that 'the emphasis in ESL classrooms is on providing opportunities for the real use of English in authentic contexts.'

Recent work into the 'accelerated learning' cycle (Smith, 1998: 23) suggests that all teachers should try to:

- create a supportive learning environment;
- connect learning to prior knowledge;
- give students the BIG picture (a summary or overview of the lesson content) before teaching the class;
- describe outcomes: 'by the end of this lesson, you will be able to …';
- provide teaching input which is stimulating, well paced and multisensory;
- use visuals;
- focus on understanding and comprehension;
- demonstrate or model the skills and learning strategies they wish to teach;
- enable students to perform tasks to practise skills and consolidate knowledge, with manipulatives, if necessary;
- design collaborative and communicative situations and share these with colleagues so they can adapt them to suit different subjects;
- review the key concepts, through concept or mind maps;
- teach memory techniques, e.g. mnemonics and metaphors.

Many EAL teachers advocate and support their colleagues with 'sheltered instruction' (Schifini, 1994), in which subject teachers modify the content of the curriculum to make their teaching comprehensible to EAL students. Teachers can also encourage interaction by using pair work, group work and jigsaw techniques. They can provide opportunities for EAL students to have 'time out' from concentrating by varying activities during the course of a lesson.

Liaison between EAL, class and subject teachers

Colleagues will have to agree and be clear about the school's procedures for establishing the most efficient and effective lines of communication between EAL specialists and subject or class teachers. Some schools use a progress log or ring binder which the EAL student carries around. Setting specific targets with the EAL student can be very helpful, e.g. 'My next goals are …; My target for next month is …'. Any teacher working with the student can then contribute to this profile. It can include samples of work, test results and assessment proformas. EAL staff need to find unthreatening ways to audit staff practices and to identify staff development needs with regard to EAL.

Staff development within the EAL department

Ideally, EAL colleagues will meet together across the age phases on a regular basis to exchange ideas and experiences and to plan appropriate and school-wide support for EAL students and their families. This is too important to be left to chance, however, and it is a management responsibility to see that it happens. Manageable ways can be sought by EAL colleagues to appraise the quality of their own work within the department through activities such as inviting each other to observe lessons, moderating students' written work and planning departmental INSET (in-service training).

Managing colleagues and a staff development programme

The Swann Report (1985) emphasised that ESL pupils should be regarded as the responsibility of all teachers. This has implications for school-wide staff development, and also, therefore, a corresponding management implication.

There are several opportunities for such development in international schools. Many schools run a rolling rota of staff attendance at the annual ECIS conferences. IB teachers are offered a supportive network and international-specific INSET, and there are several courses in Britain and the USA designed to meet international teachers' professional needs, for example the Master of Arts (MA) programmes at the universities of Bath and Oxford Brookes. For EAL specialists, there are also the Teaching English to Speakers of Other Languages of the US (TESOL), the International Association of Teachers of English as a Foreign Language of the UK (IATEFL) and Primary English Teachers' Association of Australia (PETA) conferences each year. Many EAL teachers attend the biennial, international Society for Effective Affective Learning (SEAL) conference as well. Journals, organisations and websites which may be useful are listed at the end of this chapter.

Before the EAL department can identify colleagues' professional needs and useful staff development opportunities, it is essential to address possible areas of resistance (for example 'I'm a Maths teacher – language issues don't affect me ... or my students', or 'I tried group work once but it didn't work for the ESL-ers') and to try to understand colleagues' reluctance towards changes in practice. If a need for INSET on EAL support has been identified and provided, it is helpful to use a simple, colleague-friendly feedback form to assess colleagues' responses to the INSET initiative after 1 and then 3 months.

Managing inspection

Internationally based inspectors will be looking for evidence of quality in the planning and assessment of EAL students. It is therefore vital that EAL colleagues maintain detailed profiles or records of achievement, with assessment proformas of individual children, examples of long-, medium- and short-term plans, target-setting and photocopies of student work. Students' work should be annotated with the date and the context in which it was produced.

Inspectors will expect to see a departmental development plan which looks backwards to identify achievements and forwards to identify priorities for the future. It is a management task to see that this plan has been developed and shared with all the relevant staff so that the EAL department's achievements are acknowledged and its vision for the future is a collegial one. An example of an EAL development plan format is given in Figure 4.2.

Managing relationships with governors and the school board

Because the success of the EAL department depends to a great extent on the human and material resources available, it is imperative that those responsible for the school budget appreciate the scale of the endeavour.

There are several possible avenues:

- Ask someone to come and 'teach' the board to do something in a 'foreign' language to illustrate the challenges faced by EAL students.

EAL in international schools: a development plan	Last year	Current year	Future: next 3 years?
Management of EAL			
Staff development			
Teaching approaches			
Resources			
Planning/assessment			
Multicultural factors/diversity			
Home–school links			
New arrivals			
BICS – communicative level			
CALP – academic level			

Figure 4.2 A possible format for a development plan for EAL in international schools.

- Ask if you can share your knowledge and concerns with the school board.
- Demand the best for the EAL students. Suggest increasing the EAL staffing and resources budgets, if necessary.
- Arrange school-wide INSET in EAL and invite the board members and governors to come along.
- Make opportunities for EAL students to contribute to school life, e.g. staging plays, creating an EAL newsletter, participating in assemblies, sharing early feelings about learning in an additional language.
- Organise 'international' events. Encourage the involvement of EAL parents in school life.
- Hold workshops on supporting EAL students within mainstream classrooms and send copies of materials used to the board of governors.

Managing resources

The EAL co-ordinator will need to keep up to date with resources from a wide range of fields:

- mother tongue publishing, e.g. readers, textbooks, supplementary materials;
- EAL/ESL and EFL books and materials.

The school library is clearly an important resource for EAL teachers and students. The ECIS Guide to School Evaluation and Accreditation recommends that 'the Library, ESL Department and classrooms are well stocked with appropriate reading material at all levels of proficiency in ESL' (ECIS 1997: 99).

Working with parents

All children learn best when there are good home–school links and when parents see themselves as co-educators. EAL children are no exception, although contact with parents whose own English is insecure can be difficult. Meakin (1995: 96) stresses that goodwill on the part of the school is insufficient. What is required is 'an informed and consistent set of systems for keeping open the communication between school and parents' (Meakin, 1995: 96).

Many schools hold special parent evenings for EAL students' families, on a termly basis. Teachers have found it beneficial to change the traditional format of the evening, moving away from merely reporting about progress towards setting targets for the children at home and at school, such as 'read every day in English at home' or 'contribute more in group activities'. At a school in Asia, the parent–teacher association (PTA) works with the EAL department to provide a newcomers' 'club' corner, to settle and integrate newly arrived families.

Summary and Recommendations

International schools are interlingual and intercultural institutions and this is their main strength. The pedagogical and management skills of the EAL co-ordinator and the EAL team are central to an international school's commitment to being international. EAL needs to be liberated from the broom cupboard or withdrawal class and be valued for what its advocates may contribute to the whole school and its ethos. EAL is wider than its language remit. It involves the teaching of culture and the development of complex cognitive/bilingual strategies.

One of the main challenges to school management is ensuring that EVERY international school teacher sees him- or herself as an EAL teacher. Another management goal is to support teachers through INSET and team teaching if mainstream teachers are to provide effective support to EAL students in their lessons.

In summary, the aims of any international schoolteacher must be to help children:

- love learning;
- learn 'survival English' and adapt to the new school;
- develop transferable learning skills;
- celebrate diversity and develop tolerance and understanding towards others;
- appreciate connections;
- make as meaningful and as rapid progress as possible;
- enjoy access to the full curriculum;
- participate confidently in the social life of the school and feel part of the school community;
- enable the student to extend his knowledge and use of English because, as Wittgenstein (1917, 115) pointed out,

  The limits of language mean the limits of my world.

References

Baker, C. (1993) *Foundations of Bilingual Education and Bilingualism*, Clevedon: Multilingual Matters.

Baker, C. (1995) *A Parent's and Teacher's Guide to Bilingualism*, Clevedon: Multilingual Matters.

Bourne, J. (1994) *Partnership Teaching*, London: Routledge NFER.

Cummins, J. (1986) *Bilingualism in Education: Aspects of Theory, Research and Practice*, London: Longman.

ECIS (European Council for International Schools) (1997) *The ECIS Guide to School Evaluation and Accreditation*, Petersfield, Hants: CI.

Ellis, R. (1985) *Classroom Second Language Development*, Oxford: British Council with Pergamon Press.

Eriksen, M. (1997) 'International middle school students' viewpoints from abroad', unpublished MA dissertation, Oxford Brookes University.

Genesee, F. (ed.) (1994) *Educating Second Language Children: the Whole Child, the Whole Curriculum, the Whole Community*, Cambridge: Cambridge University Press.

Gibbons, P. (1991) *Learning to Learn in a Second Language*, Australia: Primary English Teaching Association.

Hester, H. (1983) *Stories in the Multilingual Primary Classroom: Supporting Children's Learning*, London: ILEA/Harcourt Brace Jovanovich.

IBO (International Baccalaureate Organisation) (1995) *Middle Years Programme*, Geneva: IBO.

IBO (International Baccalaureate Organisation) (1998) *Primary Years Programme*, Geneva: IBO.

ISCP (International Schools Curriculum Project) (1996) *Making it Happen in the Classroom*, ISCP.

Levine, J. (ed.) (1990) *Bilingual Learners and the Mainstream Curriculum*, London: Falmer Press.

Levine, J. and Meek, M. (1996) *Developing Pedagogies in the Multilingual Classroom*, Stoke-on-Trent: Trentham Books.

McCaig, N.M. (1992) 'Birth of a Nation', *The Global Nomad Quarterly* 1: 1–2.

Meakin, S. (1995) *Languages and Cultures in English-based International Schools*, Clevedon: Multilingual Matters.

Mills, R.W. and Mills, J. (1993) *Bilingualism in the Primary School*, London: Routledge.

Murphy, E. (ed.) (1990) *ESL: A Handbook for Teachers and Administrators in International Schools*, Clevedon: Multilingual Matters.

QCA (Qualifications and Curriculum Authority) (1999) *Target-setting*, London: DfEE.

Schifini, A. (1994) 'Language, literacy and content instruction: strategies for teachers', in K. Spangenberg-Urbschat and R. Pritchard (eds) *Kids Come in All Languages: Reading Instruction for ESL Students*, Alexandria, VA: International Reading Association.

Sears, C. (1998) *Second Language Students in Mainstream Classrooms: A Handbook for Teachers in International Schools*, Clevedon: Multilingual Matters.

Sherman, S. (1993) 'Learning English naturally in Emelia Parker's classroom,' in K. Samway and D. McKeon (eds) *Common Threads of Practice: Teaching English to Children around the World*, Alexandria, VA: TESOL.

Singleton, D. (1989) *Language Acquisition: The Age Factor*, Clevedon: Multilingual Matters.

Smith, A. (1998) *Accelerated Learning*, Stafford: Network Educational Press.

Spangenberg-Urbschat, K. and Pritchard, R. (eds) (1994) *Kids Come in all Languages: Reading Instruction for ESL Students*, International Reading Association.

Swann Report (1985) *Education for All*, London: Department for Education.

Syanen, C. (1993) 'Team teaching in second grade (don't pull out the kid – pull in the teacher)', in K. Samway, and D. McKeon (eds) *Common Threads of Practice: Teaching English to Children around the World*, Alexandria, VA: TESOL.

Wittgenstein, L. (1917) *Tractatus Logico-Philosophicus*, reprinted 1961, London: Routledge.

Further information

On-line EAL and English teaching resources

ECIS: http://www.ecis.org/
ESL home page: http://www.lang.uiuc.edu/esl/
ESL links and resources: http://www.educ.wsu.edu/esl/professionallink.html
ESL resources – general: http://www.prairienet.org/community/esl/GenESL.htm
ESL café: http://www.eslcafe.com/
ESL In the Mainstream (Australia) (1999) Department of Education and Employment, PB Box 33, Campbelltown, SA 5074, Australia; e-mail rmatwiejcke@nexus.edu.au

IATEFL(International Association of English as a Foreign Language): http://www.iatefl.org
NATE (UK) (National Association for the Teaching of English): http://www.nate.org.uk
TESOL: http://www.tesol.edu/

Journals

ELT journal: e-mail 100641.33compuserve.com
English in education (NATE – UK): e-mail nate.hq@campus.bt.com
English language teaching professional: e-mail 101723.563@compuserve.com
ISSUES (IATEFL): e-mail iatefl@compuserve.com

5

LEARNING TO CHANGE AND CHANGING TO LEARN

Dean Fink

Introduction

In the 1980s, Peters and Waterman (1982) advised business people in their bestseller *Search for Excellence* to 'stick to their knitting' – attend to their core business. For educators internationally in a rapidly changing world, and in international schools in particular, this raises the question 'what is our knitting?' 'What is our core business?' In my interactions with people involved in international schools, I have heard such answers as 'achieving predetermined achievement targets', 'getting a high percentage of students through the International Baccalaureate', 'enrolling more students than our competitors', 'pleasing the school's parent governors', 'meeting the challenge of non-native speakers of the language of instruction' and 'satisfying the "influential" parents'.

If these responses are representative of answers one might get to my question, I would suggest that international schools and the policies that direct their activities require reassessment. Somewhere along the way, in the name of educational reform, educators, both public and private, have confused structure with purpose, measurement with accomplishment, management with leadership, means with ends, compliance with commitment and teaching with learning. Schools have not failed to accomplish their traditional mandate, but there is increasing evidence that schools are out of step with the changing nature of society (Rifkin, 2000). Ironically, in an attempt to shape schools for a post-modern world of diversity, complexity, indeterminacy and innovation, policy-makers around the world, state and private, seem determined to 'polish yesterday's educational paradigm' (Peters, 1999) by 'looking in the rear-view-mirror' to find answers to contemporary problems. Innovation requires creativity, imagination, autonomy and risk taking. To respond to these needs schools must possess the same characteristics.

This chapter argues that the agenda for reform in all schools, regardless of type and location, must focus on the essential purpose of education, i.e. students' learning – their learning to create, to solve problems, to think critically, to unlearn and relearn and to care about others and the environment. To do this, schools will need to change the way they do things – *changing to learn*. They will also need to forget – forget obsolete structures, dated techniques and technologies, and educational philosophies that prepare pupils for another century, the twentieth. As my former boss used to say, 'innovation is something you do instead of – not on top of '. The very large question for change agents then is what change initiatives to adopt, what to oppose and what to colonise and what to subvert – *learning to change*. Sorting out such issues in times of powerful and paradoxical social forces requires higher order strategies than schools have historically used. It will be the purpose of the remainder of this chapter to describe some of the competing social forces that affect schools, and suggest ways they confuse the purposes of schools. It will then provide insight into ways my colleagues and I have found to help schools 'sort' out these change issues and finally suggest some ways to sustain change over time.

Chaos and complexity

I travel a great deal. In the past four years I have made presentations in twenty-seven different countries. Like most travellers the first thing I do when I enter a hotel room is to turn on the television set, if one exists. Invariably I find CNN, the American international network. I can discover within hours how my favourite teams have fared, and what is newsworthy in virtually every part of the world. Our world is indeed getting smaller. In many ways globalisation defines our world (Grieder, 1997; Friedman, 1999). The European nations are joining together, not only economically but also politically. North America has its free trade agreement. The North Atlantic Treaty Organisation (NATO) now includes nations of the former Communist Bloc. The internet binds the world together in ways unimagined only a few short years ago. Companies transcend national borders and spend a great deal of time merging to avoid national taxes, regulations and environmental laws. Ironically, as our world is getting smaller and connections established, we are breaking up into tribes (Lasch, 1995). As the free market approach gives full rein to our most individualistic impulses, people search for relationships that give their lives meaning (Lerner, 1996). One need only look at Bosnia, Russia, Ireland and my own country, Canada, to see this fragmentation. Even within nations, peoples' attraction to non-mainstream religions, cults and partisan spectator sports, for example, reflects this yearning for connection to others.

This paradox of globalisation and individualism on the one hand and tribalism and the search for meaningful connections on the other is but one of the more obvious and pervasive paradoxes that has an impact on our societies, and makes the purposes and policies of education confused and contentious (Barber, 1995; Hargreaves, A. 1995). Are we as educators, for example, in the business of promoting citizenship, or feeding human capital to the engines of international corporatism, or both, or neither? Is it the purpose of education to encourage the three gods of the global market place – competition, efficiency and the free market – or is it a school's purpose to help students find meaning in their lives? Does a school teach more science and mathematics as business-oriented parents might demand or history, geography, literature and the arts? 'What is our 'knitting?'

For brevity let me list a few other paradoxes that develop this theme of complexity and diversity and its impact on schools:

- Schools have been severely criticised by the business community for being irrelevant and not preparing students for the information age (Drucker, 1993) while, paradoxically, this same business community works energetically to make wholesale reductions in jobs. Rifkin (1996) argues that technology will mean that large segments of our society will never have a job, as we have understood the term. For the first time in history the new technology does not create more jobs than the technology it has replaced. Permanent unemployment, it would appear, will be part of our social landscape for many years to come. Perhaps we should spend as much time preparing students for leisure time activities as we do helping them to develop the skills to make a living. Are we, therefore, in the business of preparing our pupils for life or just to make a living?

- As our societies become more complex, and computers and advanced technologies change even our most ordinary day-to-day activities, many people respond by yearning for some halcyon days when things were simple and easily understood. The popularity of fundamentalism in most of the world's great religions is a reflection of this longing. At the same time as we introduce high technology into our classrooms, we are often pressured to implement a 'back to the basics', 'low tech' curriculum and testing procedures which examine only splinter skills and low levels of cognitive functioning. Attempts by schools to prepare students for an information age often run head on into parental expectations that schools should look very much like they did when they went to school. As I have indicated elsewhere (Fink, 2000), educators' conceptions of a 'good' school can often conflict with parents' conceptions of a 'real' school. Do we, therefore, emphasise critical inquiry skills or the kind of low-level skills that can be tested by multiple choice or mere recall tests? Are we interested in developing the whole child or advancing our school's reputation on narrow measures of intellectual accounting? Do we move forward to the new fundamentals or look backward to 'the basics'? In the words of a teacher to a parent, 'do you want me to prepare your child for her future or your past?' (Stoll and Fink, 1996).

- Policy-makers declare that teachers are professionals, and therefore should behave like professionals, especially when it comes to collective action. Professionals make decisions to benefit their clients, yet increasingly decision-making about what students learn, how they learn it and how their learning is to be evaluated is taken away from the local setting and determined by administrators and others with no real recent experience in the classroom. Experience and intuition are of no account, only the rationalism of the technocratic, bureaucratic mind counts. Teaching is seen as a technical activity that can be defined, prescribed and mandated, and those who fail to implement others' plans are lazy, incompetent or both. This technical view of teaching is pervasive in society, but fails to account for the 'deep' emotional and social aspects of teaching (Hargreaves and Fink, 2000). Teachers in many places have become increasingly deskilled (Apple, 1986), and teaching has been reduced to a semi-skilled trade. Are we professionals or unionised skilled-trades people? The mind-set is important for teachers and their students.

- Our societies are built on a fundamental paradox. The market is an essential ingredient of an economic system based on the concept of the 'survival of the fittest'. By its very nature the market creates inequalities:

> People are paid unequal amounts because they have unequal talents, because they have made unequal investments in their skills, because they have unequal interests in devoting their time and attention to earning money, because they start from different positions (rich or poor), because they face unequal opportunities (black versus white, as well as connected versus the unconnected), and because ... they have unequal amounts of luck.
>
> (Thurow, 1996: 243)

Conversely, democracy is based on the premise that power in society should be distributed more equitably – one person, one vote. Democratic governments, theoretically, represent society's collective aspirations for what it wants society to become. It focuses on the 'public good'. In contrast, the market is more concerned with the 'private good'. This suggests the fundamental paradox that has an impact on the purposes of education. Democracy represents political equality, and the public good. The market promotes social inequality, requires adaptation to its inegalitarianism and is concerned with what is good for individuals. When the market is applied to education it creates winners and losers, and that flies in the face of the egalitarianism of democracy (Gerwitz et al., 1995; Whitty, 1997). Where do we draw the line between education as a public good and a private good? Are schools in the business of producing good citizens or good consumers?

Changing to learn

Elsewhere, my colleague Louise Stoll and I have tried to address the 'big' change issue – the 'why' question (Stoll and Fink, 1996): why should we adopt this or that change? We argue that some changes require enthusiastic support, some require concerted opposition and others can be adapted or 'colonised' to local conditions, or, if necessary, subverted. This raises the next question: how do we know what to support, oppose, colonise or subvert? Our answer was, and is, that it depends on your school's purposes. What is it that you want your students to learn? 'What is your 'knitting?' Rather than debating over whose national curriculum to use, I suggest each international school community might engage in the following process to address these questions.

First, the school and its community might begin by arriving at some decisions on what they want the pupils of the school 'to be' when they leave the school. In other words, what are the purposes of the school? The best, yet most concise, statement of what students of the twenty-first century should learn comes from a report to the United Nations Educational, Scientific and Cultural Organisation (Unesco) of the International Commission on Education for the Twenty-first Century, entitled 'Learning: the treasure within'. Jacques Delors and his co-authors argue that:

> traditional responses to the demand for education that are essentially quantitative and knowledge-based are no longer appropriate. It is not enough to supply each child with a store of knowledge to be drawn on from then on. Each individual must be equipped to seize learning opportunities throughout life, both to broaden her or his knowledge, skills and attitudes, and to adapt to a changing, complex and interdependent world.
>
> (Delors et al., 1996: 85)

To this end, the Commission proposes 'four fundamental types of learning which, throughout a person's life, will in a way be the pillars of knowledge' (ibid.: 86):

- *Learning to know:* acquiring a broad general knowledge, intellectual curiosity, the instruments of understanding, independence of judgement, and the impetus and foundation for being able to continue learning throughout life. Additionally, learning to know 'presupposes learning to learn, calling upon the power of concentration, memory and thought' (ibid.: 87).
- *Learning to do:* the competence to put what one has learned into practice, even when it is unclear how future work will evolve, to deal with many situations and to act creatively on one's environment. This involves higher skills at all levels, being able to process information and communicate with others, teamwork, initiative, readiness to take risks, and manage and resolve conflicts.
- *Learning to live together:* developing understanding of and respect for other people – their cultures and spiritual values, empathy for others' points of view, understanding diversity and similarities between people, appreciating

interdependence and being able to dialogue and debate in order to participate and co-operate with others, enhance relationships, and combat violence and conflict.

- *Learning to be:* developing the 'all-round' person who possesses greater autonomy, judgement and personal responsibility, through attending to all aspects of a person's potential – mind and body, intelligence, sensitivity, aesthetic sense and spiritual values – such that they can understand themselves and their world, and solve their own problems, i.e. 'to give people the freedom of thought, judgement, feeling and imagination they need in order to develop their talents and remain as much as possible in control of their lives' (ibid.: 94).

As the Unesco authors and others have argued, formal education has generally concentrated on the first two, leaving the others to chance or assuming that they will result from the other two. Constantly shifting global forces, however, will have an impact not only on what we need to learn but also on our thinking about the very role of learning and make 'learning to live together' and 'learning to be' as basic as 'learning to know' and 'learning to do'.

A second step for the school and its community is to determine what specific learnings are important in the twenty-first century. I suggest we combine learning categories from Unesco with our understanding of the shifting social forces which affect our lives. If we engaged in such an analysis we would have a curriculum which is more holistic, connected, flexible and suitable for a changing world than what presently exists. It could, of course, never be static because the human condition changes. To provide one example of this emergent approach to what students should learn, let us focus on 'learning to live together'. As the earlier discussion indicates, two paradoxical and competing social forces, globalisation and tribalism, increasingly influence our daily lives. If we combine 'learning to live together' in a 'globalized–tribalized' world we might want to focus our teaching on the following learnings:

Students should be able to:

- look at and approach problems as a member of a global society;
- work with others in a co-operative way;
- understand, accept, appreciate and tolerate cultural differences;
- develop the capacity to think in a critical and systematic way;
- be willing to resolve conflict in a non-violent way;
- be sensitive towards and defend human rights (Parker et al., 1999).

Such learnings may not fit the rational–linear model because they would be very difficult to assess in large-scale tests, but, in a shrinking world, survival as a species will depend on people with these kinds of learnings. The stakeholders in each school – teachers, parents and students – must address issues such as 'what do we do in this school and this community to achieve these learnings' and 'what do we do in each classroom to prepare each pupil with the knowledge and skills to accomplish these learnings?' This challenging content requires alternative approaches to teaching, deeper insight into the emotional–social dynamics of classrooms and, perhaps, a total rethinking of what education and schooling are all about (Hargreaves, 1994; Stoll and Fink, 1996; Fink and Stoll, 1998; Hargreaves and Fink, 2000). This quantum shift in thinking will not only require educators to inquire more deeply into teaching, learning and caring for students but also to develop greater capacity to understand and deal with the forces of global change (Fullan, 1993, 1999).

Learning to change

Over time, societal change has been about the interplay of change and continuity. For the most part it is about continuity. Changes are constantly occurring, but so slowly and incrementally that they are almost imperceptible at any point in time. Compare a 2001 automobile with a 1960s model. They are dramatically different. Few, except car aficionados, can remember when and how these changes occurred. In spite of rhetoric to the contrary, education has changed significantly since the 1960s, but most of these changes have been hardly discernible. Educators have for many years responded, albeit gradually and perhaps even begrudgingly, to the changing needs of their students. But the pace of societal change in the past 20 years has accelerated, and expectations for education have increased exponentially and raced past schools' ability to respond.

Periodically in the human experience social forces coalesce in such a way as to change profoundly every aspect of society. The enlightenment of the eighteenth century that ushered in an age of science, political dislocation and the industrial revolution is perhaps the most notable example in the history of Western society. There is a compelling argument to suggest that we are presently in just such a period of rapid, indeed revolutionary, change – continuity and incremental changes appear to be inadequate for contemporary challenges. For most people today the sheer speed to say nothing of the substantive changes which we see around us are very scary. As my writing partner, Louise Stoll, is fond of saying, 'the only people who welcome change are babies with a wet nappy [diaper]'. Regardless of your outlook on change, it is fair to say that the complexity, of the previously described paradoxes, suggests that our world, and therefore the world of school leadership, has become less predictable and more problematical. We live in a world in which, for the most part, the best that we can do is anticipate and deal with probabilities not predictabilities. Increasingly we find ourselves confronted by issues for which we have not been trained, and perhaps never experienced before, and for which there are no ready-made answers. There are, however, proven strategies that will help to make the 'journey' less perilous.

The parable of the boiled frog

Senge (1990) explains that if you put a frog in boiling water it will adapt and jump out. If, however, you put a frog in lukewarm water and gradually increase the heat to the boiling point it will remain in the water and boil to death. Schools that are unaware of shifts in their context and leaders who do not systematically 'take the temperature' of their context are inviting difficulties (McLaughlin, 1990; Cohen, 1995; Elmore, 1995). The first commandment of the change journey is 'know thy context'.

Context may be defined as 'the whole situation, background, or environment relevant to some happening' (Grossman and Stodolsky, 1994: 181). Internal context in schools includes the students, subjects, departments and the school itself. The external context for an international school encompasses, among others, the school's parents, school governors/board, the neighbouring community, the state and the government in which the school is located and the central agencies for international schools (McLaughlin and Talbert, 1993). As the preamble to this chapter suggests, one could add other international contexts as well. Educational polices have clearly become international and are therefore affected by changing international conditions.

The research evidence is fairly clear that schools can only be understood in their context (Hallinger and Murphy, 1986; Teddlie and Stringfield, 1993). Attempts to determine effectiveness from one country to another, for example, have for the most part been unsuccessful (Reynolds et al., 1994). Broadly based restructuring efforts in state schools have made little difference in classrooms (Cohen, 1995; Elmore, 1995; Gerwitz et al., 1995) because different contexts bring diverse and often contradictory values, beliefs and purposes for education. It is vitally important that school leaders understand the interactions among various strands of a school's internal and external contexts, and constantly monitor the influence of a school's external contexts on its internal contexts (see Fink, 2000) or risk becoming a 'boiled frog'.

A framework for dealing with change

Traditional management training, what Helen Gunter (1995) has described as 'management by ringbinder', provides lots of answers to yesterday's issues. I would suggest, therefore, that if we need better answers we require better questions. This is why my colleagues and I at the International Centre for Educational Change have developed the 'change frames' (Hargreaves et al., 2000). The 'change frames' are a way for schools to look at school issues through multiple lenses. These frames do not purport to answer questions but rather to help school personnel to ask better questions of the changes they face in their context. We have identified seven frames.

- *The purpose frame* is about meanings that people bring to a change effort. This frame requires an investigation of the purposes of the change and the sources of the change, and asks the essential question: 'does the change make a positive difference for students?' Although this may sound like an easy and perhaps common-sense task, few change efforts ever truly get behind the rhetoric of the proponents of the change. Most change efforts fail because of unclear purposes, conflicting purposes or overly ambitious purposes.

- *The passion frame* is about emotions, yours and the other peoples'. Schools are intensely passionate places. Most people go into teaching because of deep feelings that they can make a difference. It certainly is not because they wanted to get rich quick. As anyone who has spent any amount of time in a school knows, teaching and learning are intensely emotional activities. This frame requires participants in a change effort to inquire into how change affects the emotions of the people involved – teachers, students and parents – and other important stakeholders.

- *The political frame* deals with power and its distribution in a school. Power is pervasive in education. Teachers exercise power over students, principals exercise power over teachers and the smarter teachers know how to manipulate and manoeuvre around principals to exercise power. As a young teacher, I learned that real power such as control of resources often resides with the head secretary and chief custodian (caretaker). Politics is about acquiring and using power and influence. Micropolitics have always existed in schools as in any other organisation. The issue is not 'how do we eliminate micropolitics?' but rather 'how do we encourage people to interact positively to promote the interests of the school?' This frame therefore turns the light of awareness on how the competition for power affects various individuals and interest groups in and outside the school.

- *The structural frame* is about time and space, roles and relationships – how organisations bring people together and keep them apart. Structures shape relationships. Structures are what change efforts usually attend to because they are visible. There is no question that changing structures are important but such change is insufficient and often simplistic. As a Canadian, I know something about icebergs. You only see a small part of them. The danger for ships is what is unseen. Structures are but the tip of an iceberg. You can see and therefore quickly change them, but the unseen – the purposes, passion, politics, culture, learning and leadership of change – are more problematical. Perhaps the question to ask of all structures is 'do our present use of time and space and our roles and relationships still make sense?'

- Structures are inextricably linked to school culture: change in one affects the other because cultures do not exist in a vacuum; they are embedded in time and space. The *cultural frame* attends to what Deal and Kennedy (1983) describe as 'the way we do things around here'. Culture is a 'way of life' (Hargreaves, D.H. 1995: 14). It defines reality for those who work in an organisation; it also provides support, identity and 'forms a framework for occupational learning' (Hargreaves, 1994: 165). 'Culture is an uncontrollable, indefinable sea in which we all swim' (Saul, 1997: 75). The content and form of a school's culture will tend to dictate the success or failure of a change initiative, as discussed further in Shaw's chapter.

- *The learning frame* is about creating better learning for pupils, better professional learning for teachers and ways for parents to learn from each other. It's where people continually expand their capacity to create the results they desire. A simple but useful equation is that the learning (L) must be equal to or greater than the rate of change (C), so $L \geq C$ (Garratt, 1987) if an organisation is to thrive and grow.
- *The leadership frame* is concerned with both formal and informal school leaders and how they do or do not promote organisational development and learning. It is this frame that I want to develop because, in my view, it is the key to attending to the other frames in positive and productive ways.

This approach encourages change agents to look beyond the traditional school improvement agenda to consider the variables that affect a school's capacity to deal with change (Louis et al., 1998). In a sense one could describe these variables as 'lenses', 'images' or 'frames' through which to view and therefore open up to scrutiny 'the black box' of the school (Bolman and Deal, 1997; Morgan, 1997; Mintzberg et al., 1998). For researchers and practitioners alike, the idea of 'framing change' enables them to understand the multidimensionality and therefore the complexity of change in schools (Fink, 2000) and address the real contextual issues that help or hinder change.

Sustaining change

Unfortunately, in spite of the best efforts of highly talented and committed people, most change efforts fail (Senge et al., 1999). This assertion is not only true in the business world but also in the field of education. Publications with titles such as *The Predictable Failure of Educational Reform* (Sarason, 1990), 'Reforming again and again and again' (Cuban, 1990), 'Educational change: easier said than done' (Fink and Stoll, 1998) and *Good Schools/Real Schools: Why School Reform Doesn't Last* (Fink, 2000) speak eloquently of the difficulty of effecting and sustaining changes that make a difference to learning, caring and teaching in classrooms and schools. The library shelves of schools of education are filled with books advocating one change or another, chronicling promising initiatives and even a few describing the implementation of changes. The shelves containing books on changes that have been sustained over time, however, are relatively sparse. In the interplay between change and continuity, continuity, often for very good reasons, seems to win out. Change agentry (Fullan, 1999) requires more than just strategies to promote change, it also needs ways to anticipate and overcome limitations to sustaining change over time.

To determine why school reform does not last, I reviewed the international literature on new and innovative schools, as well as examining in some detail one of Canada's most innovative schools in the 1970s which, by the 1990s, had become no different from other Canadian secondary schools. The evidence indicates that most, if not all, innovative schools, over time, experience what I have called 'the attrition of change' (Fink, 2000). They have begun life as dynamic, innovative and creative places and over time become ordinary or worse (Gold and Miles, 1981; Fletcher et al., 1985; Smith et al., 1987; Fink, 2000). There appear to be a number of crucial 'warning signs' or 'turning points' that suggest that schools are losing momentum and regressing to the mean.

Leaders of dynamic, innovative schools, for example, require exceptional organisational, political and interpersonal skills. They tend to hire creative, imaginative people who provide leadership within the school. It is this critical mass of leadership that moves schools forward. Succeeding these exceptional leaders and replacing the 'critical mass' of leaders when they inevitably move on presents a significant challenge for an innovative school. The question arises as to what kind of person and what kind of approach is needed in such situations. This loss of leadership suggests that succession planning of key leaders is an important component of sustaining change. This would be a particular problem for international schools. School leaders and governors would be well advised to have a process for succession planning of key personnel in place.

As innovative schools evolve, incumbent staff members depart and new staff members are appointed. The recruitment and induction of new staff appear to be crucial ingredients in sustaining change beyond the initial euphoric stages and are particularly important in international schools, where turnover is frequent and predictable. It does not take many poor choices to contribute to a school's poor public image. Similarly, considerable time, effort and expense must go into induction processes if a school is to maintain its edge. The meanings that new staff members bring to a school can become quite different from those of the existing staff. The clear evidence from both the school effectiveness and school improvement literatures is that 'shared purpose' is a crucial ingredient for school growth and development (Stoll and Fink, 1996).

In addition, attention to the delicate micropolitics of a school staff is important to sustain change over time. Schools are filled with micropolitical groupings based on age, experience, subject expertise, nationality, ethnicity and, in international schools, expatriates and the indigenous teacher populations. Sustainability therefore necessitates directing the natural micropolitical activities in school in ways that promote the purposes of the organisation as opposed to corrosive and destructive animosity (Ball, 1987; Blase, 1998). With constant staff turnover, different wage scales between expatriates and indigenous staff and continually changing formal leaders and governors, this dilemma of sustainability is particularly appropriate for international schools.

The solution to this quandary is to maintain a sense of shared purpose among all the key stakeholders in the school. The school staff's image of a 'good' school can often diverge from the image held by its parents and larger community of what a 'real' school looks like. There is evidence that suggests that a 'real' school looks something like the one we went to in our own school days. Moving or dynamic schools must, of necessity, create some disequilibrium if they are to break out of the old 'grammar', but they must be cautious that they don't get too far ahead of what their important communities can understand and support. Issues of leadership, recruitment, induction, shared purpose and community relations are but a few of the warning signs that change agents must monitor to ensure the sustainability of changes in the teaching–learning environment. I have developed this in more detail elsewhere (Fink, 1999, 2000; Hargreaves and Fink, 2000).

In a world of rapidly changing social forces in which every aspect of society is experiencing pressures to change, schools must keep their mandate to promote student learning as the 'holy grail' towards which all their efforts are directed. To this end, this chapter has suggested that school communities need to review continually what it takes to prepare students for this shifting world into which they have been born. To achieve the changes necessary to promote new and more challenging approaches to learning, schools will have to learn how to change through asking better questions as the change frames model indicates and being vigilant to anticipate forces which might curtail necessary changes prematurely.

References

Apple, M. (1986) *Teachers and Texts*, New York: Routledge and Kegan Paul.

Ball, S. (1987) *Micropolitics of the School*, London: Methuen/Routledge and Kegan Press.

Barber, B. (1995) *Jihad vs. McWorld: How Globalism and Tribalism are Reshaping the World*, New York: Ballentine Books.

Blase, J. (1998) 'The micropolitics of educational change', in A. Hargreaves, A. Lieberman, M. Fullan and D. Hopkins (eds) *International Handbook of Educational Change*, Dordrecht, The Netherlands: Kluwer Press.

Bolman, L. and Deal, T. (1997) *Reframing Organizations: Artistry, Choice and Leadership*, 2nd edn, San Francisco: Jossey-Bass.

Cohen, D.K. (1995) 'What is the systems in systemic reform?', *Educational Researcher* 24 (9): 11–17; 31.

Cuban, L. (1990) 'Reforming again and again and again', *Educational Researcher* 19: 2–13.

Deal, T.E. and Kennedy, A. (1983) 'Culture and school performance', *Educational Leadership* 40 (5): 140–1.

Delors, J., Al Mufti, I., Amagi, A., Carneiro, R., Chung, F., Geremek, B., Gorham, W., Kornhauser, A., Manley, M., Padrón Quero, M., Savané, M.-A., Singh, K., Stavenhagen, R., Suhr, M.W. and Nanzhao, Z. (1996) *Learning: The Treasure Within – Report to UNESCO of the International Commission on Education for the Twenty-first Century*, Paris: Unesco.

Drucker, P. (1993) *Post Capitalist Society*, New York: Business.

Elmore, R. (1995) 'Structural reform in educational practice', *Educational Researcher* 24 (9): 23–6.

Fink, D. (1999) 'The attrition of change', *School Effectiveness and School Improvement* 10 (3): 269–95.

Fink, D. (2000) *Good Schools/Real Schools: Why School Reform Doesn't Last*, New York: Teachers' College Press.

Fink, D. and Stoll, L. (1998) 'Educational change: easier said than done', in A. Hargreaves, A. Lieberman, M. Fullan and D. Hopkins (eds) *International Handbook of Educational Change*, Dordrecht, The Netherlands: Kluwer Press.

Fletcher, C., Caron, M. and Williams, W. (1985) *Schools on Trial*, Milton Keynes, UK: Open University Press.

Friedman, T.(1999) *The Lexus and the Olive Tree*, New York: Anchor Books.

Fullan, M. (1999) *Change Forces: The Sequel*, London: Falmer.

Fullan, M.G. (1993) *Change Forces: Probing the Depths of Educational Reform*, London: Falmer Press.

Garratt, B. (1987) *The Learning Organization*, Glasgow: Collins Press.

Gerwirtz, S., Ball, S.J. and Bower, R. (1995) *Markets, Choice and Equity in Education*, Buckingham: Open University Press.

Gold, B.A. and Miles, M.B. (1981) *Whose School is It Anyway: Parent–Teacher Conflict Over an Innovative School*, New York: Praeger.

Grieder, W. (1997) *One World, Ready or Not: The Manic Logic of Global Capitalism*, New York: Simon & Schuster.

Grossman, P.L. and Stodolsky, S. (1994) 'Considerations of content and the circumstances of secondary school teaching', in L. Darling-Hammond (ed.) *Review of Research in Education*, vol. 20, Washington, DC: American Educational Research Association.

Gunter, H. (1995) 'Jurassic management: chaos and management development in educational institutions', *Journal of Educational Administration* 33 (4): 5–20.

Hallinger, P. and Murphy, J. (1986) 'The social context of effective schools', *American Journal of Education* 94 (3): 328–55.

Hargreaves, A. (1994) *Changing Teachers, Changing Times*, London: Cassell.

Hargreaves, A. (1995) 'Renewal in the age of paradox', *Educational Leadership* 52 (7): 14–19.

Hargreaves, A. and Fink, D. (2000) 'The three dimensions of education reform', *Educational Leadership* 57 (7): 30–4.

Hargreaves, A., Shaw, P., Fink, D., Retallick, J., Giles, C., Moore, S., Schmidt, M. and James-Wilson, S. (2000) *Change Frames: Supporting Secondary Teachers in Interpreting and Integrating Secondary School Reform*, Toronto: Ontario Institute for Studies in Education/University of Toronto.

Hargreaves, D.H. (1995) 'School culture, school effectiveness and school improvement', *School Effectiveness and School Improvement* 6: 23–46.

Lasch, C. (1995) *The Revolt of the Elites and the Betrayal of Democracy*, New York: W.W. Norton.

Lerner, M. (1996) *The Politics of Meaning*, New York: Addison-Wesley.

Louis, K., Toole, J. and Hargreaves, A. (1998) 'Rethinking school improvement', in K. Louis, J. Toole and A. Hargreaves (eds) *Handbook in Research in Education Administration*, New York: Longman.

McLaughlin, M. (1990) 'The Rand Change Agent Study: macro perspectives and micro realities', *Educational Researcher* 19 (9): 11–15.

McLaughlin, M.W. and Talbert, J.E. (1993) *Contexts That Matter for Teaching and Learning*, Palo Alto: Center for Research on the Context of Secondary School Teaching.

Mintzberg, H., Ahlstrand, B. and Lampel, J. (1998) *Strategy Safari: A Guided Tour Through the Wilds of Strategic Management*, New York: The Free Press.

Morgan, G. (1997) *Images of Organizations*, London: Sage.

Parker, W., Ninomiya, A. and Cogan, J. (1999) 'Educating world citizens: toward multinational curriculum development', *American Educational Research Journal* 36 (2): 117–45.

Peters, T. (1999) *The Circle of Innovation: You Can't Shrink Your Way to Greatness*, New York: Vintage Books.

Peters, T. and Waterman, R. (1982) *In Search of Excellence: Lessons from America's Best Run Companies*, New York: Harper and Row.

Reynolds, D., Creemers, B.P.M., Nesselrodt, P.S., Schaffer, E.C., Stringfield, S. and Teddlie, C. (1994) *Advances in School Effectiveness Research and Practice*, Oxford: Elsevier Science.

Rifkin, J. (1996) *Technology, Jobs and Your Future: The End of Work*, New York: G.P. Putnam Sons.

Rifkin, J. (2000) *The Age of Access: The New Culture of Hypercapitalism Where All of Life is a Paid-for Experience*, New York: Putnam.

Sarason, S. (1990) *The Predictable Failure of Educational Reform*, San Francisco: Jossey Bass.

Saul, J.R. (1997) *Reflections of a Siamese Twin: Canada at the End of the Twentieth Century*, Toronto: Viking.

Senge, P. (1990) *The Fifth Discipline: The Art and Practice of the Learning Organization*, New York: Doubleday.

Senge, P., Kleiner, A., Roberts, C., Ross R., Roth, G. and Smith B. (1999) *The Dance of Change*, New York: Doubleday.

Smith, L.M., Dwyer, D.C., Prunty, J.J. and Kleine, P.F. (1987) *The Fate of an Innovative School*, London: Falmer Press.

Stoll, L. and Fink, D. (1996) *Changing Our Schools: Linking School Effectiveness and School Improvement*, Buckingham: Open University Press.

Teddlie, C. and Stringfield, S. (1993) *Schools Make a Difference: Lessons Learned from a 10 Year Study of School Effects*, New York: Teachers' College Press.

Thurow, L. (1996) *The Future of Capitalism: How Today's Economic Forces Shape Tomorrow's World*, New York: Penguin Books.

Whitty, G. (1997) 'Creating quasi-markets in education: a review of recent research on parental choice and school autonomy in three countries', in M.W. Apple (ed.) *Review of Research in Education*, Washington, DC: American Educational Research Association.

6

PLANNING: THE ART OF
THE POSSIBLE

John Welton

The international school teacher, along with other habitués of airport bookstalls, will be aware of the boom in books about management and planning designed to introduce the reader to the author's favoured recipe for success. These books set out a widely varying number of essential steps, key features and common pitfalls to be avoided in order to achieve personal and corporate success. For example, the introduction to a standard book on planning, subtitled 'what every manager *must* know' states that, to function effectively in a modern planned operation, every manager must have a practical understanding of how the planning process works (Steiner, 1979). However, as Butel et al. (1998) state, some enterprises grow and prosper with very little planning, whereas others with thorough, well-laid plans disappear. Lindblom (1959) wrote a now famous article on 'the science of muddling through'.

My experience of working with senior and middle managers of international schools over the last 15 years suggests that the observation by Butel et al. holds as good in this sector as in others. Organisations can work well or badly as either loosely or tightly coupled systems (Weick, 1976). However, lack of shared planning can make it very difficult for board members, staff and parents to communicate effectively and to understand how changes in one part of a school affect other parts. Experience shows that plans are very rarely implemented as expected. Time lines in many international schools are too short for real change to take strong root. The fast turnover of senior staff, especially principals and headteachers, in the international school sector may contribute to organisational instability, as John Hardman argues in his chapter.

Although good planning may not guarantee success, Butel et al. (1998) argue persuasively on the side of the planner. They suggest that what good planning will do is increase the chance of success and reduce risk. By planning the future of a school, from money to staffing, from curriculum to governance, the chance of success is multiplied and the risk of failure is drastically reduced. The aim of planning, then, is not to predict the future precisely but to improve the chances of achieving future objectives by encouraging:

- realism and communication among stakeholders;
- a coherent and shared view of the whole school;
- managers to face up to unpleasant risks or threats;
- investigation into the market and the school's position;
- a sound business plan;
- people to make mistakes on paper rather than in reality.

However, there is an emergent view among senior staff in large corporations that whereas newly badged MBA (Master in Business Adminstration) graduates may be knowledgeable about planning and control systems they may lack shop-floor pragmatism. In school terms, lack of chalk-face 'savvy' or practical understanding of how schools work can reduce effectiveness. Bad educational business decisions can endanger a school's survival in a fast-changing business environment.

I argue in this chapter that there is potential for tension between systematic planning and spontaneity, consistency and creativity. The world-wide development of business schools and training programmes for school leaders has coincided with a broader appreciation of the need to be sensitive to uncertainty and unpredictability. While the middle manager struggles with established systems of administrative accountability, the top management of multinational countries turns to unlikely gurus of the New Science, New Age and Eastern spiritual traditions to help their senior policy-makers and planners to recognise connectivity and think outside the perceived strait-jacket of Newtonian thinking (Zohar and Marshall, 1994).

In his ground-breaking book on educational change, Fullan (1991) both laid out the elements needed for systematic and successful planned change and cast doubt on the efficacy of the whole process. Fullan suggests that the gap between policy and result is such that successful innovations and reforms are usually clear after they work, not before. Successful change agents may follow a process which is closer to 'ready, fire, aim' than to the simple linear models set out on administrator training programmes, which specify the steps from establishing vision and aims to monitoring outcomes.

It is not however the purpose of this chapter to argue against the importance of planning in international schools, but to argue that planning is a process and not an event; an art more than a science; a tool but not a solution. A football team will train according to a theory and system which they believe will be sufficient to meet all that is thrown at them by their opponents. However, once the game has started, the preplanning is put to the test in a situation of constant testing, success will depend on the ability to adapt instantly to new circumstances. The best players and teams are so good that they can make this adaptation. Once you can do something very proficiently it is easier to break the rules. World class sportspersons and musicians sometimes demonstrate idiosyncratic techniques which drive youth coaches to despair: 'do what I say, not what they do'. As a beginner sailor, I learnt the procedures for sailing my racing dinghy round a triangular course. When I was faced with preparing for my advanced sailing certificate, I needed the confidence and proficiency to sail a figure-of-eight course without a rudder, using my understanding of wind shifts and changes in weight balance and the trim of the sails. The experienced and successful school has a regularly revised strategic plan; the school managers are able to see the changes which are necessary, and some of these changes might not have been predicted when the plan was made.

Weatherley and Lipsky (1977) highlighted the gap between the planned intention of the policy-maker and policy implementation by 'street-level' workers. The gap between the former and the reality on the ground was such as to lead to the conclusion that policy is effectively what occurs, and what is do-able, rather than the blueprint of the policy-maker and planner. Walton and Welton (1976) published research into the application of rational models of curriculum planning in schools and a college of higher education. The leaders of these institutions were all seeking to apply essentially linear planning models to quite major institutional change. These school and college leaders were ahead of their time, but the research highlighted the weakness of linear models. Each case study institution had started with an analysis of the current situation and then established aims and objectives, plans for action and review; straightforward components of the planning process, restated in hundreds of ways in management texts and courses. When we visited the schools and interviewed staff we found that the written plan was largely forgotten, put away in a lower drawer of the headteacher's desk. In only one institution were there indications that the development process had kept closely to the aims and basis of the objectives model. Why? Because as soon as the staff started to implement the plan the situation had changed and the plan had become out of date. As Welton (1976: 125) noted, 'the experience of the three schools appears to have been that during the process of implementation, the practical problems of teaching and learning under the new curriculum have obscured the vision originally enshrined in the initial statement of objectives.'

Effective planning is a continual process which informs the process of review of existing practice and the improvement of performance, whether of individuals, teams or the whole school. Although all the elements of the linear model are present in the cyclical model, they are kept under regular review and may be returned to at any time.

International schools are heterogeneous in type and origin. Their approach to planning and management reflects the origins of their founders and the professional socialisation of their current managers. Teachers may react negatively to the application of management techniques from other sectors, sometimes confusing contemporary good management practice with those rooted in 'scientific management', with its emphasis on work study, time and motion exercises which set standards for performance, possibly leading to payment by results. However, scientific management was just one step in the development of management thinking and contains its own important, if partial, truths. The evolution of management thought from Frederick Taylor's scientific management to the insights of Mary Parker Follett, Mayo, Maslow, McClelland and others into the importance of understanding human behaviour and motivation laid the foundations for understanding planning and management as social processes. Planning and implementation become a process of guiding organisational energy rather than attempting to control and dominate. New conceptions of effective leadership and governance follow, and planning becomes a creative process rather than a strait-jacket.

International schools reflect different educational traditions based on the traditions established by their founders, which are in turn affected by their subsequent history, and the legal and cultural context of their host nation. International schools which developed from a North American tradition tend to differ from those which are more affected by a British tradition of educational leadership. The systematic training of school leaders and superintendents started earlier in the USA than in the school systems of the UK. Requirements for certification led to most US-trained international school principals being exposed to systematic management training and the establishment of a trained cadre of educational administrators or superintendents. International schools which are derived from the US tradition tend to appoint school principals and superintendents trained in the traditions which originated in scientific management and systematic approaches to instructional supervision. In contrast, management training for British teachers did not become common until the late 1980s. British head and senior teachers learn their management skills as professional leaders rather than as business executives, primarily from long apprenticeships in the roles of classroom teacher and as curriculum and pastoral leaders. By the time that management training became a requirement for progress to senior positions in British schools, management theory had progressed beyond the recipe-driven models of the early business schools and military academies to ways of increasing the effectiveness of schools as learning organisations (Blandford, 2000). As explored by Marian Shaw elsewhere in this book, the diverse professional roots and home cultures of teachers and managers in international schools present a particular challenge for planning and management.

With major questions being raised about the quality of universal education, national and state education systems have sought measures to impose standardisation of management practice and professional accountability in the name of equity and standards. However, international schools continue to exhibit the wide variety of characteristics which might be expected of small independent businesses, together with the strengths and weaknesses of the 'not for profits' sector. Organisations such as the European Council for International Schools (ECIS) and strongly coupled school groups such as the United World Colleges and the European Schools encourage good school planning, but, for the most part, the management practice found in international schools is dependent on the experience and quality of its board, governors and staff. The ECIS school accreditation process provides a strong incentive for schools to demonstrate effective planning and quality assurance processes.

In his last book, Cyril Poster (1999), the eminent headteacher and writer on school management, emphasised that central to any theory of school improvement and restructuring is the notion that change must be holistic: that change which is planned in one area of the school will inevitably affect all aspects of school management. In a book which is essential reading for school managers in national and international education, Poster (1999) draws together both the British and North American thinking on planning for change to determine the key factors that ensure that plans stick, that structures 'stay' structured and that schools are effective. Taking this into the specific arena of international schools, Hayden (1998), in her doctoral research into student and teacher perspectives on international education, identifies major ingredients which need to be built into a recipe for planning and delivering an international education which is distinct from the system of any one country:

- exposure to students of other cultures within school;
- teacher factors which transcend any one national tradition;
- the formal curriculum which reflects internationalism;
- informal aspects of the school which encourage internationalism, but in a culture which is grounded in links with the local community.

However, Hayden concludes that students (and perhaps by inference their parents) take a very pragmatic view of the purpose of international schools, focusing on access to higher education in other countries more than on an ideology of internationalism. She finds in her research that students in schools belonging to organisations such as the United World Colleges or the European Schools, which have strong and carefully worked out rationales for their international mission, reflect a greater awareness of a philosophy of internationalism than students who attend schools which are not associated with a particular group or tradition. She concludes that while 'the contents of a soufflé may be eggs, flour, butter and milk ... the same ingredients mixed with the same utensils and cooked in the same oven would not necessarily lead to the same outcome in her kitchen as they would in that of famous chefs such as Raymond Blanc or Marco Pierre White.' She suggests that, although her research identifies the major ingredients for the recipe for international education, how the recipe turns out in any given context will depend on the way in which the ingredients are mixed together and cooked (Hayden, 1998: 262).

So far this chapter has reflected on the developments leading to current thinking on school planning and management and concludes that, to be effective, planning should be seen as:

- a process rather than an event;
- part of a reflective cycle rather than linear in form;

- concerned with establishing recipes rather than defining blueprints;
- maintaining a holistic view of education, in that it takes account of the way change in any one aspect of the educational process affects other parts;
- requiring empowering leadership and well-informed participation by all relevant stakeholders.

Furthermore, if a school is to be truly international, considerable effort will need to be made to develop and sustain a distinctive philosophy which is shared by all its stakeholders. This philosophy must permeate all aspects of school planning and delivery, a touchstone for a distinctively international approach to education.

The isolation and instability of some small organisations, including international schools, makes it very difficult to achieve the conditions needed for successful planning on the principles discussed so far in this chapter. Rapid staff turnover, lack of investment in staff development, a tradition of school change and development based on hiring and firing, short employment contracts and time frames for implementation all lead to a culture of instability. Real change and school improvement require sufficient time, long-term investment in staff development as well as other resources and planning within a culture in which it is safe to make mistakes, to question and experiment.

Everard and Morris (1985) published an approach to school planning and implementing change that was developed with me at the University of London Institute of Education. While the approach incorporates the essential components of a linear model, it is multidimensional and based on an appreciation of the complexity of social systems. They see planning as not merely a question of defining the end, and the means and then letting others get on with it, but a process of interaction, dialogue, feedback, modifying aims and objectives, recycling plans, coping with mixed feelings and values, pragmatism, micropolitics, frustration, patience and muddle! Effective planning and implementation require the application of rationality to both planning the end and the means. Planners commonly pay insufficient attention to the means of attaining their ends. Hence Everard and Morris's model focuses on the problems of transition, the process of giving birth to the new situation, taking account of the fact that, just as in biological birth, we cannot until the last moment know what the exact outcome of the gestation process will be. In addition, the new birth is only the start of a further long and extremely unpredictable development process. A simplified version of the Everard and Morris model is set out in Figure 6.1.

The Everard and Morris model is based on gap analysis, and focuses on the processes which a school needs to undertake in order to cross the gap between where the school is and where it wants and needs to be. Their full model and approach provides a way of planning for change that 'sticks', reducing the opportunity for the process of tissue rejection associated with the transplanting of any new way of working into a school. Fullan (1991) also emphasises the

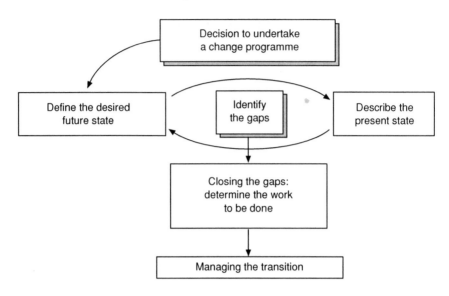

Figure 6.1 Simplified version of Everard and Morris's (1985: 184) systematic approach to change. Reproduced from Everard, K.B. and Morris, G. (1985) *Effective School Management*, London: Harper and Row, with permission from Dr B. Everard and Sage Publications.

need to pay attention to the processes of planning and implementing change. Fullan (1991: 48) describes four stages which need attention:

- initiation;
- implementation;
- continuation/routinisation/institutionalisation/incorporation;
- outcome.

The third stage is that at which real change must occur in organisational culture, changing the 'knee jerk reaction' of organisational life, the point from which there is no turning back. Everard and Morris (1985) explore ways of planning to reduce the strength of the processes of tissue rejection and achieve the critical mass for change and its full incorporation as a continuing part of the school. However, as we have noted earlier in this chapter, the short time lines and fast staff turnover of some international schools reduce the extent to which planned change can be truly embedded in the school.

Schools are also extremely complex organisations with features that complicate the assumptions about organisational behaviour found in many standard management texts. In particular, human involvement and motivation is a key aspect of both producers and product. Parents and students within international education have needs which are different from those of more monocultural, nation-state schools. Fail (1995) and others have undertaken research into the characteristics and needs of multilingual children who live simultaneously in several cultures.

Figure 6.2 illustrates the connectivity between all aspects of school planning and the way the education strategic plan derives from educational aims and objectives.

Changes which are planned in one aspect of international schooling will have an impact on other aspects, so a holistic approach to planning is needed in

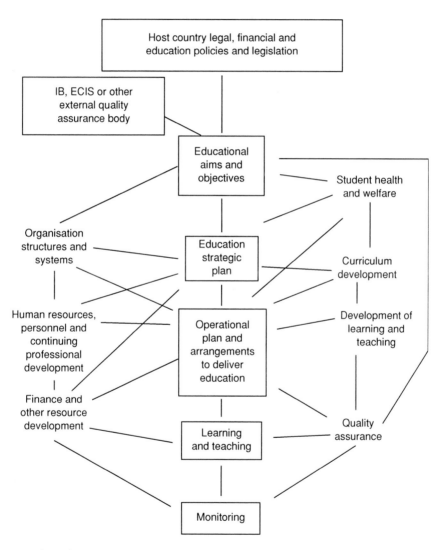

Figure 6.2 Relationships among aims and objectives, strategic planning and school planning. Adapted from Fidler, B. (1989) *Effective Local Management of Schools*, London: Financial Times Prentice Hall, with permission from Pearson Education .

order to increase the probability of successful implementation of change in any one area. The prime purpose of any change must, of course, be to enhance the effectiveness of the whole organisation to meet the needs of learners.

Or *is* this the main and only purpose of the international school? In what ways must planning take account of other needs and purposes?

One of the features of schools that differs from other organisations is that they lack manifest, early-appearing disaster criteria such as those faced by architects whose bridges fall down or surgeons whose patients die. It is said that Roman architects had to stand under the arch which they had designed while the scaffolding was being taken down. Teachers and school managers are rarely faced with the long-term consequences of their decisions in terms of the way in which their students behave in later life.

Schools share with all other organisations ways in which, in both the short and long term, their planning is crucial to the social and natural environment. At an African International Schools Association in-service programme which I attended as a speaker in Nairobi, the conference members heard a very able presentation on the impact of global warming on world climate and sea levels. At question time, a teacher reflected on how huge the issues are, and how powerless she felt to do anything about it; what could she do to help? The answer surprised everybody: 'turn off an unnecessary light'. Many textbooks on planning start by reference to a clear and shared mission for the school. 'Where there is no vision, the people perish' (Proverbs 19: 18). Little attention has been paid in the literature on school planning about the extent to which they should be reviewing their whole operation with a vision that includes enhancing the long-term quality of life, and even the survival of their community, by minimising the school's impact on the environment.

In their planning, schools like all other organisations share responsibility for considering their impact on their physical, social and economic environment. Increasingly, international schools need to take cognisance of new laws and regulations as well as market factors growing from the implementation of Agenda 21, the Rio Declaration on Environment and Development (1992). One hundred and seventy-eight countries are parties to the processes of change enshrined in Agenda 21, which set out a comprehensive plan of action to be taken globally, nationally and locally by organisations of the United Nations System, governments and major groups in every area in which human beings have an impact on the environment. The Commission on Sustainable Development (CSD) was created in December 1992 to ensure effective follow-up, and to monitor and report on implementation of the agreements at the local, national, regional and international levels.

Concern for sustainability is important both in terms of the impact of the school as an organisation on the environment and in the messages which it gives to its students, parents and the neighbourhood community. As the international school teachers heard in Nairobi, concern for sustainability is not a distant matter, involved with world economics and the operation of multinational companies. Planning for sustainability involves the enlightened self-interest of the school community, and an opportunity to educate the wider community, including the purchaser–provider chain. School planning needs to take account of the 'triple bottom line' of environmental, societal and economic sustainability. This would involve schools and other organisations judging their activities against a number of criteria, including whether the way in which they operate:

- *educates* their stakeholders both directly and by example to plan their lives and work, which makes it possible for future generations to enjoy lives of at least equal quality;
- *protects* and, if possible, enhances the earth's non-human resources;
- *optimises* the use of physical and human resources to meet current and future needs/aspirations;
- *optimises human relationships* to meet present and future needs and/or aspirations;
- *encourages*, or indeed requires, suppliers to use production and distribution methods which do not harm the social and natural environment.

Fraze and Hetzel (1990: 33), in their textbook *School Management by Wandering About*, note that purposes and strategies must be based on the core values of the school. Writing at the end of the 1980s, they recorded IBM's core value as 'respect for the individual' and Hewlett-Packard's as to 'consider the need of the person at the next desk'. Under pressure from Agenda 21, scientific evidence and both political and consumer pressure, many large companies have extended their core value statements to include issues of sustainability. International schools have a part to play in this matter, both as organisations that have an impact on the environment and as educators of future national and international leaders.

A number of international standards have been established, and organisations such as 'The Natural Step' and the 'Forum for the Future' have arisen to help organisations develop positive solutions to problems of sustainability. National and international accreditation agencies for schools might well consider the extent to which sustainability criteria feature sufficiently within their requirements. Studies are needed of the extent to which international schools are incorporating sustainability into their planning and monitoring processes and into their informal (or hidden) as well as formal curriculum.

The philosophy of this book is that the reader should have unambiguous 'takeaways' from each chapter. This chapter started with the view that, although planning is essential, plans can become strait-jackets rather than 'flexible friends'. Extending the nautical metaphor used earlier, it is argued that schools, no less than other organisations, are to be sailed rather than driven. As Dwight D. Eisenhower is alleged to have asserted, 'planning is everything, plans are nothing'.

Second, planning without very careful and sensitive attention to the process of implementation will almost certainly turn out to be a symbolic rather than serious attempt to run schools rationally and effectively. Planning and management are processes of successive approximations. When planners become really effective, they have a greater chance of achieving something like their original intention. However, without the courage and ability to be flexible in response to new conditions, and without sufficient time, the gap between intent and outcome will continue to be great. We have noted that with the characteristic 'short-termism' of some international school staffing policies it is difficult for effective planning to take place. However, for the individual child, the outcomes of such planning are crucial. School-age years are not repeatable, and children need schools to respond as flexibly as possible to meet their individual needs as they occur.

References

Blandford, S. (2000) *Managing Professional Development in Schools*, London: Routledge Falmer.

Butel, L., Curtis, T., McIntyre, J., Pearce, J., Rainbow, S., Smith, D., Swales, C. (1998) *Business Functions*, Oxford: Blackwell.

Everard, K.B. and Morris, G. (1985) *Effective School Management*, London: Harper and Row.

Fail, H. (1995) 'Some of the outcomes of international schooling', thesis submitted for the degree of M.A. in Education, Oxford Brookes University.

Fidler, B. (1989) 'Strategic management in schools', in B. Fidler and G. Bowles (eds) *Effective Local Management of Schools*, London: Longman.

Fraze, L. and Hetzel, R. (1990) *School Management by Wandering About*, Lancaster, PA: Technomic Publishing.

Fullan, M. (1991) *The New Meaning of Educational Change*, 2nd edn, London: Cassell.

Hayden, M. (1998) *International Education: A Study of Student and Teacher Perspectives*, thesis submitted for the degree of Ph.D. of the University of Bath.

Lindblom, C.E. (1959) 'The science of muddling through', *Public Administration Review* 10 (Spring): 79–88.

Poster, C. (1999) *Restructuring Schools*, London: Routledge.

Rio Declaration on Environment and Development (1992) *Rio Declaration on Environment and Development*, Rio de Janeiro, Brazil, 3–14 June 1992.

Steiner, G.A. (1979) *Strategic Planning: What Every Manager Must Know*, New York: The Free Press, Collier Macmillan.

Walton, J. and Welton, J. (eds) (1976) *Rational Curriculum Planning*, London: Ward Lock Educational.

Weatherley, R. and Lipsky, P. (1977) 'Street level bureaucrats and institutional innovation: implementing special education reform', *Harvard Education Review* 47 (2): 171–97.

Welton, J. (1976) 'Innovation as a social process', in J. Walton and J. Welton (eds) *Rational Curriculum Planning*, London: Ward Lock Educational.

Weick, K.E. (1976) 'Educational organisations as loosely coupled systems', *Administrative Science Quarterly* 21: 1–19.

Zohar, D. and Marshall, I.N. (1994) *The Quantum Society*, London: Bloomsbury.

7

SCHOOL IMPROVEMENT AND PROFESSIONAL DEVELOPMENT IN INTERNATIONAL SCHOOLS

Linda Squire

Introduction

This chapter is practically based and sets out to explore a model based on the concept of concentricity, where 'best value' principles of economy, effectiveness and efficiency are met through the careful alignment of individual, professional and institutional development goals. It also examines the ways in which schools that choose to do so may become 'learning organisations' through their approaches to professional development. The sections of the chapter cover:

- the rationale for investing in continuing professional development (CPD);
- a specimen school policy for CPD;
- key skills for school leaders in the management of CPD;
- harmonising school and individual needs: the concept of 'concentricity';
- international schools as 'learning organisations';
- from the staff member's viewpoint: personal professional development planning.

It's a good investment: the rationale for continuing professional development (CPD)

School effectiveness and improvement literature and research impresses upon us the centrality of 'the learning organisation' where staff embrace every opportunity to discover the truth about their workplace and use that information to develop themselves and their educational offer in the pursuit of carefully chosen and defined priorities for achievement. Few schools, international or otherwise, would deny the attractions of this model, but equally few would lay claim to matching it. Most, though, consider carefully and frequently the ways in which they can maximise the chances of giving the best possible opportunities to their pupils and students and have a strong awareness that recruiting,

1) Recruit
2) Develop
3) Return

developing and retaining the best possible human resource is vital. 'Learning organisation' attributes are, or can be made, a natural part of these processes.

For international schools the human resource challenges faced by all schools are augmented by those of staff mobility and staff fragmentation. The majority of teachers from overseas working in international schools are on short-term contracts of 1 or 2 years, moving on frequently from country to country and school to school; school leaders, too, are notable for their brief tenure (Hawley, 1994, 1995). In many schools conditions of service for locally recruited staff differ markedly from those offered to 'fly-ins'. And international schools are businesses: why should owners invest money in the professional development of teachers who within a couple of terms will be looking at the atlas and booking tickets to the next hiring fair?

The reason, of course, is that the business of schools is to provide the quality to which customers – the children and their families – are entitled. School improvement and pupil achievement relies on the energy and efforts of the staff. If owners and directors fail to be convinced, despite the advocacy of senior professionals, that investment in professional development is crucial, it is certainly the job of school principals and management teams to look for successful and cost-effective ways of meeting the development needs of their staff – which will have the additional effect of making the school more attractive in recruitment and retention terms. Schools typically invest a minimum of 80 per cent of their financial resources in staffing, so there is a financial imperative to prove efficiency by taking CPD seriously.

Start as you mean to go on: recruitment and retention

Successful human resource development begins at the point of recruitment, with clarity about the school's requirements set out in the job description and person specification provided for candidates. Every word counts in an advertisement and recruiting pack, so it is important to make sure that they are always drafted to attract, and describe, the person you need and want. Assuming that few new staff members, heads included, spring fully and perfectly formed to match the ideal set out in the specification, there is a need, on appointment, for both sides to think about the induction and development that will be necessary to help the new staff member to advance from a state of, say, 60 per cent readiness to occupy the role to the 90 per cent or more state that most people have the potential to achieve most of the time.

All new staff members, however experienced and however senior, have induction needs. The process can usefully begin by asking as soon as possible after appointment 'how can we help you do the job that's in the description as well and as quickly as possible?' Basic provision might include a staff handbook including practical information about school routines and policies, an initial needs analysis discussion, an induction seminar with an experienced senior staff member, with plenty of time for questions and answers, and a mentor or professional partner.

A school professional development policy

Agreeing and setting up a framework for staff development is not a complex or time-consuming matter provided there is a belief in the value of the enterprise. As a minimum, a specimen professional development policy, drawn from best practice in international and other schools, is set out in Box 7.1. It is important that school leaders consider carefully which senior colleague should carry responsibility for CPD. Some principals prefer to hold this post themselves but, whatever the final choice, it is symbolic of the importance placed on this area of management and leadership activity.

Box 7.1 Example of a professional development policy

Professional development policy at school Z

Rationale and purpose: The purpose of this policy is to ensure the highest possible standards of teaching and learning by providing staff members with a wide range of opportunities to develop and enhance their professional skills in relation to the aims and priorities of the school.

Who is entitled: All staff members, teaching and non-teaching, are entitled to participate in the school's staff development activities.

Who is responsible: Continuing professional development (CPD) in the school is co-ordinated by the deputy principal, who also has responsibility for leading the review and revision of this policy.

Induction and mentoring: All new staff members are entitled to a period of induction on arrival in the school. In addition to the staff handbook, which sets out details such as staffing structures, the school calendar, meetings, daily routines and school policies, all new staff members are allocated a mentor. In the first few days the mentor will be available for a daily meeting at which queries about school processes and practicalities can be raised. Following this early period of frequent meetings it is expected that the mentor and new member will continue to meet weekly to discuss any needs and queries that arise during the induction period, including training and development needs. After the first term meetings will be arranged as necessary. Throughout the induction period new staff members are urged to take advantage of the mentor system rather than 'struggle on'. We believe that everyone in a new job needs information and support in the early stages – and beyond.

Methods of assessing professional development needs: Professional development needs are assessed in a number of ways:

- by reference to the current priorities of the school improvement plan;
- by reference to departmental development priorities;
- through discussions during the induction stage of employment at the school;
- in relation to the requirements of individual job descriptions;
- in relation to curriculum and other initiatives undertaken by the school;
- emerging from the regular appraisal and performance review process;
- as part of whole-school or team self-evaluation;
- using data from external inspection or assessment processes;
- a competencies list derived from the leadership competencies movements such as the US-based National Association of Secondary School Principals, the UK-based National Education Assessment Centre or the Department for Education and Employment.

Range of activities: Externally provided and led training activities and events are only one part of our professional development programme. Throughout the school year training and development events are run in school by members of staff. We believe that equally powerful staff development opportunities arise from work-based activities, for example:

- creating, developing and reviewing policies and schemes of work;
- delegation;
- joint planning and team teaching;
- mentoring, or working with a mentor;
- monitoring and evaluation;
- team development through curricular initiatives and school events;
- role changes within the school (for example working with a different age group, change of subject responsibility, work-shadowing).

Systems of access: All staff members are encouraged to consider and identify their development needs, as are teams and departments. The Deputy Principal (Curriculum) regularly publicises development opportunities within and outside the school. Staff members are also invited to suggest ways in which their individual development, based on school needs analysis processes, can best be enhanced. Annual appraisal meetings provide a further and more formal opportunity for staff members to identify development needs.

Development portfolios: All staff members are encouraged to keep a development portfolio during their time with the school. This ring binder is divided into sections for:

- copy of the school's mission statement;
- individual statement of long-term professional aims;

- individual profiling document (experience, qualifications, etc.);
- curriculum vitae (you may also like to maintain this on disk);
- job description;
- summary of school development plan (SDP) priorities;
- copy of School Professional Development Policy;
- induction programme;
- appraisal arrangements and targets;
- details of courses and other development activities, with dates;
- developmental goals and achievements;
- exit interview pro-forma;
- other relevant documentation.

In addition to its value in supporting professional growth and development, the portfolio is useful for planning career development and change. Staff members leaving the school are encouraged to take the portfolio with them and continue using and adding to it as their careers progress. The exit interview provides the school with valuable information about how we can continue to work to support the professional growth of colleagues during the time they spend here.

School priorities for staff development: Many staff development opportunities have cost implications, whether for training fees or for release within the school. A system of resource management is therefore necessary based on the following criteria, given in order of priority:

1 current school development priorities;
2 training and development needs identified in the appraisal process;
3 sudden and urgent demands generated by external forces, e.g. the demands of changing statute;
4 development contributing to the improvement of teaching and learning in ways not currently specified in the SDP or identified through appraisal;
5 leadership and management development issues not currently specified in the SDP or identified through appraisal;
6 requests not covered by the other criteria.

The exit interview: This is an optional meeting offered to members of staff who are about to leave the school. Conducted by the Principal or a senior manager nominated by you it usually lasts between 40 minutes and an hour and consists of a review, from your perspective, of the ways in which working at this school has contributed to your professional growth and understanding. We hope that all staff members who move on from the school will opt for an exit interview, thus helping us to continue to improve our staff support and development systems.

Policy review
Review of this policy was completed on 12.v.00.
The next review is due in April/May 2002.

Key skills for school leaders in managing CPD

Understanding how adults learn

In managing change, leaders need to be aware that people are more likely to embrace change readily if they can see the relevance, if they know how and if they feel supported. The same is true of learning (indeed, learning is change) and so the same principles can be applied to issues of professional development. Just as people have different responses to change, and have, at different times, a range of commitment and motivation levels, so we each have preferred learning styles. Variants on Kolb's 'learning cycle' (Figure 7.1), covering preferences for active, reflective, theoretical and pragmatic approaches, or combinations of these, are commonly cited, although there are others.

Most people neither learn nor change solely on the basis of being presented with information: Joyce and Showers (1980) describe several levels and components of training, stressing that internalisation and 'ownership' of the content, and thus real change in the classroom, are likely to occur only when awareness and concepts are synthesised in the practice of actual skills (see Figure 7.2).

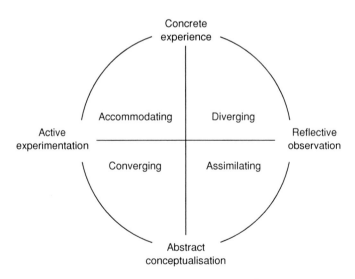

Figure 7.1 Stages of learning in Kolb's 'learning cycle' (1999). © Experience-Based Learning Systems, Inc., 1999. Developed by David A. Kolb. Reproduced with permission from Hay/McBer, 116 Huntington Ave., Boston, MA 02116, USA.

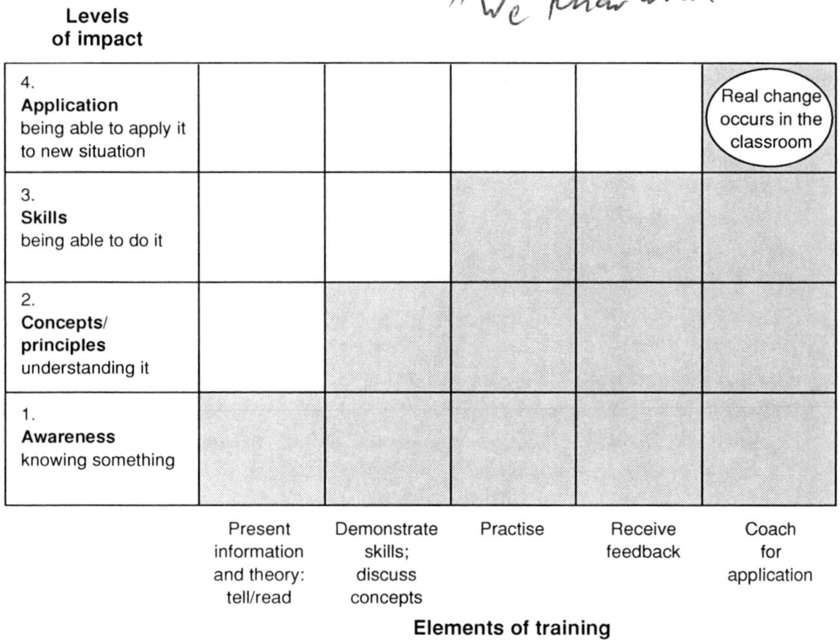

" We Know what we teach "

**Levels
of impact**

	Present information and theory: tell/read	Demonstrate skills; discuss concepts	Practise	Receive feedback	Coach for application
4. Application being able to apply it to new situation					*Real change occurs in the classroom*
3. Skills being able to do it					
2. Concepts/ principles understanding it					
1. Awareness knowing something					

Elements of training

Figure 7.2 Relationship between levels of impact and elements of training (adapted from the research of Joyce and Showers, 1980).

In planning professional development opportunities it is important to consider methods and approaches that are likely, over time, to resonate with the full range of staff members, and to monitor staff responses to the styles and patterns presented.

Internal PD

Identifying and emphasising workplace-based opportunities

Many education professionals still interpret 'staff development' as courses or conferences run outside, or sometimes within, school by professional trainers. A key skill for school leaders is in helping colleagues to widen their understanding of continuing professional development (CPD). Not only is externally provided development often expensive, it is not necessarily the best or only way to bring about professional growth. A wider definition of CPD is more likely to embrace the range of development and learning needs present in the staff of a school.

Hoyle and McCormick's (1976) concept of the extended professional describes an educator who learns constantly through a process of action and reflection, who seeks and enjoys collaboration with colleagues and identifies and pursues opportunities for professional self-development. Good, lively schools provide an environment full of promise for extended professionality, for CPD and, by the same tokens, for the growth of a learning organisation. Each school will, at different times, have its own list of possibilities; the job of the leader is to identify consciously the potential in each, and to maximise it.

Among the regular opportunities for development in the day-to-day working of the school are:

- *Agreement trials, moderation of work, examining sets or cross-section samples of pupils' work:* considering and discussing work across a subject or an age range and coming to agreements about relative standards of achievement and expectation can help to ensure consistency and continuity of provision. It strengthens the confidence of teachers in their own judgements and expectations and those of colleagues. Such professional dialogue makes a major contribution to the growth of learning organisations.
- *Change of management responsibility or age range, working with pupils of different needs and abilities; visits to other departments, activities, classrooms; job shadowing:* extending the experience and expertise of staff members is valuable both to the school and the individuals concerned. Where full-time change of responsibility, age or ability range is not feasible then visits or temporary attachments to other departments, activities or classrooms can be worthwhile. Similarly job shadowing, when a staff member spends time accompanying and observing a peer or senior colleague in action, can provide developmental insights and understandings about the demands of other roles and work types. For maximum benefit all these opportunities need to be carefully structured with intended outcomes identified.
- *Teamwork:* shared planning, team teaching, creating policies and schemes of work, projects such as curriculum initiatives (for example Primary Years Programme or Early Years Programme), school events, developing and considering and choosing new resources, contributing to the school development planning process.
- *Day-to-day teaching:* including planning, assessing, record-keeping, preparing and making reports.
- *Delegation:* Among the most misunderstood and misused of management tools, well-structured delegation offers a rich seam of work-based professional development opportunities. It is a skill that many managers learn by trial and error: it is vital to bear in mind that people often need to be taught how to take on the tasks that are delegated to them. Committed and ambitious professionals often feel that they should appear confident even when they are not. The development elements of delegation consist of giving, at the outset, terms of reference that include a clear description of the outcome required from the delegated task and the processes through which it should be achieved, together with the framework for action (such as timescale, budget and other resources, and who needs to be involved).

Offering to be available for review and support along the way are essential, unless the colleague concerned is already highly experienced and confident – and maybe even then. Good delegation takes time at the outset but in the longer term offers time benefits to senior managers as well as learning opportunities to 'delegatees'. Poor or misunderstood delegation on the other hand is a source of frustration and leads to the complaint that 'It's quicker to do it myself!'

- *Monitoring and evaluation:* participating in these activities can greatly enhance a range of skills, including data collection and analysis, observation, feedback to colleagues, planning, prioritisation, and enable a 'whole-school perspective' on standards of provision, expectation and achievement.
- *Planned reading:* there is always something new for educators to read, consider and internalise and very little time to do it. It can be helpful for such reading to be shared out between a group of colleagues and the main points and issues summarised and disseminated as a briefing, on a side of A4 or as a seminar.
- *Staff discussion:* much learning takes place through discussion, both formally in meetings and more informally through everyday contacts.
- *Staff seminars and workshops:* these can take place as part of the staff meetings cycle or as and when a particular topic of interest is current. A staff member may have existing expertise to share, lead a session to disseminate skills acquired in training or lead discussion on key points from reading. As with any form of training or meeting, it is important to ensure that the appropriate room setting, resources and furniture are used to provide a suitably professional environment without discomforts, distractions or interruptions.
- *Working as, or with, a mentor or coach:* all staff members, however senior, need induction into a new job or role. A mentor or coach can be invaluable both as a guide to 'learning the ropes' and as a sounding board for ideas and questions. The mentor, as well as the 'mentee', can benefit immensely from this way of working.

Externally provided opportunities

School-based CPD cannot entirely replace externally provided courses and conferences, Although, depending on geography, such opportunities may be limited for some international schools, other schools are well placed for external CPD. A plethora of courses, however, makes choice bewildering, and they are often costly in time and budget. In selecting the right training experience, Joyce and Showers (1980), as discussed earlier, urge the importance of ensuring that the desired level of impact is achieved.

Achieving balance

A careful match between externally provided training and the needs and priorities of the school is essential in ensuring value for money. A system of criteria such as those suggested in Box 7.1 will help in that process. Ensuring that the skills and understandings gained by individuals and staff groups bear fruit in school processes requires effective CPD evaluation processes.

Evaluating CPD

Although principles of best value demand that investment in CPD is judged in relation to its effectiveness, forms of evaluation which seek to measure the effects of CPD on the achievement of pupils remain rare.

Universally familiar is the use of 'happy hour' evaluation, which tends to take place in the last few minutes of a training event. Such evaluation is of limited value since it can be influenced not only by the content and style of the provision itself but also by a range of other factors, such as the venue, the personality of the trainers, good weather or catering or the time of day or term. Happy hour evaluations are not usually appropriate for work-based development activities.

More helpful in gauging the effectiveness of all forms of CPD, whether externally provided or school-based, is the form of evaluation where classroom or other intended professional activities resulting from or based on the CPD are monitored and evaluated. Another medium-term approach to evaluation is the 'time lapsed' evaluation, when participants are asked for their reflections on the provision and any related changes in attitude, understanding or practice, after a period of weeks or months.

Full 'impact' evaluation, of increasing interest in UK accountability processes and elsewhere, is the type that sets out to track over an extended period the effects of training or professional development on pupils' learning and achievements. This is a difficult enterprise and rarely attempted in relation to external provision; however, within the environment of a learning organisation it may become increasingly feasible.

Securing motivation and commitment

In their model of 'situational leadership' Blanchard et al. (1985) identify motivation, alongside confidence, as one of the key components of commitment; its importance in securing teacher willingness cannot be overemphasised. Over a period of 12 years, The Oxford Centre for Education Management (OxCEM) has worked on postgraduate management courses with many teachers from international schools. During this time, specific practical activities, exercises and observations have borne out overwhelmingly the motivation theories of Herzberg (1968) and McGregor (1987), i.e. that workplace commitment is better secured by appreciation, trust, communication, encouragement, interesting work and responsibility than by hard-driving approaches, criticism or material reward.

Most international schools are staffed by a combination of local and overseas staff, sometimes with differing conditions of service or cultural behaviour and value systems. These are likely to have an impact on issues of motivation and commitment. Shaw's chapter offers further insights on the privileges and challenges of managing mixed-culture teams and will also be of value in considering CPD management.

Staff development audit

Auditing the strengths and needs of the staff as a whole can be a good way of beginning a fresh focus on CPD. Ideas for an audit can be drawn from the section on 'Methods of assessing development needs' in Box 7.1, the sample policy. Why invest time in making an audit?

- So as to maximise available expertise and experience to the benefit of the pupils' learning.
- To define ways in which all members of staff can be further enabled to develop their professional skills.
- To ensure that the school has sufficient expertise to guarantee the pupils' curriculum entitlement and to meet the demands of statute.
- To support implementation of the school development plan (SDP) and bring about necessary improvements in school effectiveness and efficiency.
- To facilitate the creation of carefully structured staff development provision to meet the needs of the school and the individuals within it.
- To enable effective prioritisation and budget decisions in line with school policy.

SDP power and the school as a learning organisation

The shared vision, aims and priorities expressed and pursued through a school development plan (SDP) are, for most schools, the major pathway to school improvement, and they provide a focus for the teamwork required by learning organisations. A number of factors are crucial to an SDP's success; among them are:

- the involvement of stakeholders in the planning process;
- a limited number of priorities;
- clear criteria for success;
- detailed action plans with timescales and lines of accountability; and
- transparent links with the school budget.

Most important of all in relation to CPD is the understanding that SDP priorities can only be achieved through the efforts and commitment of staff members. SDP priorities present a focus for professional development needs that are harnessed to institutional targets. The school development process relates closely to classic models of change management, although the real-life process itself can nevertheless be challenging, as discussed further in Fink's chapter.

Schools are becoming increasingly skilled at setting improvement priorities and targets with the necessary emphasis on data gathering and analysis, and therefore on the processes of monitoring and evaluation in schools. These processes have the potential to make a massive contribution to CPD in any 'learning organisation'.

Senge (1992) sees teams, rather than individuals, as the learning unit in improving organisations, and the synergy that is possible within a developing team can be a source of strong motivation and learning for team members. Sammons et al. (1995) and Stoll and Fink (1996) also emphasise the value of a teamwork culture in the pursuit of school effectiveness and improvement.

However, in the international school setting, where there are many and frequent team changes as well as cross-cultural implications, it is important for managers and leaders to understand that careful planning and building are necessary to create teams that perform well; as Maddux (1994) explains, a group of individuals doesn't necessarily constitute a team. Certain behaviours and attitudes, such as communication, trust, the sharing of skills learned in training, conflict resolution and interdependence, have consciously to be practised and developed for that to happen. Tuckman's (1965) model of the stages of team development offers a sequence of the phases that a group of people will go through in becoming a team: (1) forming, (2) storming, (3) norming then, ideally, though by no means inevitably, (4) performing. Changes in the constitution of a team – members leave, or join, or a new task is set – mean that the development cycle must start again. Understanding the reasons for these stages, and accepting that they are normal, is likely to result in a style of management that short-cuts the earlier stages and brings the team back quickly to the 'performing' level, with learning taking place throughout the process.

Total Quality Management (TQM) as a philosophy and a system has much to offer organisations of many types, including schools (Murgatroyd and Morgan, 1992), and resonates strongly with the concept of the learning organisation. In a TQM organisation:

- people throughout the organisation are committed to a vision of quality that is clearly defined and agreed by all;
- the culture is one of continuous improvement fuelled by continuous reflection and feedback;
- communication and teamwork are promoted and highly valued;

- the customer's needs and entitlements take precedence (and staff members are seen as 'internal customers');
- there is an organisational imperative for leaders and managers to provide the support (including training and development) that staff need to develop total quality.

The Investors in People (IiP) award – now spreading from the UK to other parts of the world – lays claim to similar values and processes; the four key IiP principles (IiP, 1995) and their related standards (revised in 2000) are described as being linked in a cycle of:

- *Commitment* from the top levels of the organisation to develop all employees to meet strategic objectives.
- *Planning and reviewing* the training and development needs of employees.
- *Action* to train and develop individuals on recruitment and throughout their employment with the organisation.
- *Evaluation* to assess the achievement resulting from investment in training and development, and to improve future effectiveness (DfEE, 1997).

Aspinwall (1996) suggests four key characteristics for a learning school:

- a commitment to lifelong learning for all those within the school;
- an emphasis on collaborative learning including the creative and positive use of difference and conflict;
- a holistic understanding of the school as an organisation;
- strong connections and relationships with the community and the world outside the school.

These echo the features of TQM and IiP, and contribute strongly towards the concept of the school as a learning organisation. But a school also needs to know whether or not the measures it is taking to improve are working, and the next sections address this.

Monitoring and evaluation of school improvement goals and processes

Monitoring and evaluating the school's improvement goals and processes are addressed more fully in Skelton's chapter. They are separate but interconnected processes that call for the involvement and understanding of all staff members. They are instruments of development, measurement, accountability and change, and both provide information essential to identifying development priorities and planning for further improvement. They relate to these four accountability questions:

- Does our school make a difference?
- What difference does it make?
- Is it the difference we intend?
- How do we know?

There are many easily accessible sources of data including school aims, plans, policies, prospectuses; the school's curriculum plan and offer; teacher's plans; children's/students' work in books, folders, practical sessions, and in displays; marking in books; test and examinations outcomes and assessments; records and reports; classroom activities. Collecting and analysing this information and making the resultant improvement plans offers a rich agenda for shared experience, team development and the growth of the learning organisation.

Appraisal and performance management

Appraisal and performance management systems can make a valuable contribution to CPD systems and structures, although they continue to be suspected as potentially punitive by some. Indeed, in some international schools there is good cause for such suspicion, as the appraisal systems really do seem to be used as a control mechanism – especially when linked to financial reward. Nevertheless, an encouraging and developmental approach is the only option for truly effective staff development.

The best systems involve structured observation, evidence collection and developmental feedback, followed by the negotiation of a small number of mutually agreed targets that will be met within a timescale, supported as and when necessary by appropriate professional development provision. Good systems will always involve genuine appreciation of strengths and achievements alongside the new goals that are agreed. Managers in international schools, however, would do well to take heed of Kraiger and Ford's (1985) findings that highlight the dangers inherent in mixed-culture performance management: appraisers were consistently found to give more favourable outcomes to appraisees of their own culture.

From the teacher's viewpoint: personal professional development planning

Many teachers working in the international schools arena have in mind some sort of career pathway, although this is less frequently formalised as a 'personal professional development plan'. With the move in many countries towards the concept of continuing professional development from initial training to retirement the idea of an individual plan, revised and modified over time, is a logical one, particularly for teachers whose oyster is, literally, the world. The plan need not be a complex one and could take the form of a professional development portfolio set out in sections in a ring binder, as described in the example of a professional development policy in Box 7.1.

Encouraged by schools, such plans will not only support teachers through changes of international schools but can also be used to help them contribute as fully as possible to the current school no matter how brief the engagement.

Where teachers are hesitant about working with the school on making an individual plan for professional development it can be useful for managers to have some persuasive responses to the question 'Why make a PDP?' These responses might include:

- Planning for the future, and the sort of professional life you want to have in the longer term, benefits the teacher at least as much as it benefits the school.
- Being clear about your strengths and achievements, and the further strengths and achievements you mean to add to them, allows you to retain the initiative in times of change.
- A plan based on reflection provides you with a structured view of the range of options open to you at any given time.
- You'll have a clearer picture of long-term possibilities.
- You'll be in a position to set definite and realistic goals.
- Positive reflection offers the enjoyment of savouring your many achievements.
- You can plan a career that fits with your overall life plan.

Harmonising school and individual needs: the concept of concentricity

Sheridan (1995) provides pointers that principals may find thought-provoking and helpful. Researching professional development opportunities for British teachers overseas, he found that, alongside their high level of concern about their own professional development and the undervaluing in the UK of overseas experience, they reported limited opportunities for access to relevant training, little notion of an entitlement to professional development, isolation because of the lack of liaison between schools about professional development and that sharing within the school of knowledge and skills gained in training was rare. Two-thirds of his respondents said that their schools did not encourage INSET. Sheridan's focus was on external professional development opportunities; might a broader view of what constitutes CPD have been useful to the schools and staff represented in his sample? Undoubtedly it is in the interests of international schools to develop and promote CPD for the purposes of school improvement and business success; do they also have a broader duty to staff moving on and planning re-entry, at some stage, to their own national systems of education? Alongside these considerations, and of equal importance with them, are those of making fair and appropriate provision for local staff members: bringing together the strategies outlined in this chapter and the concentricity model outlined in Figure 7.3 can harmonise individual and institutional professional development to the ultimate benefit of all.

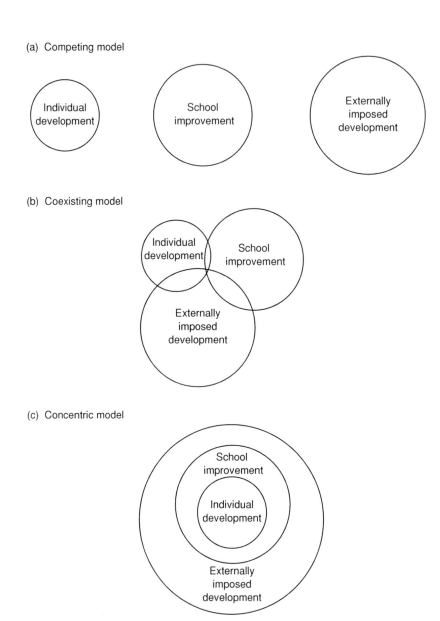

Figure 7.3 Towards a 'concentricity' model for professional development.

Figure 7.3 offers in diagrammatic form three possible relationships among individual, institutional and wider external priorities. The competing model (Figure 7.3a) is a 'worst case' scenario and illustrates the position in a school where there is no co-ordinated CPD policy or practice. Here the three sets of needs are not perceived as related; they exist separately and possibly in competition. This tension is likely to result in institutional ineffectiveness and inefficiency and lack of staff motivation.

In the coexisting model (Figure 7.3b) there is coexistence and even some overlap between the three sets of priorities, although this may sometimes be more by accident than design. However, there are possibilities in this situation for the development of co-ordinated policy and practice and, therefore, the beginnings of a learning organisation.

A 'bull's eye' structure of concentric circles is shown in the concentric model (Figure 7.3c). Here the three sets of needs are, more or less and for most of the time, in harmony. This configuration is likely to occur in schools where people and their professional development are understood to be the budget's major necessary investment. In such a school, CPD policy and practice will be led at a senior and strategic level with the contributions and achievements of individuals and teams overtly valued and celebrated and their professional needs and aspirations supported. The model demonstrates the leader's awareness that it is staff members who are central to the work of school improvement and of answering to wider accountability; it signals a development culture which stresses synthesis and synergy, hallmarks of a learning organisation where each individual in each team has the power, and is enabled, to 'make the difference we intend'.

Summary

This chapter has explored some concepts and activities that relate to effective professional development provision, suggesting some models from literature, research and practice that may be useful to leaders and managers in international school settings. It has suggested some 'key skills' for leaders in the management of continuing professional development. It has also offered a 'best value' rationale for use in persuading funders, administrators, budget holders and directors that structured investment in the development of human resources is crucial to the success of schools as businesses and has set out an easily memorised concentricity model that supports the harmonisation of school and individual needs in the steady move towards educational improvement and excellence.

References

Aspinwall, K. (1996) 'Becoming a learning organisation: the implications for professional development', *Management in Education* 10 (4, September/October).

Blanchard, K., Zigarmi, P. and Zigarmi, D. (1985) *Leadership and the One Minute Manager*, Glasgow: Fontana/Collins.

DfEE (Department for Education and Employment) (1997) *Investors in People and School Self-improvement*, London: DfEE.

Hawley, D. (1994) 'How long do international school heads survive? A research analysis (part 1)', *International Schools Journal* 14, no. 1: 8–21.

Hawley, D. (1995) 'How long do international school heads survive? A research analysis (part 2)', *International Schools Journal* 14, no. 2: 23–36.

Herzberg, F. (1968) 'One more time: how do you motivate employees?', *Harvard Business Review* 46: 53–62.

Hoyle, E. and McCormick, R. (1976) *Innovation and the Teacher*, Milton Keynes: Open University Press.

IiP (Investors in People) (1995) *Investors in People Standard*, London: IiP.

Joyce, B. and Showers, B. (1980) 'Improving inservice training: the messages of research', *Educational Leadership* 37 (5): 379–85.

Kolb, D. (1999) *Learning Style Inventory*, Boston: McBer and Co.

Kraiger, K. and Ford, J. (1985) 'A meta-analysis of Ratee race effects in performance ratings', *Journal of Applied Psychology* 70: 56–65.

McGregor, D. (1987) *The Human Side of Enterprise*, London: Penguin.

Maddux, R.B. (1994) *Teambuilding: an Exercise in Leadership*, 2nd edn, London: Kogan Page.

Murgatroyd, S. and Morgan, C. (1992) *Total Quality Management and the School*, Milton Keynes: Open University Press.

Sammons, P., Hillman, J. and Mortimore, P. (1995) *Key Characteristics of Effective Schools: a Review of Effectiveness Research*, London: OfSTED.

Senge, P.M. (1992) *The Fifth Discipline*, London: Century.

Sheridan, J. (1995) *INSET Opportunities for Teachers Working Overseas*, MA Dissertation, Oxford Brookes University.

Stoll, L. and Fink, D. (1996) *Changing our Schools*, Buckingham: Open University Press.

Tuckman, B. (1965) 'Development sequence in small groups', *Psychological Bulletin* 63: 384–99.

8

IMPROVING RECRUITMENT
AND RETENTION OF QUALITY
OVERSEAS TEACHERS

John Hardman

Introduction

Events appear to run far in advance of the ability of human beings to change and adapt to them. How much more true this must be for our children.

(Akram 1995)

Outside the home, international children's most important relationships and activities are centred around the school, with their classmates and their teachers. Akram (1995) affirms that, for expatriate families, 'the international school, in time and place, represents the only stable environment. For the children, the international school and its microcosm, the classroom, is their community.' But how stable and consistent *is* this community if the teachers themselves are part of a transient population, rarely in any one school for more than two years? Can quality teachers be persuaded to work at the school, and then be retained beyond their short contract? If so, how?

This chapter seeks to address this issue; it offers some research-based insights into the successful staffing of international schools, arguably one of the most important functions in any manager's job description. In 1996–7 I carried out a small research project to try to identify the incentives and conditions that might motivate good teachers to remain in a school beyond their original contract and to become keenly involved in school affairs within and outside the classroom, in order to promote that desired sense of stability and consistency. In the process, there emerged a pattern in the profiles of these teachers, which made it possible to identify various categories of teachers applying to work in international schools and to formulate some practical guidelines that may serve to increase managers' effectiveness in recruiting, sustaining and retaining good overseas staff.

JOHN HARDMAN

Challenges for managers in the current practice for recruiting teachers

General information on recruitment may be obtained elsewhere, and it is not the aim of this chapter to do more than mention some of the more common practices in this area. Teachers and administrators will be familiar with the international fairs, placement agencies, conferences, direct contacts, paper and electronic educational media. Quite recently, isolated cases on the World Wide Web would appear to reveal a growing trend towards the development of informal e-mail distribution lists linking heads of schools, sectors and departments for purposes of job searching and recruitment.

However, at a deeper level, the manner in which recruitment and retention are managed is pivotal to their success. Conditions of service begin some time before a teacher takes up a new position. Taken chronologically, they begin the moment a school begins a recruitment process, continue throughout the teacher's tenure and conclude on his/her departure to a new posting. There exist numerous opportunities for a school to make certain that it obtains the teachers most suited to its unique characteristics and environment, some of which are:

- advertising the position in a way that genuinely reflects the school's profile and its requirements;
- providing effective initial support and induction;
- creating and sustaining a working climate at professional, social and emotional levels that will preserve teachers' morale and build up their commitment to the school and its community;
- offering opportunities for professional appraisal, development and advancement that will further teachers' careers both at and beyond the school;
- supporting teachers at end of contract by means of references and sound counsel.

That said, conditions of service cannot be divorced from appropriate financial incentives that will serve to attract quality teachers from the outset, such as:

- competitive salaries;
- working opportunities for spouses;
- retirement schemes;
- free or subsidised quality education for children;
- housing and housing allowance;
- health insurance;
- hard currency bonus at end of each year, or at end of contract.

A third perspective is more subtle and underpins the previous two, as it has significant implications for the working climate of the school: what are the policies, practices and beliefs as embodied in the management style of the school? That is to say, what are the school's manifest and hidden values?

So what sort of staff do international schools seek, and how does this have an impact on a school's values? If, for example, we accept that stability and continuity are important to the personal and social development of international students, is the length of contract significant?

According to the ECIS, international schools seek:

> … flexible teachers who can adjust to the frustrations and stimulation of working in another culture, and who are prepared to contribute to the school as a whole by assisting with extra-curricular activities such as sports or after-school clubs. Most contracts are for two years.
>
> (ECIS, 1997)

It may be argued that the loss of good teachers after a two-year contract leaves a vacuum which replacements can never fill entirely. This is not even two years of optimal teaching because new teachers require precious time to adjust to change: they are often unfamiliar with the culture of the country, the school and the classrooms they are entering. Additionally, part of the way through their second year their energies are focusing on securing their next post. To what extent, under these circumstances, are they able to 'contribute to the school as a whole by assisting with extra-curricular activities'? Furthermore, relocated children, too, need time to adapt to their new school – a period which Akram (1995) found to be at least eight months. Given the transient nature of the school population, then, continuity in the learning environment may be quite disrupted. While the movement of the students may be beyond the control of school managers, it is worth examining those elements, such as the length of short-term contracts, that they can influence.

Challenges for international schools in providing educational continuity through effective recruitment and selection of staff might include:

- From the school's perspective:
  - What are the key skills needed for the curriculum, both formal and non-formal?
  - What balance of long-term/short-term contracts is best for the staff?
  - Is there an educationally optimal contract length?
  - If we want to keep good teachers longer, how could we persuade them to extend contracts?
- From the applicant's perspective:
  - What am I looking for in a teaching job in an international school?
  - Why should I apply to *this* school? What has this school got to offer *me*?
  - Might I be tempted to stay longer than my contract (if offered)? What might tempt me?

If these questions are valid, a manager needs to be aware at the recruitment and selection stage of how to get the right teachers for the long-term benefit of the school, and this was the purpose of the research study.

The study

In order to examine some of these management challenges, the study (Hardman, 1997) collected by questionnaire the views of thirty practising teachers and managers from international schools as widely spread as Indonesia, Tanzania, Egypt and Argentina. In addition, a balanced cross-section of staff from five major international schools in Buenos Aires were interviewed to provide more in-depth understanding of the factors that influenced the choices for both employer and employee at international schools. The length of contracts of the teachers in the survey may be seen in Box 8.1.

The aim of the research was to determine, from personal and educational perspectives, views on length of contract and its impact on students' learning, which factors motivated teachers to take up posts at international schools and which of these might encourage them to remain in school beyond their original term of service.

What do teachers look for in international schools?

International school teachers make career choices that remove them from the normal run of teachers who have elected to remain in their home country for the duration of their working lives, so what attracts them?

Table 8.1 indicates, in rank order, the incentives and conditions that teachers considered were their strongest motivators when seeking to join and/or remain in an international school.

Box 8.1 Contractual experience of teachers in the survey

> The survey sample
>
> 22 per cent had less than 11 years' teaching experience
> 78 per cent had more than 11 years' teaching experience
>
> 37 per cent had worked abroad for less than 10 years
> 63 per cent had worked abroad for more than 10 years
>
> 11 per cent had worked at only one international school
> 89 per cent had worked at two or more international schools
>
> 52 per cent had never renewed contracts for more than 2 years
> 48 per cent had renewed contracts for 3–10 years

Table 8.1 Incentives and conditions motivating teachers to join and/or remain in an international school

Factors influencing motivation to join, and remain in, an international school	% of sample
Professional advancement in school	88.5
Financial incentives	84.6
Happy working climate of school	84.6
Strong sense of job challenge	84.6
Strong staff development programme	76.9
High quality of staff, students and parents	73.1
High expectations of staff	69.2
High ideals and values of staff	65.4
School strongly centred on student learning	61.5
Staff empowerment through collaborative decision-making	57.7
Strong personal/family induction and integration programme	57.7
Positive staff appraisal programme	53.8
Strong staff involvement in students' personal and social development	50.0
Strong staff induction programme	46.2
High prestige of the school	38.5
Strong staff involvement in extracurricular activities	23.1
Other: sane administration and Board of Governors	3.85
Other: sense of staff community	3.85
Other: sense of adventure and need for change	3.85
Other: good relationship between administration and staff	3.85

[Handwritten annotations in right margin: "89%" bracketing the top four entries; "80%" bracketing the fifth entry]

Taking the most powerful motivators identified here, and exploring the issue of contracts, the rest of the chapter now debates the implications of the findings for managers in staffing their international schools. The discussion is not compartmentalised, as the factors are all inter-related.

The investigation showed that the *working climate* in the school was a recurring, if relatively undefined, theme that was important to all teachers, and this was closely identified with a strong sense of *job challenge* and opportunities for *professional advancement* in the form of new responsibilities. *Financial incentives* were also important, especially to married teachers and senior teachers when deciding on a new job, but the majority affirmed that if they were not happy in a school they would be unwilling to stay on: 'You teach not for the money. Anyone who's a teacher is a teacher for the love of the job. If I wanted to earn a lot of money I would be in a different profession' (head of department).

So, what were the important features of the school's working climate? In their own words, an appropriate atmosphere was created by 'feeling appreciated and respected' by colleagues and authorities, 'being an important member of the team' and having a 'well-communicated sense of purpose and shared aims'. Others remarked on the importance of 'a sense of security, feeling valued, good relationship with staff/pupils, able to exert some influence'. Another mentioned

Tension betw int'l tchers & local staff

'positive encouragement from the Head for innovations' and the associated job challenge.

In contrast, the downside of this was that all expatriate teachers interviewed raised the issue of hidden resentment towards overseas teachers by local members of staff, most commonly the result of differential pay scales and special benefits paid to teachers they saw doing equal jobs to themselves. This is not an uncommon situation in international schools, and results in friction, and sometimes overt conflict, creating a negative impact on the working environment. Once local teachers see themselves treated as 'inferiors', their suppressed resentment may emerge through different attitudes and behaviours which adversely affect the atmosphere in the staffroom. This is particularly so during times of innovation and change, during activities requiring teamwork, at a time when new staff are being integrated into a department, and during the general social adjustment, both for single and married teachers. The heads in the survey, although willing to acknowledge this cause of conflict, admitted in some cases to a feeling of powerlessness in the matter, whereas others were unwilling to alter the *status quo*.

The level of appointment of overseas contract staff is another factor which contributes to ill feeling: they are often appointed to middle and senior management positions that 'locals' may rarely aspire to, in spite of long and faithful service to the school. While such posts tempt quality staff to the school and provide them with the opportunity for professional advancement, they also serve to create a barrier to willing co-operation and support from colleagues, or to the integration of new teachers and their families in the local community. The 'change factor' is also a significant one; in-coming staff are frequently used by senior managers to become change agents in the school – not a role that necessarily appeals to long-established staff who may vote for static conditions at school.

In motivational terms, money never came far behind more highly valued conditions or incentives in the survey, but it was not the only priority: most teachers articulated more subtle aspects of teacher motivation in international schools, such as having 'many opportunities I couldn't try in different schools: being a housemaster, debating with teachers on the debating team, playing Santa Claus in Kindergarten, talking in assemblies, making speeches, preparing plays, working across the curriculum.' Other teachers expressed that they were attracted to teaching as it gave them the opportunity to make a difference, to have personal contact with young people, the chance to influence their lives. In his study of schoolteachers, Lortie (1975) affirmed that, among the attractions of teaching as a profession, second after personal contact came 'the idea of service', but job challenge and professional advancement were to be highlighted as stronger motivators in this study.

In exploring what else moves an international teacher, other studies note how powerful a multicultural setting can be:

Observing in other contexts makes you stop and think about the way you do things. You don't go to a new place to decide who is doing 'it' right and who is doing 'it' wrong. You go to get new ideas, to question what we are doing here at home. You may not be able to do anything about the problems here because one person is not going to change the whole system, but travel does change you in a way because you get to think in different ways.

(Cole and Knowles, 1995: 127)

The diversity of teachers' nationalities, backgrounds and experiences contributes significantly to the successful evolution of international education. This highly desirable aspect of the international teacher's profile may well be associated with the term Hayden and Thompson (1995) define as 'worldmindedness'. What's more, this trait would appear to be becoming increasingly recognised as a major factor in the success of transnational organisations world-wide (Trompenaars, 1993).

It is unlikely that managers will be able to ensure that all of the major conditions and incentives are in operation for all of their staff all of the time, but it is important for senior staff to be aware of what motivates their staff and to do everything in their power to ensure the consistent quality of the educational provision offered by the school because this increases the likelihood of good teachers being willing to remain in the school beyond their original contract. So is there an ideal length for the contract?

Is there an ideal length of contract?

The issue of contract length showed an interesting discrepancy between beliefs and behaviours. No one considered that the customary 2-year contract offered the greatest benefits to student learning:

All my previous posts have involved moving into a post where there has been a lack of continuity in the staff. This previous lack of continuity gave rise to haphazard curriculum delivery, and children were unsure and demotivated as a result. With time, a relationship can build up and the children feel more secure in their work and achievement increases.

(Head of department)

In the words of a deputy headteacher, 'it is very difficult to accurately measure true academic learning, particularly over relatively short periods of time, say, three to five years.' Despite this belief, fewer than half the teachers in the sample had renewed their contracts more than once (some never). So is there an ideal length of contract?

Bearing in mind the inevitable extended settling-in period and the less productive last few months, where thoughts of 'new pastures green' affect performance, one senior manager in an international school remarked that 'five to six years should be viewed as minimum term of service', reflecting the belief of an overwhelming majority of teachers that extending beyond the two-year contract was beneficial to children's learning, and that the optimal length of service was five to six years. But the benefits of an extended contract to the school go beyond a teacher's contribution to the formal curriculum:

> My experience has clearly shown that longer serving members of staff are able to impart certain invaluable 'ingredients' to the students such as: discipline, school spirit, values, non-academic skills/activities. In addition, INSET courses led by overseas staff for locally trained staff are often well received.
>
> (Deputy head)

On a school management level, where change today is the norm rather than the exception, a further forceful argument is provided by the time-span considered necessary by change experts to implement change effectively: 'for change to be successful, you need to think in terms of three years as a minimum' (Martin-Kniep, 1997). This is true in many settings. In classroom practice, for instance, a teacher may determine what needs to be changed in the first year, plans and implements the change the second year, and assesses and improves on the change process in the third year.

One simple explanation for the discrepancy between beliefs and practice, was voiced by senior teachers and heads. Despite their conviction that extending contracts was a good thing, some teachers simply did not wish to renew contract once they had experienced everything they felt a country had to offer them: as free and independent spirits, often 'mavericks', the novelty of their situation had worn off. So, in spite of the belief they may have expressed regarding the value of extending quality teachers' contracts, they were not willing to follow through with this conviction in their own practice.

Looking at the other end of the scale, is it possible to overextend contracts beyond their useful value? None of the teachers in the study believed that renewing contracts beyond eight years was particularly useful, as 'too long a stay can make you, the teacher, less self-critical and become too set in your ways' (head of department). After eight years' tenure teachers become 'jaded', losing that edge which is initially one of their major assets, both in terms of their specialist subject and the currency of the language and culture they brought to the school. This means that they no longer provide students with the prized freshness and state-of-the-art expertise for which they were hired. In metaphorical terms, they become 'Penelopes'; faithful to the country they had adopted.[1] The value of this type of teacher tends to diminish with the passage of time as the teachers become more comfortable in their adopted environment. In order to limit this tendency, some schools have developed policies that discourage international teachers from remaining in their position beyond a pre-established number of years. In several of the schools consulted maximum tenure was 10 years, after which, if they wished to continue working in the school, teachers would lose their international status and with it their expatriate benefits.

So, how can this information be useful to international school managers? In hearing what teachers and school leaders had to say about their jobs and teachers' attitudes to them, it seemed possible to categorise teachers according to what motivates them and what they offer the school (see Table 8.2). Mathews (1989) developed this to some extent, and what is clear from his account and the findings of the study would appear to confirm that there is no single 'right' type of teacher. Each individual brings something unique, and every school has its own special assortment of contract teachers. By identifying types it is hoped that senior managers may become more skilled when interviewing potential staff, and therefore more able to select the right staff for the mix they consider to be ideal. If, for example, teachers from the first two categories – which may appear to be very similar at first glance – are not differentiated, a school may easily appoint an unsatisfactory teacher. Similarly, there is much to be said in favour of careful screening by the employing agent or the school itself before investing considerable sums in bringing out a teacher with a family. Some schools go to the very healthy extent of flying short-listed candidates out to the school before final interview in order to ensure that, should they take up a position, they do so in full knowledge of the host country.

From an employer's perspective all categories of teachers offer interesting and valuable qualities. Careful and comprehensive preparation of the requirements for positions at any level of responsibility set against the above categorisations should contribute significantly to reducing the risk of failure when recruiting, and thereby to fulfilling the aforementioned educational imperative that the children's best interests be kept at the heart of all school business.

Effective induction practices

We turn finally to the question of what schools can do to make the new teacher, once in-country, feel comfortable and therefore settled as soon as possible. It was clear from the study that, while not all the schools studied offered an induction and/or a mentoring programme, where these did occur they had become a valued part of practice that benefited both the new teacher and the school.

Recommendations for induction of new overseas staff

The best induction processes begin at the time short-listed teachers are being interviewed, as they may be provided with practical information on the host

Table 8.2 Categories of overseas teachers applying for posts at international schools

Category of teacher	Motivators	Advantages to school	Potential disadvantages
Childless career professional	Happy working climate Feeling valued New teaching Exciting activities Involvement with students	Dedication Experience May extend contract Welcomes change No expense of children	Few – ideal teachers! May eventually turn into a Penelope?
Maverick	Change of country Global travel New school location Possible escape from own national system	Enthusiasm and creativity Embraces change and responsibility No expense of children Easy rapport with students Cheap Easy to acquire	Unlikely to extend contract May break off contract unexpectedly if personal circumstances are unsatisfactory Superficial commitment to school development plan (seen as 'educational tourist')
Career professional with family	Prestigious school (rather than location) Whole financial package (insurance, accommodation, pension, education for their own children) Commitment of school to innovation and improvement Happy working climate	Stability – less likely to leave on whim Can create conditions for innovation in school May bring two staff (with spouse) Likely to extend contract, if conditions suitable for family Regards this post as stepping stone for the next, so gives much to school	Expensive: huge investment with whole family Disaffected spouse or children may influence teacher's own decision to stay

Senior teacher (older, children left home): Senior Penelope	Social integration into community more important than job challenge	Stability in school Plenty of experience	Change may be threatening and can become 'resisters' May not move when outlived their value
Senior career professional	Job challenge and stimulation Life-long learning	Experienced in innovation No ties Maturity in dealing with staff	
Senior maverick	Freedom from family life Urge to travel again	Experience Curiosity	Working towards retirement plans Desire 'to see it all before I retire'

country and the school and informed of the school's induction practices before final decisions are made. Issues to cover at this time and once the teacher has been hired are:

1   The host country.
    –   Its culture, basic functional language, strategies for coping with change.
    –   Main systems: government, finance, transport, entertainment. A booklet outlining these is a practical way of putting it all together under one cover.
2   The school: staff, parents and students, culture and curriculum.
    –   Educational provision of school, school manual, departmental handbooks.

George

    –   New teachers may be paired off with experienced colleagues in order to become familiarised with the practical day-to-day running of the school, to get a feel for the culture of the classroom through observation of lessons and to understand appropriate and accepted behaviours.
    –   Heads of sector and selected members of staff can provide informal gatherings, dinners or cocktail parties to introduce new teachers to other staff, members of their department, to help them to settle in.
    –   Provision of photographs of staff for quicker identification of colleagues.
    –   Introduction to students at the first opportunity in circumstances that promote informal exchange.
    –   Interviews with the headteacher and administrator for information on accommodation, salary scale, health scheme, school policies and procedures, rules and regulations.
    –   Assignation to a House and introduction to Head of House.
    –   Provision of special lessons in the language of the country.
    –   Provision of a map of the school and of the area surrounding the school, indicating shops and services.

Conclusion

While bearing in mind that this study was small, we can nevertheless make some generalisations about recruiting and retaining quality teachers into international schools from overseas. First, teachers strongly agreed that in order to sustain the quality of learning in any school quality teachers should be retained beyond a first two-year period. Second, the study identified certain conditions and incentives that would motivate teachers most strongly to continue working at the same school: opportunities for professional advancement within the school, financial incentives, a happy working climate of the school, a powerful sense of job challenge and a strong staff development programme. There is no simple formula, however; teachers are people as well, they have families and different needs, all of which produce a unique combination of factors that influence them when deciding to take up, or remain in, any one teaching position. Schools have to take risks. But if the relevant factors are scrutinised carefully by both employers and placement services when recruiting new staff, the risk may be minimised. Finally, once appointed, a coherent induction and mentoring programme is crucial to the effective, successful incorporation of new teachers and their families.

Note

1   'Penelope' is a term loosely based on the character of Ulysses' wife in Homer's *Odyssey*, who spent 20 years marking time as she waited for her beloved husband, the errant King of Ithaca, to return to her side from the Trojan war. During this time she would spend her days knitting for her husband, with the promise that she would marry the pretender to the throne once the garment was finished. Every night, Penelope would undo all the work she had done that day, thereby postponing her fate for two decades, after which time Ulysses did in fact return to reclaim his throne and his queen.

References

Akram, C. (1995) 'Change and adaptation: children and curriculum in international schools', *International Schools Journal* 15, no. 1: 39–53.

Cole, A.L. and Knowles, J.G. (1995) 'Crossing borders for professional development', in D. Thomas (ed.) *Teachers' Stories*, Buckingham: Open University Press.

ECIS (1997) http://www.ecis.org/htm/genen.htm – June, p. 4.

Hardman, J. (1997) *Neither Mavericks nor Penelopes: Sustaining and Retaining Quality Overseas Teachers Through School Conditions and Incentives*, MA Dissertation, Oxford Brookes University.

Hayden, M. and Thompson, J. (1995) 'International education: the crossing of frontiers', *International Schools Journal* 15, no. 1: 13–20.

Lortie, D. (1975) *Schoolteacher: A Sociological Study*, Chicago: University of Chicago Press.

Martin-Kniep, G.O. (1997) 'Supporting quality curriculum and assessment: an administrative perspective', seminar given to IB Americas Regional Conference, Puerto Rico, July.

Mathews, M. (1989) 'The uniqueness of international education, Part 2', *International Schools Journal* 18, Autumn: 24–34.

Trompenaars, F. (1993) *Riding the Waves of Culture*, London: Nicholas Brealey Publishing.

9

MIDDLE MANAGEMENT IN INTERNATIONAL SCHOOLS

Sonia Blandford

Introduction

This chapter is based on educational research and practice; it focuses on middle management in international schools, and, as such, it relates to all staff. It begins with a brief introduction to management and the international school setting, leading to a description of middle management. This is followed by a discussion on practical issues relating to the role of middle managers with a particular focus on team leadership and management. The chapter concludes with a framework for practice.

Education management is the achievement of objectives through people; managers are responsible for the work of others. Bush and West-Burnham (1994) define the principles of management, which encompass *planning, resourcing, controlling, organising, leading and evaluating*. In brief, these involve:

Leadership	Values, missions and vision.
Management	Planning, organisation, execution and deployment.
Administration	Operational details.

In brief, managers lead, manage and administrate; they keep things going, cope with breakdown, initiate new activities and bring teams and activities together. More specifically, the essential functions of school management are to manage policy, learning, people and resources; school managers create, maintain and develop conditions that enable effective learning to take place.

It is axiomatic that management in education has to happen; curriculum, finance, resources, buildings, pupils, staff and the wider community all need management. One might consider to what extent the emergence of middle management in schools is either a reflection of practice or the cultural influence of hierarchical structures in society (Blandford, 1997). In the Victorian period, increased bureaucracy and administration contributed to the creation of the middle classes. Has increased bureaucracy in schools led to the creation of middle management? Does the same phenomenon apply to all schools?

International schools

Because of the huge range of constitutions, structures and practices in international schools, there is no simple definition, and management at board or trustee level is just as diverse. As Hardman discusses in Chapter 8, staffs employed by international schools are often transient with a maximum of two years' guaranteed employment. The curriculum they deliver (see Chapter 2) can vary from the International Baccalaureate to programmes of learning from the host countries' national curricula, such as USA, UK or any other nationality represented in the school. What is evident is that teachers need to be managed in order to provide the necessary support for each other and their pupils.

The importance of middle managers in this context cannot be overstated. Education reflects society, and as society becomes increasingly more complex education managers encounter many new (and challenging) values and expectations. The process of middle management is to get things done within the framework of practice, as determined by the school as a community and organisation. Harrison (1995: 8) comments that 'managers live in a practical world'. Not unlike schools across the world, an international school will reflect its environment. As a community, each school is self-centred, self-reliant and culturally 'different' from any other school. As an organisation, each school can work within existing structures or create new structures; as Greenfield and Ribbins (1993: 54) state, 'the self cannot escape organisations'.

Throughout their summary of the work of management gurus since the nineteenth century, Pugh and Hickson in *Writers on Organisations* (1989) emphasise the need to place individuals in the workplace within an identifiable structure. This is particularly relevant to middle managers, who first need to locate themselves within a school structure and second need to locate their managers and teams.

Middle management defined

The essential functions of international school management are the management of learning, policy, people and resources. The management of learning, as a central purpose, unites all international schools. Divisions of responsibility within a school are determined by the needs of:

- all pupils to learn;
- all teachers to teach.

As such, teachers are classroom managers, managing the development of knowledge and understanding, skills and abilities of pupils. In addition, a middle manager is a team manager, managing the knowledge and understanding, skills and abilities of both colleagues and pupils. The role of a middle manager is to work with other people within the context of teaching and learning. This involves working with individual values and beliefs manifested in the ethos of the school. As will be discussed later in this chapter, a middle manager has contrasting roles within management teams. Middle management requires individuals to identify, and identify with, different tasks and different people: teacher, leader and team member. This hybrid role within school management provides the framework for the daily practice of the middle manager. Figure 9.1 places the middle manager in context, as a teacher, leader and team member.

Why middle management?

As described earlier, the culture of management in international schools is changing from a 'top down' hierarchical model to a flatter structure, involving the majority of staff in the management of international schools. From this scenario evolves the need for middle managers with responsibility for a range of teams, including:

- subject teams;
- year teams;

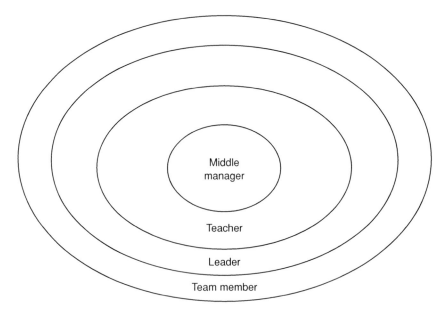

Figure 9.1 Middle management in context. Reprinted from Blandford, S. (1997) *Middle Management in Schools – How to Harmonise Managing and Teaching for an Effective School*, London: Pitman, with permission from Pearson Education Ltd.

138

- curriculum;
- faculty;
- department teams.

In practical terms, school managers have been unable to meet the demands of the changes in management practice, including the management of resources, inspections, recruitment and assessment, curriculum and pastoral matters. Within the international school setting, all teachers have to consider management to be part of their daily practice.

Central to effective middle management is the ability of the middle manager to identify his/her role at any given moment in the school day. An 'effective manager' would differentiate between each management role as required. It is therefore essential that a middle manager understand the nature of his/her job.

What is management?

Understanding the purpose of management within the international school context is fundamental to effective practice. Generally school leaders (boards, principals, headteachers and heads of section) develop vision and mission statements (school aims and objectives) which identify the purpose and direction of the school. Available to all, these statements provide a starting point for all management activities within the school. The shared development of vision and mission statements is critical to determining key objectives and policies, which will provide a framework for education which is specifically suited to each international school community.

In practice, a manager is someone who gets the job done, through people. Everard (1986: 6) defines a manager as someone who:

- knows what he or she wants to happen and causes it to happen;
- is responsible for controlling resources and ensuring that they are put to good use;
- promotes effectiveness in work done, and a search for continual improvement;
- is accountable for the performance of the unit he or she is managing, of which he or she is a part;
- sets a climate or tone conducive to enabling people to give of their best.

Management is therefore the achievement of objectives through people, as managers are responsible for the work of others. These require policies at the macro- and microlevels of the school board, senior management and staff committees. Such policies might include:

- assessment and reporting procedures;

- staff development;
- learning and teaching styles;
- language;
- support;
- equal opportunities;
- care (of both students and staff).

Middle management in practice

If a school is to be effective, managers need to adopt good practice. Rutter et al. (1979: 25) suggest that middle managers should have the following attributes:

1 Strong positive leadership.
2 Staff involvement.
3 Positive school ethos.

Essentially, middle managers should aim to enjoy and encourage good practice directed towards developing and retaining the above if their team (and school) is to be effective. However, being a middle manager does not mean being 'all things to all people'. Effective international schools will need the necessary flexibility in order that middle managers can develop their own management style to fulfil the requirements of the post. Knowing what is required is the key. It is essential for middle managers to identify their roles in terms of:

- tasks;
- responsibilities;
- relationships;
- working conditions;
- external influences.

Middle managers need an understanding of their role as detailed in their job description, negotiated with the senior management team and approved by governors. Clarity is essential if ambiguities, which lead to confusion, are to be avoided. In sum, the role of the middle manager in international schools is to teach, lead teams and be a team member.

Therefore, middle managers are responsible for:

1 Implementing school-wide strategies, structures and intentions. In this process, middle managers 'fine tune' these strategies to suit the real world.
2 Being role models for their staff. A middle manager's daily behaviour must represent the people-centred culture of the school as an organisation.
3 Passing on practices that are learnt as a consequence of operational wisdom.

As practising teachers, a middle manager's timetable will have a greater number of contact hours with classes than the number of hours allocated to those employed as senior managers. To understand the nature of their job, middle managers need to consider their teaching commitment within the context of their middle-management role. This is not merely an issue of time management, but also of the compatibility between the two roles. If practitioner values and beliefs are transferable to management practice, teaching and middle management may coexist quite successfully. If, however, individuals adopt values and beliefs in their management role that differ from their values and beliefs as a practitioner, this will be problematic. The values displayed by middle managers will determine their management style and the nature of their relationship with their colleagues.

However, in the context of organisational structures it would be difficult to define middle management in absolute terms. Comparison of middle management in different countries (Blandford, 1998) has revealed that all teachers have management responsibilities for curriculum and/or pastoral areas. In many cases pastoral and curriculum responsibilities overlap. It was also found that the introduction of a more collegial approach to management in the majority of schools studies results in organisational structures which are flatter, less hierarchical and more inclusive. Interestingly, within the profession the author found that teachers considered management to be part of their daily practice.

Moving towards middle management

Not necessarily true ??·¿

Handy and Aitken (1986: 41) state that 'the assumption behind the promotion structure in schools is that the best teachers make the best managers. Career success means moving upwards to an increasingly managerial role.'

Middle management is in its infancy in schools. Teachers find themselves in management positions without having received appropriate training and development. Management activities often detract from teaching responsibilities. The process by which teachers become managers in the past has been unstructured, yet many teachers are now managers.

When moving to middle management a period of reflection is required in order to analyse the implications of the new position within the school management structure. It is worth repeating that all teachers are managers of the practices that take place in their classrooms. In contrast, *middle* managers are responsible for the policies and practices of their team within the school as an organisation. Middle managers may find it difficult to adapt to their new position, that of manager and teacher.

Player–manager

teaching while administration !!

Middle managers in international schools are very much 'players–managers', participating in the daily tasks of teaching while fulfilling the role of team

141

leaders/managers. It is important for a player–manager to know the role of a middle manager in relation to both leaders and team. A school middle manager is led by a senior management team, the school board, advisory/inspection teams and (depending on where the job is in the management structure) their line manager.

There is a distinctive status to being a manager. It is important to identify what this means early in a management career. Equally, there is a distinct status attached to team membership. As a middle manager, there is every likelihood that a teacher will join teams with responsibility for the management of the school. It is therefore essential for middle managers to know their role, know their team and know their managers.

Evaluating practice

To know how to manage is an ongoing process. The development of the knowledge and understanding, skills and abilities required to manage others takes time. Good middle managers are aware of the need to reflect on and learn from their own practice. Professional managers constantly evaluate their roles within an institution, which is a two-way process: managers developing the skill to know themselves and their team members, and the team knowing its manager. Inconsistency will lead to bad practice; clear evaluations are respected and valued.

To enable evaluations to take place there is also a need to create opportunities for middle managers to meet and to develop management skills and abilities. Time for such meetings would be desirable for managers as individuals, and invaluable to the school. This would also allow middle managers to develop self-evaluation skills within a 'safe' environment. Indeed, the forging and strengthening of a middle-management *team* is one of the most powerful ways in which the role of the middle manager can contribute fully to the life of the school – and yet this is one of the most underdeveloped teams in many international schools.

Problems and dilemmas

For many teachers, involvement in management is not desirable. Whether because of poor management experiences or the view that management and teaching are not compatible, teachers may prefer to teach and leave others to manage. Role conflict is a critical issue for middle managers to address; a middle manager may encounter management dilemmas, which generally arise out of the conflict between management of learning and management of people. Hall and Oldroyd (1990a: 38) identify role strain as a difficult area for all teachers. Sources of role strain were considered to be:

Role ambiguity: when you are unclear about what is expected.
Role conflict: when one of the roles you have is in conflict with another.
Role overload: when more is expected of you in a role than you could manage.
Role underload: when you feel underutilised in your role.

Handy and Aitken suggest a possible method of reducing strains imposed by role problems:

> The more positive approach would be to reduce the ambiguity by agreeing with everyone what the job is all about ... to reduce the conflict by dropping some roles or at least putting clear boundaries around each so that they interfere with each other as little as possible; ... and to reduce the overload by thinking out the priorities properly instead of coping with the crises as they occur.
>
> (Handy and Aitken, 1986: 60)

Defining what the job is all about may only go part way to solving the problem, it may also produce its own set of dilemmas. As Holmes (1993: 38) identifies, 'maintaining a healthy professional community while focusing on learning can create its own conflict.' As a solution, Holmes suggests *trade-offs* when required, which would seem to be a more pragmatic approach to resolving conflict than defining roles. In practice, this will mean defining responsibilities in order to delegate.

Ultimately, the job of a middle manager will always have problems and dilemmas. Choices will need to be made and difficult people confronted, although in practice confronting colleagues who are 'difficult' can itself be problematic. To be an effective middle manager it is important to resolve difficulties as they arise, as merely by withholding goodwill and co-operation a 'difficult' colleague can destroy the learning environment. Courage, in measured doses, is required to deal with situations in a non-confrontational manner. How a middle manager approaches such situations often reflects his/her own personal integrity. Middle managers are constantly watched by colleagues, so personal integrity is very important. Holmes (1993: 104) advises: 'if the leader misleads, mistreats or misrepresents his or her colleagues in any serious way, he or she forfeits trust, respect and, in extreme cases, collaboration.'

When dealing with problems and dilemmas, listening skills are important, and a middle manager will need to listen and use information sensitively. Persistence is also a valuable tool. As a middle manager has many audiences in his/her role, it may be difficult to resolve dilemmas quickly. Persistence without being overbearing will produce changes which will benefit the middle manager and his/her team.

What the job entails

Specifically the job of being a middle manager entails knowledge and understanding, skills and abilities. A checklist of practice might include:

- leadership;
- participation and delegation;
- stress management;
- conflict management;
- knowledge of schools as organisations;
- communication – interpersonal relationships;
- understanding of teams;
- time management;
- appraisal;
- strategic planning;
- operational planning;
- decision-making;
- monitoring and evaluation;
- financial management;
- management of change;
- staff development;
- recruitment and selection;
- self-evaluation.

With each of these, a middle manager will need to consider the most appropriate management style. Tannenbaum and Schmidt (1973) found that management styles differ according to several factors. These can be identified as:

- *the leader:* his or her personality and preferred style;
- *the led:* the needs, attitudes and skills of the subordinates or colleagues;
- *the task:* the requirements and goals of the job to be done;
- *the contact:* the school, its values and beliefs, visions and missions.

Selection of the 'best or preferred' style appropriate to the individual is critical to the success of the manager and team. A middle manager will need to adopt a style that is applicable or sustainable.

Team leadership

Effective team leadership will produce effective teams and an effective school. A team leader has to be able to work in an open and honest manner. As professionals, teachers should value effective teamwork; schools are dependent on teamwork. An effective middle manager will avoid the pitfalls of weak management, which include:

- overemphasis on people, at the expense of task achievement;
- overemphasis on task, at the expense of the people in the team;
- overemphasis on agendas, not processes;
- reacting to events, not anticipating them.

In the majority of settings, the process of managing a team is often dependent on the task. The characteristics of effective teams are (Hall and Oldroyd, 1990b: 34–5):

- *Clear objectives and goals* – according to task.
- *Openness and confrontation* – dependent on effective communication and interpersonal relationships.
- *Support and trust* – requiring active listening and understanding.
- *Co-operation and conflict* – working together, sharing and developing ideas in a democratic and creative manner.
- *Sound procedures* – enable everyone to contribute to decision-making.
- *Appropriate leadership* – knowing and understanding team members, their beliefs and values.
- *Regular review* – monitoring and evaluating in a rigorous manner.
- *Individual development* – enabling individuals to develop strengths, involving appraisal and staff development.
- *Sound intergroup relations* – a commitment to teaching pupils through openness and trust.

However, a middle manager may find identifying the characteristics of his/ her team difficult. The nature of the task and the culture of the school will influence the working habits of team members. Equally, pressure from external agencies will affect the quality of teams in schools. Family commitments, hobbies and political initiatives are areas of influence on teachers' lives; these, in turn, will influence the individual's commitment to the team. In essence, the quality of the relationships within the team will determine the quality of the task. A professional view of the school as a learning organisation is also helpful in developing such relationships, as discussed further in Chapter 7.

Participation and delegation

The opportunity to participate in decision-making teams, which influence school management, is a relatively new phenomenon in the context of international schools. For some middle managers, participation and delegation can be difficult to manage. Reliance and dependency on colleagues can be perceived as a weakness. However, these are not insurmountable problems. If a team is effective and has the characteristics and strengths listed above, participation and delegation will be necessary parts of team management.

Participation

A confident, open middle manager encourages participation, which has meaning and relevance to daily practice. Middle managers might function in any of these forms:

Consultation: team members are invited to suggest ideas; decision-making remains the responsibility of the middle manager.

Consent: team members, as a group, can consent to or veto any decision made by the middle manager.

Consensus: team members are consulted, followed by whole team involvement in decision-making through majority vote.

A middle manager should be able to identify which style is applicable to any specific task or situation. Democracy is fine if applicable; equally, autocracy is acceptable for some tasks and can work in the right circumstances. A middle manager will need to decide which of the above styles to adopt in which situations.

In practice, decisions may be beyond the mandate of the middle manager and his/her team. Senior management may be responsible for the initiation of policies, expecting middle management to implement decisions that have been made by others. In this situation, participation is at an operational rather than strategic level.

Delegation

Being led and leading will involve the middle manager in the process of delegation. Managers can save time by delegating tasks to colleagues or teams. There are several factors to be considered by middle managers in the delegation process:

- Quality of the result – will the outcome be good enough?
- The ability of the individual – how capable is the individual of completing the task?
- Relationship – will the manager be able to coach the individual or leave him/her to the task? Either could cause problems.
- Time – have staff the time to complete the task?

It is essential that any delegated work be clearly understood. A middle manager will need to ensure that they have the knowledge and understanding, skills and abilities to complete the task. When delegating, a middle manager should retain control over the work delegated, whether by instruction or participation.

In essence, delegation will enhance the quality of a middle manager's work and that of his/her team. It will demonstrate a move from an autocratic style to a democratic style of management. It is worth noting that reluctant and poor delegation is often worse than no delegation at all. Box 9.1 is an example of delegation in practice.

Department/faculty management

The size of the department or faculty accommodating each subject area is determined by the size of the international school. For a middle manager responsible for a department or faculty, the number of staff within each academic team will reflect the number of pupils attending the school. The size of the academic team will also determine the financial incentive allocated to the post and the level of delegation possible. The situation is more complex still if, as in bilingual international schools, language and cultural difficulties divide teams.

Communication, written or oral, is essential for the success of the team – and this has language implications. A middle manager is a disseminator and gatherer of information, acting as the 'gatekeeper' for the team. A middle manager will need to be aware of the team's needs; in the majority of cases teachers will want to be informed of policies that affect their practice. They will also wish to be informed of staff development opportunities. In essence, a middle manager should try not to be too protective of staff, but to impart information on a 'need-to-know' basis.

Box 9.1 Delegation in practice

Task:	annual stock take.
Process:	team member asked to:
	(a) audit stock used in current academic year;
	(b) forecast stock budget for forthcoming year;
	(c) plan implementation, e.g. stock control and storage.
Time scale:	3 weeks.
Number of staff:	four.
Accountable to:	subject co-ordinator.
Report to:	subject meeting.
Outcome:	budget plan for stock including:
	budget review;
	budget forecast;
	budget implementation;
	stock-keeping record procedures.

Pastoral management

Every teacher has, to some extent, a pastoral responsibility for pupils. Heads of year/house teams manage this area, which involves regular contact with parents, members of the community and external agencies. Areas of responsibility should be well defined within the management structure of the school. This is occasionally a neglected area within international school management, and it is inevitably made more complex by the management of different national cultures under one roof (see Chapter 10). A framework for practice of the pastoral care management should therefore:

- be workable;
- recognise the needs of the school;
- be understood and acknowledged by all staff;
- relate to the school's vision and mission;
- allow middle and senior managers to develop knowledge and understanding, skills and abilities;
- allow middle managers to participate in and develop continuing professional development (CPD) programmes.

Just as teachers have pastoral care responsibility for their pupils, so managers have pastoral care duties towards their staff. One cannot expect loyalty and pastoral care from staff towards pupils if they themselves are not treated with respect.

Management accountability

A middle manager is accountable to his/her leaders and to those he/she leads. Accountability takes many forms, as shown in Box 9.2.

Middle management can use accountability in a positive manner, and celebrate success. A middle manager will need to understand accountability. There is little to be gained from viewing the tools of accountability with fear and anxiety.

Conclusion – a framework for practice

In order to bring together the role of a middle manager in an international school, the author has constructed a framework for practice. This was provided by a number of sources. Research by Brown and Rutherford (1996) focused on heads of departments in secondary schools in England. Using Murphy's (1992) typology, Brown and Rutherford applied the descriptors to the head of department role:

- servant leader;
- organisational architect;

Box 9.2 Accountability relationships

- **Pupils:** lesson content, examination results and attendance.
- **Parents:** reporting, consultation and pupil support.
- **Colleagues:**   teaching, management of staff and situations.
- **Senior management:** participation and delegation, team effectiveness, teaching, results – examination tables.
- **School Board and/or owner:** results – examination tables.

- moral educator;
- social architect;
- leading professional.

Having observed and interviewed six heads of department, Brown and Rutherford (1996) defined each of the above as follows:

- *Head of department as servant leader:* there was evidence of heads of department serving the needs of the department, such as the head of department who was organising staffing requests, e.g. who teaches what to which class for the following year, involving making plans, building consensus and making decisions through a constant process of informal discussion.
- *Head of department as organisational architect:* the heads of department acted as managers of their own departments within the overall organisational structures of the school, providing the systems to accommodate and develop both departmental issues and staff.
- *Head of department as moral educator:* a head of department was observed working together with a teacher of special educational needs in that teacher's classroom. The teacher hoped, by personal example, to extend the practice to the entire department. This, the researchers believed, was an obvious example of a head of department exercising leadership through the modelling of deeply held values.
- *Head of department as social architect:* an example of a caring head of department was observed when a member of the department collapsed with stress at the beginning of the morning and was unable to teach (and eventually had to go home). The head of department supported and counselled the teacher throughout the morning and was able to prevent the situation deteriorating further.
- *Head of department as leading professional:* heads of department spent at least 80 per cent of their time actually teaching, this is their main professional role. Much of the rest of their time was spent leading and managing the department. There appeared to be little time left for initiatives to improve teaching, learning and achievement.

If Murphy's typology is put alongside the qualities of middle management found in the National Council for Administration and Teacher Education (NCATE) management literature, and those in the Teacher Training Agency (TTA) subject leader training programmes, we have a framework for practice (Box 9.3).

The framework for practice raises the following key issues.

- *Context-based issues.* The diversity of practice that exists serves to illuminate the complexity of defining middle management. In some international schools, middle managers are emerging in every facet of school management. In others, headteachers or heads of section could be considered to be middle managers. In smaller schools, the practice is so collegial that all teachers have management responsibilities.

Box 9.3 Framework for practice: middle management

Brown and Rutherford (1996):
    Servant leader.
    Organisational architect.
    Moral educator.
    Social architect.
    Leading professional.

NCATE (1994):
    Professional and ethical leadership.
    Information management and evaluation.
    Organisational management.
    Interpersonal relationships.
    Financial management and resource allocation.
    Technology and information systems.
    Curriculum – all aspects.
    Professional development.
    Student personnel services.
    Community and media relations.
    Education law, public policy and political systems.
    Internship.

TTA (1997):
    Strategic direction and development of subject.
    Teaching and learning.
    Leading and managing staff.
    Development and deployment of resources.

- *Specific needs in each school system.* Divisions of responsibility within international schools are determined by the needs of:
  - all pupils to learn;
  - all teachers to teach.

  There is a need to develop a management culture in international schools. This chapter also indicated that a middle manager, or class teacher, as a member of the school teaching team, needs to have knowledge of all operational aspects of the school, which encompass:
  - curriculum issues;
  - pastoral issues;
  - research and development;
  - policy and practice.
- *Common issues leading to a generic framework.* Management activities take place in all international schools, and there appear to be generic responsibilities that apply to all schools regardless of the identification of roles within a given organisational structure. The specific role of the middle manager, however, is not always recognised in its own right in some international schools. The role might be enhanced by formal recognition, training and the development of a supportive and decision-making middle-management team.
- *Cultural and organisational issues.* In identifying that teachers in international schools have management responsibilities, the author has identified the need to locate management within differing individual and organisational cultural contexts. Emerging management and organisational issues are relevant to educational practice in all international schools.

Summary

It can be concluded that within each international school setting middle managers are very much players/managers, participating in the daily tasks of teaching while fulfilling the role of team leaders/managers. This demonstrates how important it is for a player/manager to know his/her role as a middle manager in relation to both leaders and team. To know how to manage is an ongoing process; the development of the knowledge and understanding, skills and abilities required to manage others takes time. Education managers need to be aware of the need to reflect on, and learn from, their practice, constantly evaluating their roles within an institution. This is a two-way process: managers knowing themselves and their team members, and teams knowing their managers.

Irrespective of culture and differences in practice, for all teachers training and development is important, and knowing what is required is the key.

References

Blandford, S. (1997) *Middle Management in Schools – How to Harmonise Managing and Teaching for an Effective School*, London: Pitman.

Blandford, S. (1998) 'Middle management in schools, an international perspective', presented to the European Conference on Educational Research, Slovenia.

Brown, M. and Rutherford, D. (1996) 'Leadership for school improvement: the changing role of the head of department', presented to the British Educational Management and Administration Society 'Partners in change – shaping the future' conference, 22–7 March, Cambridge.

Bush, T. and West-Burnham, J. (eds) (1994) *The Principles of Educational Management*, Harlow: Longman.

Everard, K.B. (1986) *Developing Management in Schools*, Oxford: Blackwell.

Greenfield, T. and Ribbins, P. (1993) *Greenfield on Educational Administration: Towards a Humane Science*, London: Routledge.

Hall, V. and Oldroyd, D. (1990a) *Management Self-development for Staff in Secondary Schools, Unit 1: Self-development for Effective Management*, Bristol: National Development Centre for Education Management and Policy.

Hall, V. and Oldroyd, D. (1990b) *Management Self-development for Staff in Secondary Schools, Unit 3: Team Development for Effective Schools*, Bristol: National Development Centre for Education Management and Policy.

Handy, C. and Aitken, R. (1986) *Understanding Schools as Organisations*, Harmondsworth: Penguin.

Harrison, B.T. (1995) Revaluing leadership and service in educational management', in J. Bell and B.T. Harrison (eds) *Vision and Values in Managing Education*, London: David Fulton.

Holmes, G. (1993) *Essential School Leadership*, London: Kogan Page.

Murphy, P. (1992) *The Landscape of Leadership Preparation*, Thousand Oaks, CA: Corwin Press.

NCATE (National Council for Administration and Teacher Education) (1994) *Advanced Programmes in Educational Leadership*, New York: NCATE.

Pugh, D.S. and Hickson, D.J. (1989) *Writers on Organisations*, 4th edn, Harmondsworth: Penguin.

Rutter, M., Maughan, B., Mortimore, P. and Ouston, J. (1979) *Fifteen Thousand Hours: Secondary Schools and Their Effects on Children*, London: Open Books.

Tannenbaum, R. and Schmidt, W.H. (1973) 'How to choose a leadership pattern', *Harvard Business Review* 36 (2): 95–101.

TTA (Teacher Training Agency) (1997) *National Standards for Subject Leaders*, London: TTA.

10

MANAGING MIXED-CULTURE TEAMS IN INTERNATIONAL SCHOOLS

Marian Shaw

Introduction

One of the key characteristics of international schools, whatever their size, philosophy or constitution, is almost certain to be the mix of cultures represented among the staff and students. In the true spirit of international education, this can be hugely broadening, producing unexpected delights and sociological advantages. But this same characteristic can also present considerable management challenges. Managers in international schools need to understand the motivations and values of the staff working with them, and may often interrogate their own behaviours and those of others around them: Why did he react like that? What is the best way to address a sensitive topic with someone from a different culture? Am I being fair?

This chapter, emerging from management training and consultancy experiences in many international schools, explores management implications in obtaining the best from mixed-culture teams of students and teachers. It first identifies the concept of school culture or climate, and then presents ten scenarios from international schools where there have been misunderstandings at least partly attributable to the mix of different national cultures in the team or the school. These are followed by a discussion on how cross-cultural theory might help with such situations, and the scenarios are then examined in the light of this theory. The chapter is designed so that it can be used as the basis for a practical training session: this approach, applied sensitively, has been found useful in raising awareness in international schools.

The field of cross-cultural research is a most fertile one at the present time, and this chapter does not have space to do justice to it; if the situations presented here are all too familiar, a deeper trawl through some of the literature mentioned will be both fascinating and rewarding.

Whole-school context

A central feature of school life which is frequently overlooked, or rather ignored on the grounds that it is diffuse, complex and difficult to address in a scientific and logical manner, is the ethos of the school – the organisational climate which provides the environment for all the business of the school. Most international schools, whatever their particular constitution, have clear and unambiguous purposes, usually expressed as mission, values or aims, many of which relate directly to the aims of the International Baccalaureate Organisation (IBO) in providing a broad education suitable for young people in the twenty-first century (Box 10.1).

Each of these IBO statements aspires to the development of students as confident young people, able to relate to others in the world. There is little here that most international schools would not subscribe to, and examples of mission statements and aims taken at random from the websites of a sample of international schools across the world reflect similar sentiments:

- 'We foster independent inquiry, critical thinking, open-mindedness and service to others.'
- 'The curriculum and learning strategies encourage the development of responsible, democratic citizens.'
- 'The school strives to embody the finest spirit of international co-operation.'
- 'We are committed to honesty and responsibility in all relationships, respecting the legitimate rights of individuals and stressing the importance of social awareness and sensitivity.'
- 'We will seek to promote equal opportunity and social justice.'

Box 10.1 Excerpts from IBO Guides (author's emphases) *Suitable for young people in the 21st Century*

- Students as *risk-takers* should be able to 'approach unfamiliar situations without anxiety and have the confidence and independence of spirit to explore new roles, ideas and strategies' (IBO, 1998: 5).
- Encouraging *open-mindedness*, they should 'respect the views, values and traditions of other cultures, and [be] accustomed to seeking and considering a range of points of view' (IBO, 1998: 5).
- '*Intercultural awareness* goes beyond mere tolerance or a polite attitude towards the ideas and artefacts of other cultures. It is positive, empathetic movement towards others, a readiness to act co-operatively in genuine exchange and shared effort … it promotes the unarguably universal values common to civilised society' (IBO, 1994: 5).
- 'The IBO aims to assist schools in their endeavours to help young people and teach them to relate their experiences of the classroom to the realities of the world outside. Beyond intellectual rigour and high academic standards, strong emphasis is placed on the *ideals of international understanding* and responsible citizenship' (IBO, 1997: 3).

But the reality of meeting such aims is a different matter. In many of the workshops that we have run, headteachers have identified a significant gap between rhetoric and practice. So where does this gap come from? How does a school meet objectives beyond the 'intellectual rigour and high academic standards'? What sort of learning environment does an international school need in order to promote values such as 'co-operation', 'international understanding', 'unarguably universal values' and 'responsible citizenship'?

Underpinning how students learn in school is the way the school itself operates – the 'hidden curriculum'. It has long been recognised that the best educational outcomes derive from students perceiving consonance between the formal and hidden curriculum. But the issue is broader than students and their learning. Staff, too, react to – and are shaped by – the way the school operates, and this is both a concern and a responsibility of managers. The atmosphere in the school defines the school (organisational) culture, henceforth referred to in this chapter as 'climate' to avoid confusion with culture in the national sense. It affects the manner in which *all* members of the school community relate to each other. The school culture may be visible and explicit, or vague and implicit. It may be strong and dominant, or virtually impotent. A helpful climate of an international school might be defined as *the way in which all of us in this school agree to work together in order to provide the best service for the learners.* It affects everything from the way decisions are made to the way students learn, and is in turn affected by these factors, as the research of Rutter et al. (1979) demonstrated.

Attempting to analyse this further, one might categorise the elements which affect school climate into three groups:

- The *social environment*, i.e. the background against which the school processes take place. This includes the national cultures represented in the school, the gender balance, the maturity and experience of staff, the geographical position and physical nature of the school, and the nature of the community from which the school draws its intake. It has an underlying effect on the way people work, affecting teachers' and students' expectations of each other, thus having an impact on the extent to which school aims are achieved. In international schools, the cultural aspect of the social environment clearly has more significance than in most national schools.
- The formal *management systems, policies and structures* also affect organisational climate. Implicit and unintentional messages may be conveyed by the answers to questions such as these:
  - To what extent do the pastoral and academic systems cohere?
  - Are there differential levels of pay for people of different culture?
  - Who gets appointed or promoted to leadership positions?
  - Is there an assumption that one national culture will dominate in the school management?

- What length is the standard contract? Does this give teachers sufficient time to build mutually beneficial relationships in the school?
- To what extent does the educational (as opposed to the profit) agenda drive decisions?
- Are staff encouraged to develop 'on the job', or are teachers treated as expendable items that must be replaced with a model that is already trained for the latest development?

• A third element influencing the organisational climate is the *actions and behaviours* of the people in the school, as these determine ultimately how policy is implemented. This is hard to legislate for because it depends on willingness and ability – and therefore also on attitude and skills. As people are inevitably influenced by, and respond to, the way they themselves are treated, the responsibility of the school leadership to set an example and to create a conducive atmosphere is pivotal.

Together, these three elements affect the school climate, and are, in turn, influenced by it (see Figure 10.1).

The relationships among the elements in Figure 10.1 determine the degree of consonance operating in the school. Where there is a high degree of consonance, or consistency, the school values are more recognisable, and the

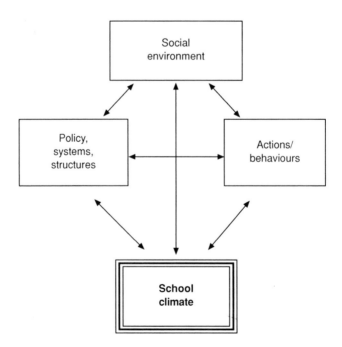

Figure 10.1 Factors influencing school climate.

school is likely to provide an agreeable and productive atmosphere for learning. But where there is dissonance, or disharmony, between these elements, energy gets diverted away from the central educational task: it is expended on such activities as mediating conflict or counteracting the consequences of suppressed resentment.

The potential for dissonance through misunderstanding exists in every school, but in an *international* school this potential is increased when people of different culture have differing expectations of each other. Actions may be taken, and behaviours exhibited, which are misinterpreted by others, and this can be a source of confusion or distress within a team, and a challenge to the team leader. It both reflects and – eventually – influences interactions in the wider world, affecting the degree to which the aims of the IBO are achievable. As Rodger notes in his study of an international school, *Developing Moral Community in a Pluralist School Setting*:

> it will be a great advantage to have a framework for decision making which requires to be **applied** by individuals and groups to their given circumstances; which permits and does not lament the possibilities of different decisions; which encourages the distinction to be recognised between decisions which are merely different and those which express disagreements; and which enables the disagreements to be discussed within an agreed, principled framework.
>
> (Rodger, 1996: 64)

It is by way of exploring how dissonance through misunderstanding might occur that the scenarios given in Table 10.1, all drawn from real international schools, are now presented, later to be analysed through the cross-cultural theory.

Cases of misunderstanding in international schools

Misunderstandings are created by complex situations, and usually cannot be attributed to a single cause, but the situations detailed in Table 10.1 have all been chosen because they are partly attributable to cultural elements.

As well as illustrating the points about cross-cultural teams, they can also be used as a training exercise to stimulate discussion about why the situations might have arisen, and what might be done about them.

While these are fragmented incidents, each has the potential to influence both school climate and school effectiveness, and therefore needs to be better understood. The reasons for these situations could be attributed in each case to various factors, depending on the circumstances of the school and the people concerned, but the common feature is that in each case *the situation arose by people not understanding, or not conforming to, what was expected of them in those circumstances.* They judged the situation from within their own culture, and

Table 10.1 Ten cases of misunderstanding in international schools

School	Situation
A	In an international school in the Far East, an appraisal system has been introduced by its Western managers with the prime function of improving staff development. It requires that heads of department (HoDs) provide frank feedback to their staff, discussing areas for improvement as well as recognising and praising achievement. Many of the HoDs from the local culture are unable to do this, although training has been provided.
B	In an international school in the Middle East, student behaviour that is regarded and encouraged as healthy curiosity in some classes, typically led by expatriate teachers, is perceived as insubordination in other classes, typically led by local teachers, and treated as such.
C	The Principal of an international school returns from a leadership course, and, with change management in mind, sets up a structure of greater decentralisation, delegating more to her mixed-culture middle-management staff. She has delineated the new roles and responsibilities for HoDs in a new handbook, but is frustrated by some staff who seem unwilling or unable to take the decisions that they are now entitled to take, constantly referring back up to her.
D	A new teacher to a bicultural school in Indonesia, recruited from the UK to her first international school appointment, uses her tried-and-tested technique of whole-class discussion to check for understanding and to challenge the thinking of the class. She is frustrated by the domination of the relatively few British students in the class, and she cannot find a way of getting the other students in the class to contribute to the discussion.
E	Following an overhaul of the appraisal system in an international school in Africa, HoDs are encouraged to use appropriate styles of 'situational leadership'* with individual teachers in order to help them develop and to face the imminent changes in school. A workshop is held for the HoDs. A year later the coaching and mentoring appears to be less successful where there is a big cultural difference between the HoD and the teacher.
F	In a bicultural 'British-style' school in Latin America the managers, mostly European, are frustrated that, in spite of clear procedural guidelines, the local teachers sometimes seem to be demotivated from carrying out their school duties. These teachers, on the other hand, are upset that their managers ignore their own traditional celebrations, such as Teachers' Day, when managers are expected to fête their teachers.
G	A teacher from Europe has just joined his first international school. His African colleagues in the curriculum team, however, are quietly upset by his apparently outspoken behaviour in meetings.
H	In an international school in Japan, when asked a question by a student from a local family, an Australian teacher suggests that the student finds out the answer and tells the rest of the class. The student's parent complains to the Principal that her teachers are not properly qualified, as they don't seem to be able to answer questions in class.

I   The Board introduced performance-related pay in order to reward those teachers whose teaching is outstanding, and to motivate others to achieve financial reward by better teaching. Conversely, 18 months later, the morale in the mixed-culture staffroom has dropped significantly.

J   An international school in Asia is increasing its intake of local children, but the Headteacher is finding it difficult to engage the parents in school life. The more he tries to improve communication, the harder it becomes. He calls a meeting, and the parents appear to agree with his suggestions, but he receives feedback via the community that they resent what he is trying to do.

Note
*Situational leadership implies that managers will think carefully about the skills of each individual member of staff and give them appropriate personal direction, support or coaching in performing specific elements of their roles (Blanchard et al., 1985).

may have had their own preconceived ideas about what they should be doing. Because culture is implicit, and therefore not discussed a great deal, we tend to make assumptions about what is, or is not, appropriate behaviour in given situations. So what is it that influences the behaviour of the individuals within the school? Where do they get their guidance on how to behave/respond in any given circumstance? Cross-cultural research and theory is useful, and will be referred to next before we examine each of the cases described.

How can theory help to clarify cross-cultural misunderstandings?

There are numerous theories about how people respond and react to each other at work. They are concerned with attributes such as character, situation, organisational climate, race, gender, tradition and so on. While acknowledging that factors influencing behaviour are extremely complex, this chapter focuses in particular on *cross-cultural theory*. This suggests that people from different cultural backgrounds work in different ways, and that therefore culture is central to the way organisations work. While it is valuable in opening up understanding, and also in providing objective explanations for when misunderstandings actually occur, it cannot, nevertheless, provide a complete picture.

One group of 'culture-free' theories argues that all organisations, regardless of where they are in the world, should be able to operate best with a single set of principles, as long as they have appropriate and similar conditions of structure (for example patterns of control, communication, co-ordination). It originates in *contingency theory* (Taylor, 1947; Fayol, 1949; Laurence and Lorsch, 1967), which searches for similarities between different organisations and uses these to identify a number of ways in which universal principles of management can be applied. This theory would argue that international schools are much the same everywhere, regardless of country, and that, as long as the same principles are applied, schools will run smoothly and each person will be able to play her/his part in this.

This approach does not give a great deal of practical help to managers trying to make sense of their worlds, as there is little linkage to the behaviour *inside* organisations, and its popularity has declined in recent years. Throughout the 1960s and 1970s there was little attention to the cross-cultural aspects of management, but Hofstede's (1980) research changed all this by looking at how national cultures affected the way organisations worked, thus initiating a new body of 'culture-bound' theory.

Hofstede's (1980, 1991) seminal work is familiar to many, but a brief summary follows as a reminder. A total of 117,000 employees in many different countries world-wide were surveyed, and Hofstede found distinct differences in basic cultural assumptions which had an effect on the way people worked, and on the way they related to each other at work. He likened culture to an onion with different layers: the outer, more visible layers, concerned with *practices* such as customs, clothing, housing, rituals and ceremonies, being relatively easy to observe and to understand, but the innermost *core values* being hidden. The latter are the *assumptions* inherent in the culture; they define the norms by which people of the same culture live, although they are rarely articulated, or even overtly recognised, as they are taken for granted. One's upbringing, particularly in the first 10 years of life, is thought to exert a powerful effect on the values one holds. This is the aspect of culture that Hofstede (1991: 5) defines as 'the collective programming of the mind which distinguishes the members of one group or category of people from another. Culture is learned, not inherited. It derives from one's social environment, not from one's genes.'

Trying to make sense of the differences in core values, Hofstede derived from his data a way of categorising cultures into various dimensions (Box 10.2), and then explored ways in which these interacted with each other. Different countries are found through the research to have different relative positions on these dimensions, and some understanding of values in that society may be deduced from their positions.

Tables of national cultural values, and the way the cultural dimensions relate to each other, can be found in Hofstede (1991). In addition to these dimensions, other relevant cross-cultural phenomena include:

- *Disconfirmed expectancies:* if people have a strong expectation, then any deviation from it is seen as greater than it really is (Helson, 1964). Brislin (1993: 44) remarks that 'disconfirmed expectancies are certain in intercultural encounters'.
- *Fundamental attribution error:* this is the mistake of making judgements about the characters of others without taking situational factors into account (Ross, 1977). Actions of other people are judged through the value system of the perceiver, who may then form incorrect conclusions about the motive for the action – often thinking the worse of them.

Box 10.2 Hofstede's five dimensions

Individualism – collectivism:
The degree to which people see themselves or their collective group as more important. Individualistic societies tend to emphasise the 'I' above the 'we', whereas collectivist societies respect the goals of their own group more than individual achievement.

Power distance (PD):
The amount of emotional distance between employers and employees. In high power distance cultures, employees tend to prefer their managers to lead visibly, and paternal–autocratic leadership styles are seen as caring. In low power distance cultures, the opposite is true; employees express a preference for consultative management styles.

Uncertainty avoidance (UA):
The degree to which people feel threatened by uncertain or unknown situations. People with a high uncertainty avoidance index tend to prefer to know where they are, with rules of precision to guide them, whereas the opposite is the case with those with a low UA index, where more risks may be taken.

Masculinity–femininity:
This is concerned with the degree of achievement–orientation built into the culture, taking its name (perhaps unhelpfully) from stereotypical gender expectations. High masculinity cultures value status, challenge and achievement, whereas high femininity cultures value good working relationships and co-operation.

Confucian dynamism (long-term versus short-term orientation):
This dimension emerged after the others following studies of entrepreneurial development in East Asia, which did not fit into the previous dimensions. It represents an emergence of the long-term orientation of 'virtue' (persistence, thrift, ordering relationships by, and observing, status, and having a sense of commitment to others) out of the more traditional short-term orientation of 'truth' (personal stability, protecting 'face', respect for tradition). The interaction between the two makes up this cultural value.

Source: Hofstede (1991).

- *Symbolism:* sometimes others do not understand the value and importance of the way people relate to the symbols inside their own culture; this can break down trust.

Cross-cultural research is complex, and not without its problems, particularly when applied to educational issues: it is largely Western-centric (Trompenaars, 1993); the research tools are not appropriate in all cultures, which means suspect validity (Lonner, 1990; Riordan and Vandenburg, 1994); it is mainly industry-based, and can be easily misused when attempt at transference is made to other areas (Jameson, 1994); and it has tended to attach stereotypes to nation states (Hofstede 1980; Trompenaars, 1993).

Nevertheless, as long as we remember that cultural stereotypes only represent an *average* of many individuals in a country, and that there is danger in labelling *individuals,* or in believing that everyone of a certain nationality thinks and behaves in the same way, the stereotypes are useful in giving us, in the words of Brislin (1993), a 'shortcut to thinking', or a starting point.

This is a very curtailed summary of some, but by no means the only, elements through which cross-cultural interactions might be analysed. It will nevertheless suffice, in the given space, to illustrate next the ten cases, which were outlined earlier in Table 10.1.

Examining the possible causes of misunderstanding in the scenarios

In discussing these cases, it will be assumed that the international schools in question have a mixed-culture staff and student body. The 'discussion' component in the following section suggests possible causes for the dissonance, some of which are cultural, while the 'ideas' section focuses in practical terms on what *might* work under the circumstances to improve the situation.

School A: providing frank feedback to staff

Discussion

Teacher appraisal can be notoriously difficult to implement in the first instance, as it involves making informed judgements about colleagues and then reflecting these back to them. Training is a prerequisite, but it also needs confidence on behalf of both appraiser and appraisee, particularly where there are substantial areas for development identified. Some individuals take such feedback more personally than others, however carefully it is delivered, and this can inhibit the appraiser, who usually does not wish to discomfort the appraisee. Such a situation may be further exaggerated in a culture high in collectivism and also in Confucian dynamism, typical in the Far East, where activity causing 'face loss' is taboo.

A high power distance (PD) might also play a part in this case, as status may get in the way of open discussion. Although individual preference plays an important role, people from individualistic cultures with low PD (such as many northern European countries) stereotypically accept open discussion of differences.

The situation in school A is not uncommon; Heads of Department (HoDs) in international schools are often appointed from European or North American cultures, whereas teachers from the local community are more likely to occupy 'ordinary' teaching posts – which increases the PD further. Nevertheless, teachers can only improve if they are helped to reflect on their own progress, so a way forward needs to be found if the whole appraisal system is not to become a superficial and time-wasting process.

Ideas

 Adopt, or design, an appraisal system overtly concerned with professional development.
- Joint training for appraisers and appraisees so that difficulties can be discussed and understood by all parties.
- Clear and agreed criteria for observations and appraisal judgements/comments.
- A mutually accepted form of words that helps people deliver constructive feedback kindly, without the recipient feeling either shamed or confronted.

School B: classroom behaviour

Discussion

The school approach to what is/is not acceptable classroom behaviour is at the centre of this dissonance. If it is not addressed, students may not always feel secure, teachers may blame each other for what they perceive to be unhelpful practices, and ultimately there is also the possibility that differences between staff will be exploited by students. In a school with a strong personal and social development policy, students may be encouraged to develop through enquiry and challenge. But the behaviour of the teachers is critical to the success of this strategy (Shaw, 1991), and national culture also plays a part. Teachers from high power distance (PD) cultures (such as Malaysia, Arabian countries, India) may incline more to didactic teaching than those from lower PD cultures (such as Britain), as it may be considered rude or insolent if students talk back to, or question, the teacher in the public forum. Teachers from low uncertainty avoidance (UA) cultures (such as Britain, USA and Scandinavia) may be more inclined to use open-ended learning situations, where students are encouraged to argue and defend their standpoint, than teachers from high UA cultures, who prefer to avoid the risks involved with handing over responsibility to students for making their own enquiries.

Ideas

- Discussions to share assumptions about classroom expectations among staff, students and parents.
- Understanding the points of view of all concerned.
- Agreement about school norms, while allowing enough flexibility for personal preference.
- Training for staff, if appropriate, in extending their range of classroom strategies.
- A management climate which encourages experimentation rather than blames failure.

School C: taking decisions at lower levels

Discussion

Change is easier to implement in schools if all staff play a full role. This implies delegation, but delegation needs the right climate in which to work. The staff need to have confidence and freedom to learn by trying things out. Simply writing about new roles and responsibilities in a handbook is not enough to build this confidence. Additionally, if the middle managers come from a high PD or a high UA culture, they may be even less likely to take the initiative in such a climate, as they will worry more about getting it wrong.

Ideas

The Head could:

- show trust;
- encourage initiative;
- praise success;
- mentor/coach for new roles;
- structure the delegated risks to limit damage caused by errors of judgement;
- open discussion about new roles/responsibilities;
- anticipate and agree in advance what to do when things go wrong;
- develop a middle-management team identity for mutual support (see Chapter 9).

School D: whole-class discussion

Discussion

The British teacher here is making an assumption that strategies which work in the UK will also work in school D, but is finding it hard to get some of the students to speak out in class. They may be shy by character, but culture might also play a significant part. Students from a collectivist culture might be inclined to behave this way, and Hofstede (1991: 62) points out the difficulty that teachers from individualist societies have in this respect. The teacher needs to understand that 'for the student who conceives of him/herself as part of a group, it is illogical to speak up without being sanctioned by the group to do so'.

This is not an uncommon problem with staff new to international schools; they expect their previous successful teaching strategies to be transportable, but some groups of students do not have the skills or confidence to work in this way. The teacher needs to recognise the problem, and then to develop a classroom atmosphere that encourages participation without pressure. The school also has a responsibility here.

Ideas

The teacher could:

- observe what students find acceptable/uncomfortable;
- structure discussions so that opinions come from small groups with rotating spokespersons who speak for the group;
- find ways of making individual contributions easy and fun.

The school could:

- induct new staff into the cultures of the students;
- open up discussion about the needs of *all* students, rather than assume that 'West is best';
- share and agree a range of appropriate classroom strategies for the cultures represented in the school.

School E: coaching and mentoring

Discussion

Although the situational leadership model is helpful in many circumstances, it is a model that makes cultural assumptions about the way teams operate, i.e. that communication inside the team is open, that team members feel relatively at ease with team leaders, that both praise and frank feedback are acceptable in the culture, and that close but objective interaction is possible between manager and each team member. In this model, team members are helped in their development when leaders (HoDs) work closely with them supporting, coaching and mentoring. But in cultures of high collectivism or high power distance there is likely to be more psychological distance between team members and their leader, particularly where there may be a racial difference too (Shaw and Welton, 1996). History, of course, also plays a role; previously oppressed people in Africa may find it hard to trust someone who represents to them the face of colonialism. In the end, a pattern of mutual avoidance may be set up so that team members and HoDs do not have to communicate too closely.

Ideas

School E may be helped by:

- the same workshop for *all* members of staff, not just the HoDs;
- an exploration of behaviours suitable for coaching and mentoring, giving a voice to each member of staff so they can express how they wish their HoDs to react and enable development.

School F: recognition of traditional celebrations

Discussion

This is a clear case of school managers not appearing to respect the cultures and traditions of staff. (It only becomes 'clear', however, after an independent consultant has heard complaints about the attitude and behaviours of each party from the other.) The European managers are perceived by their local staff, who are full of life and fun, to be cold, clinical, uncaring and lacking in humanity. They have a tendency to refer to procedural guidelines, and expect staff to do the same, assuming that non-compliance is unprofessional. Each behaviour is interpreted falsely by the other party (the 'fundamental attribution error' of Ross, 1977). There is an unrealised assumption that the other party will be aware of the other's viewpoint, and the disconfirmed expectancies make the situation more difficult. It is not surprising that staff treated in this manner are not performing at their highest motivational level.

This type of situation occurs very frequently in bicultural schools, where a critical mass of each culture ensures certain staffroom attitudes.

Ideas

Such situations, once recognised, can be discussed openly, allowing each cultural group to identify the elements of the other that irritate, as well as those that delight.

Prevention, however, is more effective, and half a day spent – sensitively – on awareness of the main cultures, and expectations of their colleagues, as well as which symbols are important to each culture, is time well spent. The dominant culture is more likely to be heard, however, and a way needs to be found to give a voice to the other(s).

School G: new European teacher in African school

Discussion

What the new teacher regards as assertiveness and straightforward communication is regarded by his colleagues as unacceptable – another case of disconfirmed expectancy. The teacher comes from a culture where individual views are welcomed and where there is less likelihood that such views will be taken personally by others. Collectivist behaviours, however, assume that colleagues will be more circumspect in offering their views, testing their feelings and opinions in the whole group first.

The situation cannot be ignored, as this will eventually destroy teamwork. African colleagues are likely to be too polite to raise the issue, and the new teacher may never realise the effect he is having on the rest of the team, solidifying a behavioural pattern that becomes chronically unhelpful.

Ideas

School G might:

- induct new staff, particularly those inexperienced in international schools, more carefully into the cultures prevalent in the school;
- provide a mentor to help with cultural adaptation;
- monitor progress and social adaptation of new staff.

School H: degree of student autonomy

Discussion

This situation arises because there is a basic misunderstanding between the Australian teacher and the Japanese culture about the purposes of education and what is expected of a 'teacher' in that society. Parents may choose to send their child to the international school for several reasons – not always because they subscribe to the way of teaching. It may represent to them a way of helping their child acquire an English-medium education, or it may be a way of selecting another educational advantage, such as IB. The broad purpose of education is often assumed, not explicated, when parents sign up to a school. Individualistic societies, such as Australia, may be more inclined to assume that, as well as acquiring knowledge and good examination results, education is about preparation for unknown future situations, and thus it focuses on learning how to learn for life.

Collectivist societies, on the other hand, may place more emphasis on learning facts (Hofstede, 1991: 63). If the student also comes from a high UA culture, s/he is more likely to want to know the single right answer from the teacher,

167

who is expected to be the guru with all the answers. If the answers are not given, this is taken as a sign of weakness, as in school H.

The Australian teacher, who is likely to be low on both collectivism and UA, *assumes* that the student will develop best through finding out; the parent *assumes* that this means that the teacher does not know. A high UA teacher with high UA students would have no dissonance in this respect – s/he would have divulged the answer, and expectations would match all round.

Ideas

Such a situation might be prevented by:

- clarifying for parents when they signed up what attendance at this school implies for their child; the school's mission or value statement is a starting point, but further explanation may be needed;
- whole-staff discussion and agreement about differing assumptions *re* the purposes of education provided by the school;
- in-service training to explore the range of classroom strategies consistent with this agreed position;
- staff encouraged to explain to students why they do what they do in class;
- parents kept in touch with school processes and expectations of homework, etc.

School I: performance-related pay

Discussion

This situation is a complex one. Performance-related pay is notoriously difficult to introduce successfully under any conditions, but in a mixed-culture team of staff it has particular dangers. While highly individualistic cultures may find it challenging to strive to better their own situation above that of their colleagues, staff from more collectivist cultures are less likely to value this form of recognition.

Much also depends on who is carrying out the assessment. Research (Kraiger and Ford, 1985) shows that performance appraisals disadvantage those employees who come from a cultural background different from that of their appraisers. In a school, judgements may be questioned – even if not overtly – in a cross-cultural appraisal where real reward results.

The masculinity dimension also plays a role in this case. Where people enjoy competition, they are more likely to feel motivated by this system. Conversely, more collaborative cultures may feel alienated by it.

Additionally, as such a system inevitably demonstrates publicly where people have succeeded, or not, it may be harder in societies where preservation of visible self-respect, or 'face', is important.

So far we have discussed culture, but gender is also significant in this case. Women typically put themselves down, or fail to rise to the bait of competition as eagerly as their male counterparts (Tannen, 1991).

It is not surprising, under the circumstances, that morale has dropped since the introduction of performance-related pay. Continuation of it may polarise staff into unhealthy factions.

Ideas

The simple answer might be not to introduce such a system.

If, however, it is inevitable, much preparation and groundwork with the whole staff is needed, including:

- a fair and agreed process;
- clear and objective criteria for judgement, collaboratively designed;
- in-service training of all concerned, but especially in matters of arriving at judgements;
- raised awareness of cultural traps;
- an appeals procedure.

However carefully it is introduced, there is inevitably the moment when an individual's competence is being judged by another, and where this has an effect on salary emotions take over.

It may be worth considering whole-team rewards instead of individual rewards.

School J: parental involvement

Discussion

It is not uncommon for an international school to develop by altering the nature of its intake, and then it becomes necessary for the management to adjust accordingly. In this school, the headteacher is doing what he would do in his own country by contacting the parents and trying to address the issue openly. Nevertheless, he is finding it difficult to meet their expectations of him, as he gets no direct feedback, and only negative indirect feedback. The more he tries, the harder it becomes.

From their perspective, the parents are not accustomed to being consulted by somebody in the position of headteacher, and, coming from a high power distance culture, are less inclined to give an opinion than parents from a low power distance culture might be. Their Eastern values of 'face' prevent them from seeming to disagree, even if in reality they do not agree. However, their strong sense of community enables them to discuss this outside school, and, once the informal feedback reaches the headteacher, he feels as though he has failed.

The situation has some similarities with school H.

Ideas

This is a difficult case. The headteacher needs to start from the perceptions of the parents, and build up their confidence in him as a person, as a leader and as a member of the community. Only then will his attempts at improving communication be accepted, but he will have to go slowly.

Conclusion

For the purposes of this chapter, the examples used here have been partly explained by reference to cross-cultural social psychology research, which has necessarily been simplified for the analysis. When managers of international schools are confronted by misunderstandings, they might adopt a three-step process:

1 Understand the possible cause(s) of the behaviour.
2 Provide relevant and culture-sensitive professional development experiences.
3 Develop a distinctive organisational climate for the school.

1 *Understand the possible cause(s) of the behaviour*
   Managers need to find a way to discover the core values of the various nationalities represented in the school, and to understand how these interact, and whether, or to what extent, this contributes towards the misunderstanding in question. Explaining reasons for differences of behaviour in a mixed-culture team, however, is merely a start. If taken no further, it is easy to take a culturally relativistic stance and allow culture to become the reason why things cannot happen.

2 *Provide relevant and culture-sensitive professional development experiences*
   The second step is to focus on professional development. This might take the form of sensitive cultural awareness raising, or it might be more formal training for some people in the team to enable them to be heard, play a full role, or provide equal opportunity to others in the team. But herein lies another potential trap: management approaches in international schools are frequently dominated by people and attitudes from high individualism and low power distance cultures. Similarly, many of the training models and processes in common use are derived from cultures rich enough to carry out the research to provide the theory that enters the textbooks sold world-wide. The hegemony of the 'West' does not stop here: consultants and management trainers have a tendency to recycle these models and

theories around the world, whereas they would do better 'to question the adequacy of their domestically-derived models' (Jackson, 1995: 27). Managers in international schools commissioning professional development experiences from outside consultants are therefore urged to make choices of training personnel, materials and ways of working that are appropriate to the context of their own school's cultural mix (Shaw and Welton, 1996).

3   *Develop a distinctive organisational climate for the school*
The third step looks constructively ahead for the whole team, or preferably the whole school. Some of the post-Hofstede research (for example Kanter and Corn, 1994; Cray and Mallory, 1998) indicates that developing a distinctive organisational climate is a powerful tool in helping people to work together *regardless* of their own cultural programming. Experience in many international schools has shown that those which have *consciously* focused on developing their own distinctive climate, starting with agreed values and bringing together the policies, systems, structures and behaviours of the school community into a state of consonance, are the ones that provide the right environment for successful management of mixed-culture teams.

It is only through such awareness of our differences that we can reach understanding through a better quality of communication, and thus perhaps help to achieve some of the ideals of the IBO mentioned at the start of this chapter. Perhaps we can best conclude with the wisdom of Alex Rodger:

> the possibility of humane communities in a pluralistic context depends on establishing the conditions possible and foster communications which serve the goal of mutual understanding. That communication, in turn, can emerge only from the kind of comm-union between human beings which begins in the acceptance of kinship as a fact to be explored; develops through recognition of the other as both strange and familiar; and leads to the framing of language which can bridge the gulf of separation, incomprehension and antagonism.
>
> (Rodger, 1996: 54)

References

Blanchard, K., Zigarmi, P. and Zigarmi, D. (1985) *Leadership and the One Minute Manager*, Glasgow: Fontana/Collins.

Brislin, R. (1993) *Understanding Culture's Influence on Behaviour*, Orlando: Harcourt Brace Jovanovich College.

Cray, D. and Mallory, G. (1998) *Making Sense of Managing Culture*, London: International Thompson Business Press.

Fadil, P. (1995) 'The effect of cultural stereotypes on leader attributions of minority subordinates', *Journal of Managerial Issues* 7 (2): 193–208.

Fayol, H. (1949) *General and Industrial Management*, London: Pitman.

Helson, H. (1964) *Adaptation Level Theory*, New York: Harper and Row.

Hofstede, G. (1980) *Culture's Consequences*, Newbury Park: Sage.

Hofstede, G. (1991) *Cultures and Organisations*, London: Harper Collins.

IBO (International Baccalaureate Organisation) (1994) *Guide to the Middle Years Programme*, Geneva: IBO.

IBO (International Baccalaureate Organisation) (1997) 'Mission statement', *Guide to Diploma Programme*, Geneva: IBO.

IBO (International Baccalaureate Organisation) (1998) *Guide to the Primary Years Programme*, Geneva: IBO.

Jackson, T. (ed.) (1995) *Cross-cultural Management*, Oxford: Butterworth Heinemann.

Jameson, D. (1994) 'Strategies for overcoming barriers inherent in cross-cultural research', *The Bulletin for the Association for Business Communications* September: 39–40.

Kanter, R.M. and Corn, R. (1994) 'Do cultural differences make a business difference? Contextual factors affecting cross-cultural relationships,' *Journal of Management Development* 13 (2): 5–23.

Kraiger, K. and Ford, J. (1985) 'A meta-analysis of Ratee race effects in performance ratings,' *Journal of Applied Psychology* 70: 56–65.

Laurence, P. and Lorsch, J. (1967) *Organisation and Environment*, Homewood: Irwin.

Lonner, W. (1990) 'An over-view of cross-cultural testing and assessment,' in R. Brislin (ed.) *Applied Cross-Cultural Psychology*, Newbury Park: Sage.

Riordan, C. and Vandenburg, R. (1994) 'A central question in cross-cultural research: do employees of different cultures interpret work-related measure in an equivalent manner?', *Journal of Management* 20 (3): 643–71.

Rodger, A. (1996) *Developing Moral Community in a Pluralist School Setting*, Aberdeen: Gordon Cook Foundation.

Ross, L. (1977) 'The intuitive psychologist and his shortcomings: distortion in the attribution process', in L. Berkovitz (ed.) *Advances in Experimental Social Psychology*, Vol. 10, New York: Academic Press.

Rutter, M., Maughan, B., Mortimore, P. and Ouston, J. (1979) *Fifteen Thousand Hours: Secondary Schools and Their Effects on Children*, London: Open Books.

Shaw, M. (1991) *Practical Tutoring*, Oxford: Oxford Polytechnic.

Shaw, M. and Welton, J. (1996) 'The application of education management models and theories to the processes of education policy making and management: a case of compound cross-cultural confusion', paper presented at the Indigenous Perspectives of Education Management conference, 19–24 August, Kuala Lumpur.

Tannen, D. (1991) *You Just Don't Understand: Women and Men in Conversation*, London: Virago.

Taylor, F. (1947) *Scientific Management*, New York: Harper and Row.

Trompenaars, F. (1993) *Riding the Waves of Culture*, London: Nicholas Brealey.

11

CREATING STANDARDS AND RAISING PERFORMANCE

Martin Skelton

Introduction

This chapter looks at the central issue for schools of raising standards and performance. It begins by identifying the difference between each of these terms and looks at some of the difficulties particular to international schools. The chapter then points the way to some of the standards and elements of consistency which might matter more to international schools than schools in other contexts. The chapter goes on to explore why standards might be raised or lowered and identifies the key questions that schools should ask themselves to determine which is necessary. The chapter concludes by exploring the different contributions that students, teachers, schools and boards can make to raising performance.

What does a 'standard' look like?

Richard Pring (1992) has defined standards as 'bench marks ... criteria whereby one assessor evaluates the quality of a particular activity or a process.' Although these standards or benchmarks can be raised or lowered, Pring reminds us that what is usually going up or down is the *performance* of students as measured by standards, not the standards themselves.

If a 'standard' means the 'benchmark against which performance can be judged', then schools need to establish a series of those benchmarks for the different age ranges of the students taught in the school. For sure, these benchmarks will be used to define a student's academic performance but they may also be used to define other things, too, such as a student's personal and social development. Standards can refer to learning in both narrow and broad senses.

In other words, they need to define what is appropriate for students to know, be able to do or understand at different points as they move through the school. Often these points will be annual, so that the standards indicate that 'By the end/beginning of Year *x* or Grade *y* students will know …; be able to do …; or understand … .' But they could also cover longer periods of time, so that the standards might indicate, for example, that 'By the time they are 8, 11, 13 or 15 students will know …, be able to do …; or understand …, etc.'

Many international schools already have some experience of this, particularly when deciding which students should be admitted to the school. It is not uncommon to find schools setting standards in relation to language ability. A typical example might be 'No student can enter XXXX school at Year *y* unless he/she has passed the basic competency tests in spoken and written English'. The school then administers a pre-entry test and entry is predetermined by whether the student does sufficiently well on this test.

The importance of standards as a means of judging *performance* is also illustrated in this example. Once a student has taken the test his/her performance can be measured or judged against that of all the other students who have taken the test. So, 'this student has performed in the top 10 per cent on this entry test'. Without the standard, performance is impossible to measure.

What standards are necessary?

Some standards already exist in most international schools. The important issue to consider is the range of standards which need to exist. This is a straightforward question to answer, if not always to implement.

Standards are required for those aspects about which the school thinks it is important to judge or measure performance.

Some of these aspects will be related to the curriculum. Most international schools already have standards relating to mathematics or English/language arts, if only because they have brought in curriculum packages which implicitly or explicitly contain those standards. What needs to be considered is whether sufficiently explicit standards also exist for other subjects of the curriculum. Does the school know, for example, the standards expected from students in Year *x* in art, history or physical education?

Other standards will not be curriculum related. For example, schools which are fundamentally committed to students' social development will want to be clear about the standards of interpersonal behaviour required by students at different ages. Schools which are committed to developing an international perspective in students will want to make clear what such a perspective might look like at different stages of schooling.

Some standards will not be directly related to students at all. Many schools will want to be clear about standards of teacher competency in the classroom, given the impact this has on student learning.

What is important is that the standards a school chooses to define represent what it is that the school considers to be of fundamental value about what it does. It is against these standards that the school will commit time, resources, physical and mental energy to measure student, teacher and organisational performance.

As long as we remember that much of the research into effective schools comes from a predominantly Western cultural tradition, the evidence provides us with useful pointers.

Murphy (1992) confirms the two key characteristics of effective schools, both of which are consistently visible in a variety of systems. They are:

- *A drive to improve student learning outcomes:* it is the word 'drive' which is important here. All schools are to some extent concerned with improving student learning outcomes. But the more effective schools are able to set this at the very heart of what they do. They seem to understand – to use a term from outside education – that improved student learning is their core business.
- *An understanding of the need to develop appropriate organisational consistency:* schools which are more effective develop a more coherent act than less effective international schools. The sense of 'this is the way we do things around here' is very strong. To use Murphy's nice line (1992: 56), these schools are much more than 'a collection of classrooms linked by a common heating and cooling system.'

If we accept this evidence, it becomes easier to see which standards and performance we should be trying to raise.

Raising *standards* means defining:

- the highest appropriate outcomes that students are expected to achieve at particular times as they pass through the school;
- the appropriate behaviours which define the consistency needed throughout the school to develop high student outcomes.

Raising *performance* means working hard to:

- increase the levels of attainment that students reach against those performance standards;
- increase the extent to which those working in the school comply with the appropriate standards of consistency which have been defined.

Are the Standards Appropriate for All Levels of Ability and Experience?

Once a school has clarified where standards are necessary, the next task is to ensure that the standards are appropriate for the range of aptitudes, abilities and experiences of those to whom they refer.

This applies to both teachers and students. One American school with which I work, for example, has spent considerable time developing standards of teacher competency. These have been defined in such a way that those responsible for hiring teachers understand the minimum competencies required before a teacher can be considered as suitable for employment in the school. Another set of competencies lays out the standards required of teachers who are in their first two years in the school. A third set lays out the standards required of those who have taught in the school for two years or more.

What this school is doing is establishing a set of standards which takes into account the differing contextual understandings of teachers who may move from the home country to the international setting or from one international setting to a different one. Teachers with greater experience and understanding of the context within which the school operates are judged against higher standards than those with less experience.

The same differentiation in standards should apply to students. Most international schools contain a student population of differing abilities. One set of standards for all students is unlikely to be appropriate, even if it is a good starting point. Schools need to move to devising sets of year-by-year and other standards which refer to more able and less able and those students whose abilities fall midway along the continuum.

One useful way of doing this is to think of 'must', 'should' and 'could' as the appropriate language for setting standards. 'Must' standards refer to the knowledge, skills and understanding that all students must acquire, irrespective of their ability. They represent the very core, the essence of what counts. Once students have achieved these 'must' standards – in other words, their performance has been judged appropriate against those standards – then they can move on to develop higher level attributes, knowledge, skills, etc. from the 'should' category of standards and so on into the 'could' category of standards.

In many ways *'must'*, *'should'* and *'could'* are related to the divisions between the less able, the averagely able and the more able. Where they make a strong contribution to raising of performance is that they establish the core of what counts from the very beginning. Relatively less able students are not judged against a deficit model.

Are standards explicitly stated?

Because standards are the criteria against which judgements of performance will be made they need to be stated as explicitly as possible. It is simply impossible to make good judgements of performance against standards which are unclear.

Eisner (1977) has provided two useful concepts to help us think about clarity. Eisner distinguished between two sets of objectives – 'instructional' and 'expressive'.

- An *instructional* objective – or, in our case, standard – contains clarity about success or failure within itself. So, when sent the standards for writing my chapter of this book the editors told me that it should be close to 5000 words long. It's easy for me – and them – to know whether I have succeeded or failed.

- An *expressive* standard, on the other hand, cannot contain complete clarity about its outcomes. One of the purposes of this book is 'to provide support and development for senior and middle managers in international schools'. The range and experience of senior and middle managers is so great that it is impossible for the editors of this book to be able to know definitely that all managers will benefit. But this lack of absolute clarity doesn't reduce the importance of the standard.

Instructional standards can be measured. *Expressive* standards need to be judged. When we develop expressive standards, therefore, we need success criteria. Success criteria in this context represent a number of indicators of the sorts of outcomes that will be considered appropriate if the expressive standard has been reached. (Instructional standards do not need success criteria. The success criteria of an instructional standard is already built into the wording.)

Clarity is vital in standards if they are to contribute to the raising of performance. Greater clarity makes more explicit to teachers, students, parents and others what is required. Knowing what is required enables judgements to be made more effectively and consistently across the school.

Can standards be raised?

Standards are not performance, but they can be both raised and lowered. The reason for doing so is their appropriateness for the group to whom they are being applied.

Following the Gulf War, the student population of many of the international schools in Kuwait changed considerably. Before the war, one school had a student population which was 80 per cent British and 20 per cent from other nationalities. What standards the school had created were, for the most part, based on the attributes of a British expatriate population. Immediately after the war the student population almost reversed. Eighty per cent of the students were non-British and only 20 per cent were British expatriates. The most important change was in students' abilities in spoken and written English.

For a time, this school had to 'lower' its standards for English so that the new standards were both challenging and appropriate to the student body. As time progressed and the school began to organise the effective teaching of English as an alternative language the performance of these new students rose against the standards. The 'new' standards then became inappropriate and had to be 'raised' in order to reflect the increasing abilities of the student population.

What this indicates is that speaking of 'raising' standards in the same way as talking of 'raising' performance may be unhelpful. Standards need to be raised when they no longer represent appropriate criteria against which to make judgements about the performance of students, teachers or management. But they need to be lowered sometimes for exactly the same reasons.

The implications for international schools are considerable. Standards cannot simply be set once and left alone. There needs to be consistent evaluation of the different performances against each of the standards to ensure that the standards remain appropriate.

The most important issue is who is responsible for this review of standards, particularly where board membership, senior management, faculty, students and parents change frequently.

The involvement of external agencies represents one of the best solutions to this problem. Reviews, inspections and accreditation procedures all have a chance of providing the school with a 'cool' outside view. One of the most important contributions these processes can make to an international school is to provide feedback to the school about whether the standards that the school has currently declared to be appropriate are, in fact, so.

Raising performance

Raising performance means two things. First, it means increasing the attainment of students, teachers, administration and others relative to the standards which have been set. So performance is raised when individual students or groups of students, teachers and managers do better against those standards than has previously been the case.

Second, raising performance means increasing the levels of consistency within which the school operates. In other words, performance is raised when more people are doing things similarly in those areas where it has been decided that consistency is important.

Raising performance is the responsibility of everyone in the school – students, teachers, parents, senior management and the Board. But each of these groups needs to be aware of what can and cannot be done.

Students

Raising student performance is the central goal of the school. It is meaningless to raise the performance of teachers or management if the subsequent improvement does not have an impact upon student performance.

Yet students are often in the weakest position to affect their own performance. Younger students are less able to take individual responsibility than older students. Students who move from relatively unsupportive homes into schools which are not clearly focused on how to improve their performance are at a significant disadvantage. Even where students can play a part – such as in the formulation of their own targets or goals – the school or individual teachers need to be committed to this process for it to happen. This is why an understanding of the 'core business' of education is so important for international schools dealing with a mobile student population. The school holds so many of the aces.

Student targets are important for a number of reasons. First, they provide the student with involvement in the process of their own improvement, which is motivationally beneficial.

More importantly, students in international schools are often the best source of information about the strengths and weaknesses of their achievements elsewhere. The transfer of meaningful records is not easy among international schools, partly because of the difficulty of establishing the common standards discussed above. Student self-analysis against the school's standards can be a useful part of the induction process for the student, an important provision of information for the school and the faculty and a way of focusing the student onto improvement soon after their entry into the school.

Student self-defined targets provide the most effective way for international schools to enable students to be a part of raising their own performance.

Teachers

Teachers are at the heart of the issue about raising levels of learning and consistency. Their contribution is vast and a description of all they can do is beyond the scope of this chapter. At best we can offer some pointers.

Teachers play an enormous part in the development of consistency within schools. International school teachers need to understand the relationship between their personal and professional freedoms, the extent to which the school in which they work will exist as an organisation long after they have gone and the students whose effective performance outcomes are the reason for the school's existence in the first place.

The success of much in the school depends on how teachers are able to strike this balance. Working with American international schools and teachers in Saudi Arabia, it has been thrilling to see how the formal process of defining targets for school improvement and subsequently reaching them (known in the UK and elsewhere as 'school development planning' but in many American schools as 'continuous improvement planning') has been made more successful by teachers' willingness to accept a definition of professionalism which encompasses both the individual and the collective. Increasing consistency depends so much on teacher attitudes.

More obviously, perhaps, teachers have a central involvement in raising student performance and, therefore, in improving their own performance in such a way as to contribute to this. Teaching is not an end in itself. Students do not come into school each day to watch teachers enjoy themselves. There is a direct relationship between improved teaching and improved student learning.

Among the most important areas for teachers to think about are:

- *The quality of planning* – or the extent to which teachers are themselves aware of what it is appropriate for their students to learn and how best they can make this happen.
- *The development of student self-esteem* – or the extent to which teachers enable students to take appropriate risks in their learning so that maximum progress can be made. Csikszentmihalyi (1997) calls this state 'relaxed alertness'. Some teachers are very good at enabling students to be relaxed whereas others are good at enabling students to be alert. Creating both together is the important skill.
- *The analysis of evidence* – or the extent to which teachers are willing to make assessments or judgements against the standards set and then analyse those assessments to discover the best way forward to meet students' needs.

Schools

This chapter has already mentioned many of the areas in which the school as an organisation is involved in the raising of standards. There is little point reiterating everything that is said there. But some pointers can be reinforced. What schools can do is set out below.

Establish standards

Hopefully, little now needs to be said about this other than to provide one more reminder that without appropriate standards no judgements can be made about raised performance. So whatever schools do or don't do, it is vital that some standards are established.

Focus available documentation

Most international schools already have documentation which, if clearly understood, can make a significant impact on raising levels of consistency and performance.

The main purpose of school policies, for example, is to establish consistency. A policy statement is an explicit declaration of 'how we do things round here'. The potential mobility of everyone connected with international schools means that the policy statements are one of the few measures against which people's feet can be held to the fire of consistency. In order to help everyone understand how the school works, policy statements need to be as explicit as possible.

School improvement plans, school development plans or the even more appropriate 'continuous improvement plans' should, by definition, be focused on the developmental aspects of the school rather than the maintenance. As we know that effective schools are those which focus on attainment and consistency (Murphy, 1992), schools can help to raise performance by making sure that their central planning document focuses on these two issues alone.

School improvement plans should provide the answer to two questions. First, in what ways will student and teacher performance improve over the next year? Second, how does the school as an organisation need to become more consistent? Having answered these questions through explicit targets, the rest of the plan then defines how the school will get there. But it is the explicit focus on improved performance and consistency that separates out effective school improvement plans from less effective plans.

Schemes of work, rubrics and other similar documents establish clearly what it is that students should learn at different stages of schooling. They are the documents which define the standards discussed earlier in this chapter. The most important quality of an effective scheme of work is that it focuses on what students will achieve rather than what teachers will do. Teacher activity is important, but only inasmuch as it arises from and supports what students should be learning.

Most international schools possess examples of all three of these documents. Better schools make sure that each is appropriately focused.

Develop self-analysis and review

Raising performance and consistency is impossible without knowledge of the current starting point of the school. So self-analysis and review is about raising the stock of knowledge the school has about itself so that it can decide what performance needs to be improved.

The analysis should seek to provide answers to a number of important questions, including:

- Are our standards currently appropriate?
- Would greater levels of consistency help the school improve?
- Are levels of student, teacher and management performance good enough?
- Having identified our needs, can we identify priorities for action?

These are the very same questions which need to be answered in order to create a useful school improvement plan. For schools which are unsure how, or are unable, to begin a process of self-analysis and review, the school improvement plan provides an excellent peg on which to hang this activity.

The process of self-analysis and review can also involve many other important aspects of school organisation. Staff appraisal and review, to name but one, can contribute a great deal to the stock of knowledge which the school builds up.

The raw data for school self-analysis is drawn from both *monitoring* and *evaluation.* Taylor-Fitzgibbon (1996) distinguishes between two important indicators. *Compliance indicators* are those which provide information about whether something which ought to have been done has been done. *Performance indicators* provide information about the quality of what has been done. It is helpful to see a link between compliance indicators and consistency and between performance indicators and attainment. Monitoring can be seen as the process of checking for compliance or consistency. Evaluation can be seen as the process of making judgements about the levels of attainment or performance.

The time it takes for this process to become established in an international school should not be underestimated. This is partly because establishing any activity across a school takes a long time, but it is also because the mobility of the faculty, management and board work against the development of the process of regular analysis and review which can contribute to real development.

Use external agencies

We have already mentioned how external agencies can help to focus an international school and provide continuity of evidence about the appropriateness of a school's standards, its increasing consistency and the improving performance of its students and faculty.

External agencies can be seen as the 'critical friend' of the school, helping the school to improve by, hopefully, sympathetic revelation of evidence. Different forms of critical friending have both advantages and disadvantages.

Generally speaking, accreditation procedures have concentrated more on the consistency elements of a school but less on student and teacher performance. On the other hand, inspection models such as that recently introduced into UK national schools and used by some international schools tend to concentrate more on student and teacher performance and less on elements of consistency. Both accreditation and inspection impose upon the school a set of external standards against which it will be judged.

The process of review is more likely to focus on a set of standards generated internally by the school. The process of defining these standards contributes to the process of self-analysis and review as does the self-study preceding an accreditation procedure or the creation of an action plan following an inspection.

Each method of using external agencies has its advantages and disadvantages. The most important benefit for international schools is that they provide an injection of an outside reality, often from organisations which work with other international schools. Combined with the school's own self-analysis this can be a potent stimulus towards raising standards and performance.

Develop a culture which focuses on raising standards, performance and consistency

Many schools have the sort of documents described above. Many routinely take part in self-review. Many engage the services of external agencies. Yet some schools are clearly more successful at raising standards than others. Why is this? It seems to be because the most successful schools are able to create a culture in which raising standards becomes central. These are the schools which are truly driven by the desire to raise student and teacher performance and increase consistency.

All organisations develop a culture and international schools – because of their unique position within a community and a sharing of expatriate status by most people involved in them – invariably develop strong cultures. What is important is to try and make sure that this culture is a positive one which contributes towards improvement.

The ways in which a culture develops are manifold. Everything a school does with its students, for the parents, between board members and within the teaching faculty contributes to the development of its culture, as portrayed in the previous chapter. The processes are both formal and informal. Much of the work described throughout this chapter and in other chapters of this book will formally help to create a culture of improvement if it is implemented with a professional rigour.

But cultures are also created informally, too, and the senior management team and the Board have a large responsibility in defining what sort of culture is created. What the school chooses to celebrate will say much about what counts. What principals or headteachers choose to focus on in conversations or how they choose to spend their time will do the same. I have already referred to the school improvement work of some American international schools in Saudi Arabia. Among the many simple activities that the principals of these schools have introduced to lock improvement into the culture, it is worth mentioning:

- the school which discusses progress on its improvement plan as the second item on every faculty meeting;
- the school which has displayed on every document and around the school the words 'Our mantra: Are we improving? What's the evidence?'
- the schools where staff are given and take responsibility for delivering progress on the targets and reporting on them;
- the school where the Principal has offered to be the servant for the day of the Junior High School student who shows the greatest improvement in his or her attitude to reading.

These particular instances are not examples for your school to copy. But they are instances of how small acts can work towards creating a culture of improvement.

The Board

If the role of the teacher is to create the conditions within which students can raise their performance then it could be argued that the role of the management of the school is to create the conditions within which teachers can do that. Following this principle, the role of the Board is to create the conditions within which the senior management of the school can do its job effectively and then be held responsible for it, as discussed in Chapter 1.

To help the school raise standards and performance, school boards need to:

- understand the core business of schools;
- set clear management standards relating to that core business and review management against those standards;
- make decisions based on broad rather than narrow evidence;
- understand that their own working context usually means that micromanagement is likely to be counterproductive;
- develop medium-term financial stability in order to ensure the school's survival.

Creating appropriate standards and raising levels of performance and consistency is the central task of any school. It is complex and multifaceted. The challenge for international schools is to find ways to do this within their own particular context. Some aspects of this context will naturally make a positive contribution whereas others will require skilful management and leadership. However, many of the processes which can deliver improved standards and performance already exist in international schools. The real challenge is to fine-tune each of these processes to make sure it is contributing effectively to the core business of the school.

References

Csikszentmihalyi, M. (1997) *Finding Flow, The Psychology of Everyday Life*, New York: Harper Collins.

Eisner, E. (1977) 'Instructional and expressive objectives', in D. Hamilton, B. MacDonald, C. King, D. Jenkins and M. Parlett (eds) *Beyond the Numbers Game*, Berkeley, CA: McCutchan Publishing Corporation.

Murphy, J. (1992) 'Effective schools: legacy and future directions', in D. Reynolds and P. Cuttance (eds) *School Effectiveness, Research, Policy and Practice*, London: Cassell.

Pring, R. (1992) 'Standards and quality in education', *British Journal of Educational Studies* no. 1: 4–22.

Taylor-FitzGibbon, C. (1996) *Monitoring Education – Indicators, Quality and Effectiveness*, London: Cassell.

INDEX

CPSIA information can be obtained at www.ICGtesting.com
Printed in the USA
LVOW081811130212

268519LV00002B/9/P